ON THE OTHER HAND

CHAIM BERMANT

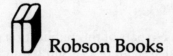

Robson Books

Acknowledgements

I am grateful to the editor of the *Jewish Chronicle* for permission to use the columns reproduced here. Also to Linda Greenlick (chief librarian), and the *Jewish Chronicle* library staff Anna Charin and Keith Feldman, who gave me the run of the library and who were so patient and helpful.

I am also indebted to Adrienne Baker, Evie Bermant, Zena Clayton, Trudy Coleman, Sally Malnick, Naomi Greenwood, Gerald Jacobs, Emma Klein, Myrna Lazarus, Marilyn Lehrer, Evelyn Stern and Vivian Wineman for looking over my selection and giving me useful feedback and comments. Thanks are also due to Dolores Baron, Liz Olivestone and Ruth Kelfa for help with proofreading.

Finally my thanks to Lorna Russell (editor) and Jeremy Robson (publisher) for their part in helping this book to see the light of day.

First published in Great Britain in 2000 by Robson Books, 10 Blenheim Court, Brewery Road, London N7 9NT

A member of the Chrysalis Group plc

British Library Cataloguing in Publication Data

A catalogue record for this title is available from the British Library

ISBN 1 86105 309 6

Printed by Butler and Tanner Ltd, Frome and London

Contents

The Way We Live Now . . . Israel

Israel and the Diaspora

Dress that Maketh Man

Freedom . . . and the Press

Personalities

The Old Wild West

Religion

The Morality of Orthodoxy

The Festivals

Gourmet

Animal Magic

Foreword

The *Jewish Chronicle*, like all newspapers, is the sum of many parts. Each of the men and women who have worked for the oldest Jewish paper in the world have left their mark on it. But of only a handful can it be said that, without them, the *JC* would have been a fundamentally different place. Chaim Bermant was one of those. Without him, the paper would not only have been fundamentally, but unrecognisably, different: duller, smaller and, in every sense, poorer.

He wrote for the *JC*, in one capacity or another, for almost four decades. But it was as our main opinion columnist – for more than a quarter-of-a-century, until his sudden death in January 1998 – that he left an ineradicable imprint on the newspaper, and on Jewish life in Britain. Over the years, we have conducted occasional reader surveys. Typically, they have yielded maddeningly mixed messages: the *JC* faithful want more foreign news (and less); bigger photos (and smaller ones); more controversy (and none at all.) On only one issue were such surveys almost always consistent: Chaim. Not all readers, by any means, agreed with what he wrote. But they all read him – often before even the front page. And more than this, they grew to love him.

In the week that Chaim died, the shock which we at the *JC* felt over his loss was at least briefly mitigated by the delightful task of paging back through his hundreds of columns and longer feature pieces, in order to prepare a fitting tribute. His subjects ranged from Israeli politics (where he advocated 'land for peace', and direct talks between Israel and her foes, when many in the community saw such talk as heresy) and the concept of the Messiah (in one column, he proposed a deal under which Elvis

Presley would get the 21st century, and the Lubavitcher Rebbe the one afterwards) to the mangling by his computer spellchecker of a letter he had written spiced with Yiddish expressions.

Nearly all his writing was enlivened by his wonderful humour. But to mistake his lightness of touch for flippancy would be to miss the meticulous care with which Chaim approached each column or article, and the essential seriousness that underpinned everthing he wrote. He could be wonderfully, gloriously funny, but almost always in the service of the core principles he held dear. And since Chaim was, above all else, intensely Jewish, many of those principles had to do with things Jewish: the need for open-mindedness and tolerance, for a Judaism which celebrates life over dogma and which delights in – rather than shuns – difficult questions, and for a Jewishness that honours and values tradition while remaining irrepressibly in touch with the modern world.

Chaim liked to describe himself as the *JC*'s 'licensed heretic.' To the editors and many others at the *JC* whose delight it was to help provide that license over a period of decades – and, indeed, his tens of thousands of *JC* readers – his absence is hugely felt. We miss his eye for detail, his ability to puncture self-righteousness and hypocrisy in communal life, his passion for justice. But his greatest gift was more complex. Chaim could write harsh things sometimes. But he satirised without savagery. He always somehow retained that sense of humanity and tolerance, vitality and good plain fun, which he urged on the community as a whole.

Judy Bermant shared, and helped animate, that vision more than anyone. In this wonderful book, she has recaptured Chaim's voice, in all its breadth, its versatility and eloquence.

Ned Temko
Editor, The *Jewish Chronicle*

Introduction

The suggestion for this book first came from the *Jewish Chronicle*'s editor, Ned Temko, and was taken up enthusiastically by publisher Jeremy Robson.

Since Chaim's sudden death in January 1998, I have been continually assailed by people demanding to know when Chaim's *Jewish Chronicle* columns would be appearing in book form. Moreover, each person had his or her own personal favourite and 'could I please include it in any forthcoming book.'

I didn't know where to start. The thought of reading through so many weekly columns dating back to the early 1960's, and assembling them into book form was a daunting prospect. Should the book be chronological, beginning with Chaim's earliest columns and charting his progress? Or should it be selected on the basis of subject, and be thematic in character? In the event, as I started reading, it resolved itself.

I spent the summer of 1999 in the *Jewish Chronicle* library poring over thirty-five years of articles recorded on microfiche (my eyes soon felt the strain), in bound volumes of past *JC*s, and photocopying them all. I emerged with a full collection on which to base this book. The library staff were wonderfully patient and understanding, though the photocopier, unused to such heavy duty, broke down constantly and the engineer was a frequent and welcome visitor.

At home, in the autumn, I waded through hundreds of columns on numerous subjects. I hadn't realised, until I began reading, how widely Chaim had cast his net and how perfectly tuned and crafted each piece was. I rarely, if ever, came across a duff column. How on earth was I going to whittle down the material to a manageable number?

xi

Once I began, I was quickly reminded how Chaim returned repeatedly to a group of familiar themes, and that I should have to give them due prominence. I gave myself several guidelines:

1. I decided to concentrate on those columns carrying Chaim's own by-line, i.e. from the late 1970s. Each of these focused on a single issue. The earlier columns each covered several different topics and did not give Chaim enough freedom to develop an argument or express himself as well as he did in the later columns.
2. Although Chaim was an outstandingly funny writer, I decided to give pride of place to some of his most serious and passionately argued polemic. These would form the central core of the book.
3. I would try not to use columns that had already appeared in previous anthologies except where they lent colour and effect to a group of articles, or amplified a particular argument.
4. Columns would be included only where they had not become obviously outdated.

I found it painfully difficult to discard much of his wittiest and most profound writing, my own favourites among them, but having to select some 150 articles from approximately 2000, made this inevitable.

This selection underlines again and again how remarkably prescient Chaim was. He argued in favour of talks with the Palestinians and the PLO at a time when most of the Jewish world regarded them as pariahs. Many views which are today widely held, or even commonplace, were so unpopular when Chaim first expressed them that he was repeatedly attacked and vilified. This was clearly reflected in the letter pages of the *Jewish Chronicle*. I found a letter, dated 1981, from Ehud Barak, today Israel's Prime Minister but then defence attaché at the Israeli Embassy in London. The letter attacked Chaim for views that are now part of the thinking of Barak's own Government. At one stage there were concerted communal efforts to have Chaim removed as columnist from the *Jewish Chronicle*, (whose editor I'm glad to say stood firmly by him). He regularly received threatening letters – including death threats.

The pieces here reflect all of Chaim's central concerns. He wrote with lyrical warmth on Jewish life and tradition, but did not shrink from exposing the absurdities, hypocrisy and corruption that can often go with them. Chaim was in a unique position, understanding the Jewish community from the inside and remaining deeply involved in it, yet able to stand back and view it objectively from the outside. He used his column to give voice to his most humane instincts and convictions. He said more than once that his column was a pulpit. 'To the habits of a journalist', he wrote, 'I have added those of a rabbi'. He believed that he had 'not only a right but a duty' to speak out against injustice, to voice his reservations regarding the Israeli occupation of the West Bank and Gaza, and his despair at the erosion of ethical standards, and basic humanity, in the name of Judaism.

Chaim was a deeply serious man, a practising Jew with an extensive knowledge of, and feeling for, Judaism and especially Jewish history. He tried hard to live up to high standards of decency and integrity in his own life and expected no less from others, especially from religious and communal leaders. He was a keen student of world affairs, and very knowledgeable about economics and politics. All of this formed a solid platform for his opinions. I believe that time will show him to have been a towering influence within post-war Jewish Britain. Changes that he had urged for so long, are now beginning to happen. Two notable examples of his lead belatedly being followed, are, the recent woman's campaign on behalf of Agunot (so-called 'chained women', whose husbands refuse to grant them a religious divorce) – culminating in an intervention by the Chief Rabbi, and the radical re-assessment of Israel – Diaspora relations. People are coming round to his way of thinking.

This, I believe, is why this collection of his writing is so timely. It is also marvellously entertaining.

Judy Bermant
February 2000

1
Speaking for Myself

'Chaim', coupled with 'Itze' (or Isaac) means 'life and laughter', and I have done my best to live up to both.

Personal Opinion

ABOUT 25 YEARS ago, almost to the day, I was invited by William Frankel, then editor of the *Jewish Chronicle*, to join a panel of contributors writing a column of 'Personal Opinion' under the collective name of Ben Azai.

Ben Azai was a great, if controversial, second-century sage, and a particularly outspoken one, but I was given no directives except to speak my own mind.

The column had by then been going for two or three years. Its mainstay was Sefton Temkin, now a Professor of English in America, while other contributors included Norman Cohen, John Gross, Wolf Mankowitz, Rabbi David Goldberg, the late Rabbi Kopul Rosen and Alfred (now Sir Alfred) Sherman. I eventually became the sole contributor, with stand-ins taking over on the frequent occasions I was away. And when I found myself under attack for opinions I didn't hold as well as opinions I did, I decided to come out under my own colours.

A number of years ago I spent a Shabbat in Stamford Hill. Nobody actually tried to lynch me for it was, as I said, Shabbat. But my reception was less than cordial and a lady felt compelled to come to my defence with the most offensive remark I have ever heard in my life: 'Why don't you leave the poor boy alone, he's only earning his living'. In other words, she thought of me as a professional hatchet-man, hired by the editor to do his dirty work for him.

The irony of the situation is that the only times either William Frankel or his successor Geoffrey Paul have interfered with the column was in their attempts to get me to tone *down* my remarks. When I was in Israel I would get almost monthly letters from Paul asking me to forget about Begin for a while because I was becoming a bore. But to his credit he allowed me to be one, for while one should try to amuse, divert and inform and perhaps even advise, one should not, if one holds an opinion strongly, be afraid to bore.

If one has built up a loyal readership it will tend to be long-

3

suffering, or at least it will suffer boredom, if only for a while. What it will not suffer is pomposity. And any columnist who takes himself too seriously and comes to regard himself as an oracle will not retain his readers for long.

One must be prepared to admit one's errors, obviously so in matters of fact, but I would say even in matters of taste and judgement, and to apologise if the occasion demands it. But again one cannot build up a readership with a series of assertions in one week and a series of withdrawals the next.

I have written more than one million words in the course of my 25 years and I would not be human if I had not committed some howlers, but I think I have kept them within tolerable limits. I have established my humanity without, I hope, impairing my credibility. Some weight and authority are obviously called for, but they should be carried lightly and displayed without *gravitas*. If one loses one's balance one depends on one's editor to maintain it.

But I cannot recall that it has been necessary in my case and my relations with both Frankel and Paul have, on the whole, been entirely happy. I am given a completely free hand. Any contretemps which may have arisen between us have been due mainly to the intervention of lawyers who are the bane of my existence. They read the most sinister implications into the most innocent remarks. If you should find a particularly flat phrase in any of my paragraphs you may be fairly certain that a lawyer has sat on it.

I am sometimes introduced as a 'controversial columnist' as if it were a commendation in its own right. I am not flattered by the description for it is no *kuntz* (great feat) to be controversial. All one has to do is to latch on to a topic on which there is universal agreement – such as that eating people is wrong – and say the opposite. I certainly do not dabble in outrage for its own sake. If I should occasionally seem controversial it is because I live by the word and regard both words and space with reverence and I feel that if a thing is worth saying it is worth saying forcefully. My views themselves, if examined in detail, are unremarkable. But I take pains to be clear, emphatic and brief and if I have built up a following at all it is largely because I say publicly what a great many people think privately.

All this can, of course, have its dangers. One is always accused of 'washing dirty linen in public', and of 'giving ammunition to our enemies'. I certainly take no pleasure in seeing my remarks picked up in the Arab press. But if linen isn't washed in public, it isn't washed in private either and is generally allowed to accumulate until it stinks to heaven. I doubt if the Arabs in the West Bank need to read the *JC* to know they're oppressed. And if my remarks, or those of any other Jewish commentators, should come to their attention, it merely tells them that some Jews have a conscience. In any case it is not the commentators who give ammunition to our enemies, but the politicians whose acts excite comment. To stay silent when one has an opportunity to speak out is to be almost an accessory after the fact.

The *JC* is widely quoted and read in America and I am, as a novelist, largely dependent on the goodwill of the American Jewish readers. And I must confess that there were moments when I was tempted to stay silent for reasons of commercial prudence. But that became impossible after the invasion of Lebanon. By now even those who have tended to regard me as a public enemy can see that I have, unfortunately, been proved right by events. As I have often remarked, one doesn't need much vision to be a prophet of doom.

The prince of columnists, the late Cassandra of the *Daily Mirror*, gave me a number of tips in his time, the most memorable of which was: 'Never praise because you will almost certainly be proved wrong.'

I take no pleasure in being, or appearing to be, a professional curmudgeon, but I hate complacency and humbug. The air is often so loud with mutual congratulations and self-praise that I feel provoked into chirping in with a word of dissent, if only to put the record straight. But in the main I like to praise where I can for I like to be liked. And if I can make some wholesome utterance about this or that institution or individual, I approach my Sabbath with a glad heart. Alas, there are few occasions for doing so.

When I was in Israel I would search around with something like desperation for something positive to comment on, if only by way of a change, and I generally found it in the landscape. But when it comes to Anglo-Jewry there isn't even the landscape to work on. As a result I have occasioned more than one passing moment of displeasure. But any journalist who writes a column for 25 years – as indeed any rabbi who occupies a pulpit for that length of time – without making enemies, is not worthy of his craft.

Manna Spring 1984

Glaswegian

I HAD A good war, as wars go, though, at first, I found it all rather confusing.

I had arrived in Glasgow from a small *shtetl* in Latvia only a few months earlier. I had already acquired a school uniform with a crest on my blazer pocket, and a further crest on my cap, which more or less made me a native. I was just beginning to get used to big-city life when the war broke out and our school was evacuated to Annan, a small town in Dumfrieshire.

We were accompanied by Old Ike, the headmaster of the local *cheder* (religious classes) (he could only have been in his forties, but anyone who devotes his life to Jewish education becomes old before his time). He came bearing a small version of the Ark of the Covenant on his shoulders to make sure that, in leaving Glasgow, we would not be leaving our faith.

He set up a kosher canteen in a church hall, where we ate on Shabbat and at lunch-time on weekdays; opened a *shul* (synagogue) in a disused furniture shop; and appointed me as *shammas* (beadle).

My duties were two, one difficult, the other impossible. The first was to guard the precious bottle of Palwin's No 4 (whatever happened to Palwin's Nos 1, 2 and 3?) for *kiddush* (ceremonial blessing over wine) and *havdalah* (ceremony marking the end of Shabbat). This was a little like appointing a cat to look after the cream. The second was to assemble a quorum for afternoon prayers on Shabbat afternoon. More than 100 boys would come to *shul* in the morning, so it should not have been impossible to bring together ten in the afternoon.

But everyone was at the pictures or playing football in the park, and I could never get more than five or six to turn up, all of them small fry, the sort of solitary little figures who tend to haunt religious gatherings because nobody asks them to play.

Minchah (afternoon prayers) was followed by *seudah shlishit* (late-afternoon meal), a frugal meal of bread and herring, washed down with Tizer (served in cups the size of thimbles).

Ike would tell us stories about the martyrdom of Rabbi Akiva and Rav Tarfon, which did not add much to our merriment, and we would then sing *zemirot* (sabbath songs) in tuneless voices in the gathering dusk, while the shrill sounds of sinners having fun wafted in with the evening mists. (Others would eventually trickle in in time for *havdalah*, if only for a swig of the Palwin's No 4.)

I didn't have much fun on Sundays, either, for I was billeted with a farmer and his two elderly sisters, all of them strict Presbyterians. They would spend much of the day reading and discussing the Bible and would sometimes consult me on the more arcane parts of Ezekiel in the hope that, with my family connections, I might know something they didn't.

They didn't like to play ball games on the Sabbath or even switch on the wireless, except for the Nine o'Clock News (which, in the course of the war, acquired a religious standing in its own right), so that it was almost like having a two-day Shabbat.

I was the first Jew they had met outside the Old Testament and they treated me with particular deference, especially after they heard I was the son of a rabbi.

They seemed unduly familiar with the Jewish dietary laws and went to excessive lengths to see that everything I ate was *kosher*.

I once came home with a bag of chips. 'I wouldn't touch those, dear,' said one of the sisters, 'they're fried in lard.'

I didn't know that, but wasn't grateful for the information because, given the level of cuisine in the *kosher* canteen, the chips were a necessary supplement.

In spite of the restrictions, I came to love the farmer and his sisters, the farm life, the cows, the sheep, the fields and woods, the nearby river, the great, open skies. It was like being back in my small *shtetl* in Latvia, without the fear of the surrounding *goyim* (gentiles).

Then, one afternoon, I was attacked by two older boys on the way home from school. I was knocked to the ground, kicked and had my face rubbed in the mud. My nose was bleeding, my face was scratched, my bones were aching, but even so I was more hurt in spirit than in body.

In fact, my whole world fell in. I was back among the *pogromchiks* of Eastern Europe. Even Scotland wasn't safe, it seemed.

The following morning, however, I discovered that there had been a concerted attack by local boys on the evacuees. I had suffered not as a Jew but as a Glaswegian. I felt redeemed.

This was the period of the phoney war. The air raids everyone had expected did not materialise. One after another, we drifted back to Glasgow. My rustic idyll was over.

5 May 1995

Beards

I RECENTLY HEARD a broadcast by Mr John Sparrow, a former Warden of All Souls, which made me bristle. It was an attack on beards, the proliferation of which he regards as a reversion to savagery. Mr Sparrow is a classical scholar and his aversion falls within the classical tradition which expected a civilised man to be shaven and regarded the unshaven as barbarians and, indeed, the literal meaning of barbarians is the bearded ones. [Not true: it derives from foreign and uncouth speech. Ed. *JC*.] I, on the other hand, grew up in a world where hairiness was next to holiness, where hairiness, indeed, was an attribute of holiness, and where bare-faced rabbis were as uncommon as bare-headed rabbi's wives. And not only rabbis. All the burghers of note, all the pillars of society were (if I may be allowed to mix my metaphors) bearded and it seems to me that the main reason why women have never been allowed a full part in Jewish communal life, derives not so much from *halachic* (Jewish religious law) injunctions as the fact that they cannot grow beards (though looking back on it, I can think of some exceptions).

I suspect that the place of the beard in Jewish lore and, indeed, law, has something to do with the belief that man was made in God's image and, in the popular imagination, the Jewish God (as distinct from the Greek ones) has always been bearded, as were all the Prophets and, with the exception of Jacob, the Patriarchs.

I have never been able to understand why the Yiddish expression for a Gentile priest is *galech*, the shaven one, for all the priests that I encountered, the *patushkas* of the Russian Orthodox Church

8

were as hirsute as the rabbis, only more so, for their beards came in huge black slabs, with every hair fixed in place as if it was tarred, whereas the rabbinical beards, truth to tell, were bedraggled and fuzzy, with ends uneven and hairs sticking out in all directions. If the Russian Orthodox beards were privet, the Jewish Orthodox ones were bramble. There is, of course, a reason for this. The Jews treat their beards as a dairymaid treats an udder: they tug at them, they worry them, they milk them for inspiration, they use them as study-aids. Open any well-used volume of the Talmud and you will find it as full of loose hairs as a cat's basket.

The only Jew of note to treat a beard with the respect it deserved was Herzl and when he appeared at the first Zionist Congress he was greeted with cries of 'he is King of Yeshunun.' I doubt if he would have provoked such ecstasy if he had been beardless.

The same was perhaps true of the late Dayan Abramsky whose fine features seemed trapped in a wilderness of hair. I once saw him in Woburn Square in conversation with Ewen Montagu. Mr Montagu (he should live to be 120) is about seven foot tall; Dayan Abramsky was nearer five, and together they represented the epitome of the Yiddish expression *Shabbos hagodol mit kurtz Freitig* (the Great Sabbath with a short Friday), with Mr Montagu in the unlikely role of *Shabbos hagodol*, but one could never think of the Dayan as a short man because his beard gave him a presence out of all proportion to his size.

In the nineteenth century when Britain was a God-fearing nation there were beards everywhere and of every shape and size, on cheek and chin, goatees and mutton-chops, side-boards and side-burns, to say nothing of dundrearies, wispy little tufts like Disraeli's (it seems to me that he worried the life out of his beard), and rich effusions like Salisbury's, but with the rise of the razor the country declined, and like Samson, it lost its might when it lost its mane.

It seems to me that a rabbi without a beard is like a high priest without his canonicals, for who will take spiritual guidance from a man without a hair to his chin? The United Synagogue tried to compensate with canonicals and has encumbered its clergy with dalmatics and copes and chasubles, but between them, they do not generate the authority of a good, honest beard. Fashions have changed and in recent years while rabbis have not quite allowed their chins to grow wild, most of them have acquired semi-beards varying in size and shape from Arafat *sephira* (the period between

Pesach and Shavuot) beards to well-kept Van Dyks. Today it is chins rather than theology that divide the denominations. The Reform movement is clean-shaven; the United Synagogue is semi-bearded; the Federation is bearded and the Adath is over-grown. (It seems to me, to judge from recent pronouncements, that Adath rabbis grow beards inside their heads as well as outside them.)

From all of which you may infer that I too am unshaven and I will confess that I am attached to beards. I have had three in my time (consecutively rather than concurrently). The first I lost when a budding Delilah clipped off half my beard and I put the other half out of its misery; the second I lost when I fell asleep in a barber's chair and woke up with a small tuft on my chin like the back end of a duck; the third is the beard I have now. I regard it as one of the tools of my trade and snatch at it every time I get stuck in a middle of a sentence. Scripture, too, regarded beards in a fairly benevolent light. 'A hoary head,' we are told, 'is a crown of glory.'

But in the main it is a form of compensation. When the head has lost its crop what is there to do except cultivate the chin?

8 June 1979

'There but for the grace of God . . .'

I GET QUITE a lot of mail, some of it flattering, most of it critical. The imbalance doesn't worry me, for one is more easily moved by wrath than by appreciation (I am myself). What does worry me (apart from the expense of replying) is the number of readers who take me for the rabbi and address their *halachic* problems to me, such as: 'I have fallen in love with aunt. May I marry her?' To which I am always tempted to reply, 'Certainly, my child, you may,' if only to counter the tendency of rabbis in general to say 'No, you mustn't.'

I suppose I am taken for a rabbi because I have been next door to *the* rabbi (may he live for many long and good years, Amen) for so long that people believe I have become one by contagion. Also, as I may have suggested a few weeks ago, I verge on the hirsute, and there seems to be a feeling at large in the community that the beard is the badge of the ecclesiastic, whereas it often hides a multitude of sins.

At which point I must confess to a secret – or not-so-secret – hankering for the cloth. It was my earliest ambition to be a rabbi and I have not abandoned it yet (though, in a sense, it has abandoned me), and where other boys played at soldiers, I played at *shuls* and would arrange chairs in a row and address them on the weekly *sidra* (reading from the Torah [law] in synagogue). I recently wrote myself a part of a rabbi in a television play, but, alas, I couldn't have it because I wasn't a member of Equity (the actors' trade union), I couldn't join Equity because I wasn't an actor, and I couldn't become an actor, because I wasn't a member of Equity – which shows that it isn't only rabbis who say no.

The nearest I got to playing the part was in America, where I was once on a prolonged lecture tour. In America the pulpit is not quite the *terra sancta* it is here, and even laymen have been known to use it without being struck dead. I must have spoken from about 30 pulpits in the course of the tour, at the end of which I felt like a common-law rabbi. (In one New England town, incidentally, they actually have a getaway pulpit; one press of a button and it sinks underground. Once, while enlarging on a point with flailing hands, I accidentally pressed the button and, like Korach, vanished from view in full spate.)

In a way, it would have been as natural (if not as lucrative) for me to go into the ministry as for a Rothschild to go into banking. I come from a rabbinical family. My father was a rabbi, my brother-in-law is a rabbi, and, but for the grace of God, I might have been a rabbi myself.

The pen, they say, is mightier than the sword, but the two must make an invincible combination. A well-known Anglo-Jewish divine once said to me: 'All those books you keep churning out, do they give you a living?' 'Of sorts,' I said. At which he drew me aside and whispered: 'Why don't you become a rabbi? You get a decent salary, subsidised housing, a good pension and all the free time in the world. Besides,' – he added by way of final inducement – 'they're so short of people they'll take *anyone*.'

He might have added that the rabbi-writer is brought into touch not only with this world, but with the next, and is thus provided with a field of exploration not available to the ordinary scribe. The American novelist, Herb Tarr, used to be a rabbi-writer until his royalties multiplied and he turned to full-time authorship, but he still lives on his rabbinical experience much as a camel lives on its hump. Isaac Bashevis Singer, who is a wunder-rabbi manqué, spent many years in *yeshivah* (Talmudical college), but also drew heavily on the experience of his father, who was a Warsaw *dayan* (rabbinical judge). He is extremely erudite and I once asked him if he had ever thought of being a rabbi, to which he replied: *Mehr fehlt mir nit* ('that's all I need').

I once lived in Tunbridge Wells (I have lived everywhere) and became friendly with an Anglican vicar. I envied him his ancient church, his spacious vicarage, his large library, his beautiful garden, his serene way of life, and sitting in front of his drawing room fire with a cup of tea one wintry afternoon I confessed that if I were to choose my reincarnation, I would probably become an English country parson.

'But why wait till then?' he asked. 'What's to stop you being one right now?'

'Several things.'

'Such as?'

'I can't accept the divinity of Christ.'

'But, my dear boy, who does?'

In other words, lack of faith need not be an obstacle to service to the faithful, at least in the Church of England. Synagogues, whether of the Orthodox or Reform variety, are less latitudinarian. There may be room for free-thinkers, there is certainly abundant room for non-thinkers, but what of someone like myself whose views would put him well to the left of Rabbi Rayner (may he live for many long and good years, Amen), while his disposition and habits would put him to the right of Rabbi Padwa (may he, too, etc . . . Amen)?

Many individuals are prone to conflicts, and the United Synagogue (and, I suspect, also the Adath) thrives on the fact that most men prefer to be sinners in a holy congregation than saints in a profane one. And so I must be content to be a mere lay rabbi with this column as my pulpit.

Here endeth the lesson.

6 July 1979

12

To be an Englishman

YOU MUST KNOW the story of the little Lithuanian Jew who, on taking out British citizenship in 1947, broke into tears.

'*Gevalt!*' he wailed, 'they've given away India.'

It's many years since I acquired British citizenship but I felt the same when they gave back Hong Kong. I was literally in tears as the Black Watch beat the retreat with pipes and drums and the very heavens seemed to weep as the rains descended.

Anne Applebaum, the writer and journalist, confessed to the same sentiments in the *Sunday Telegraph*. And she is not even British, but a foreigner, an American who happens to be working in London. Her family, however, like mine, is from Belarus, which may explain her strong feelings about Britain and British ceremonies.

A few years ago, Sir Isaiah Berlin, while analysing Chaim Weizmann's devotion to England, the English people and English institutions, came to the conclusion that he was an incurable 'Anglomaniac'.

Weizmann was, of course, born and brought up in Belarus, but I believe that the term would apply equally to Sir Isaiah himself, who is from Riga – and to everyone else who stems from what I like to call Greater Lithuania.

Lithuania, though tiny now, was once a great empire, which included all of Belarus and large chunks of Russia and Poland. But it went into decline in the sixteenth century and was absorbed by Poland in 1569.

The concept of Lita, however, remained intact in the Jewish imagination long after the place had vanished from the maps. Indeed, most of the Jews who made their homes in Britain in the past 120 years were in effect Litvaks. They also retained their Lithuanian habits of mind. They were rational, clear-headed, with a distaste for extremes and a love of tradition.

Thus they adapted readily to the British way of life and, once they acquired local habits and attitudes, they often stuck to them with greater tenacity than the Brits around them and I sometimes feel that one has to be a Lithuanian Jew in order to be a British patriot.

It is possible that I may harbour a vision of Britain which no longer exists and that some of the institutions which I particularly cherished are now largely defunct. I, for example, never spent a lot of time at school and derived much of my education from the BBC. But that was in the good old days of steam radio, when Reithian principles still prevailed and one could rarely switch on to a BBC programme without coming away a wiser and happier man.

One cannot expect the same standards from TV because television, by its very nature, is anxious to catch the eye rather than absorb the mind and tends to skate along the surface of events. But worse than that is the narky tone which some reporters feel obliged to adopt at even the most solemn occasions.

Anne Applebaum, for example, noticed that one BBC commentator in Hong Kong scoffed even at the handover ceremony. My attention must have been otherwise engaged at that moment, or I might have put my boot through the screen.

There is also what they refer to in France as *le vice anglais* and which was celebrated on Saturday by a Gay Pride Festival on Clapham Common which, according to the organisers, was attended by more than 200,000 people.

The numbers did not surprise me because a free circus will always attract a large crowd, but I was surprised that the government felt obliged to send an official representative in the person of Chris Smith, the Heritage Minister – which may suggest to anyone who may have doubts on the subject what the British heritage is about. Such events are disheartening, as are the unending revelations about sleaze in public life, but one can draw some comfort from the fact that they are revealed at all.

They are piffling compared to the levels of corruption which one finds elsewhere in Europe, to say nothing of Asia, and if they fill whole pages of our daily press, they would pass unnoticed in most other parts of the world.

We expect high levels of probity and, in the main, I think it's fair to say we receive them.

There is no paradise on this side of heaven (I'm not convinced that there is one on the other side, either). Every place has its drawbacks and Britain has its fair share of them.

But it also has more than its fair share of virtues and those of us who are still prone to Anglomania may, I think, be forgiven for it.

11 July 1997

Computer Yiddish

I CAN'T SPELL. You may think this an odd failing in a writer. It's like being an accountant who can't count. But accountants don't have to count these days, and writers don't have to spell. Their computers do it for them.

I can imagine that there will even come a time – if it hasn't come already – when doctors will have no need to know anything about medicine. All they will need to do is punch symptoms into their computer for it to come up immediately with a diagnosis, prognosis and likely cure, if any, plus any side effects which might arise from the cure.

Similarly, rabbis faced with a *halachic* problem will no longer have to turn to higher authority. They will turn to their computer instead, though I am not sure why they should bother, because the answer will always be: 'No.'

My own computer, though I got it wholesale from a good Jewish trader – Stanley Kalms, in fact – is thoroughly goyish and doesn't know a word of Yiddish, nor any Hebrew for that matter. Thus I have only to press the 'spell' key, and expressions like *booba, zeida, yenta, shadchan, mechutan, shnorrer* and *shlemiel* are instantly changed to boob, zebra, yen, shallow, machismo, scorner and shnitzel.

Shortly before Rosh Hashanah last year I wrote the following to a friend:

Dear Shmuel,
Just a line to thank you for a lovely *Shabbos*.

15

Your wife Fruma is a real *eshes chayil*. What a cook! What a *nosh*! Her *gefilte* fish, *cholent, kugel, kishke, tzimmes* and *shtrudel* were out of this world. But are you sure the *parev* cream on the *lokshenh* pudding was really *parev*?

It was so delicious that I forgive her even if it wasn't.

You've got a lovely *mishpoche*. Your Soraleh, *kin eine hora*, was a *mechayeh* to look at, while your Moishele has the makings of a real *mensch*. Even your *shvigger* was not the *alte klafte* everyone says she is, but I'll bet your *schver, olov hasholem*, feels he's happier where he is. May she live *bisken hundert und tzwanzig*.

As for your *shul*, quite frankly it wasn't worth the *shlep*. They didn't stop *shmoozing* for a minute. It was as noisy as our *shtibl*, but not half as *heimish*.

Your *chazan* was toneless, your *rov* gormless, and your *gabboim* were brainless.

Even your *shammas* was a *shmo*. The *tallis* he gave me was an *alte shmatter*, with all the *tsitsis* gone, and I doubt if he knows a *chumash* from a *siddur*.

And you'd think, as a visitor from out of town, they would have given me *maftir*, or at least an *aliyah*, but what did they offer? *Hagboh* – while I was still convalescing from a double hernia! I think they did it on purpose, the *grobbers*.

As you know I'm not one to harbour *faribbles*, but a *meessa meshunah* would be too good for them.

Wishing you all a *ksivah v'chsimah toivah*, Chaim.

I pressed the 'spell' button, and this is what I got:

Dear Shovel,
Just a line to thank you for a lovely Shabby.

Your wife Fruity is a real Eschew Chaos. What a cook! What a niche! Her gehennah fish, chalet, kudos, kibble, times and shrivel were out of this world. But are you sure the partridge cream on the lockjaw pudding really was partridge?

It was so delicious that I forgive her even if it wasn't.

You've got a lovely mishmash. Your Sore, keen eider horn, was a mechanic to look at, while your Muesli has the makings of a real menace. Even your scarifier was not the ale klan everyone says she is, but I'll bet your shower, olive hashish, feels he's happier where he is. May she live to be bisexual, hunch-backed and tantalising.

As for your sump, quite frankly it wasn't worth the scrap. They didn't stop schooling for a minute. It was as noisy as our shamble, but not half as hellish.

Your chaser was toneless, your rob gormless, and your gabble were brainless.

Even your shames was a shoe. The tallies he gave me was an ale shatter, with all the tits gone, and I doubt if he knows a chump from a sicker.

And you'd think, as a visitor from out of town, they would have given me mafia, or at least an alias, but what did they offer? Haybox – while I was still convalescing from a double hernia! I think they did it on purpose, the robbers.

As you know I'm not one to harbour fairies, but a mishap miasma would be too good for them.

Wishing you all a kelvin vaccinal toad. Chain.

5 March 1993

Alive and kicking

IT IS ROUND about two in the afternoon. And I am sitting in my local watering-hole drinking a beer and reading a paper when in walks our local Gujarati newsagent and calls us all a bunch of *shnorrers* (beggars).

I was not offended by the remark because, for all I know, it may have been true but I was intrigued by his using it. I asked whether he had picked it up in Gujarat.

'Gujarat?' he said, 'it's English isn't it?' Which, of course, it is.

Now it so happens that the paper I was reading at the time was the *Daily Telegraph* and what should it have in the news pages but two articles, the one describing, and the other lamenting, the death of Yiddish.

17

Why the *Telegraph*, of all papers, should be interested in Yiddish was a mystery to me, and I could only conclude that the proprietor's wife, the lovely Barbara Amiel, is a closet Yiddishist.

I immediately folded my paper, finished my drink, went home and wrote to the paper to say that Yiddish had outlived all its obituarists and that even when 'the last Yiddish speaker should speak his last, Yiddish will always survive through the English language.'

The English themselves are slightly closed, which is possibly why I mix mostly with Jews, Scots, Welsh, Irish and Gujaratis.

The English language, however, is marvellously open which is why it is the language of some of the greatest writers, poets and dramatists in the history of the written word and why it has become the lingua franca of the literate world.

The notion of purity is alien to the English tongue. There is no academy to scrutinise new entries or give them English forms. The language is utterly promiscuous.

If it is short of an expression to describe a particular situation or give voice to a particular sentiment, it will not hesitate to borrow or steal from any language within earshot, including Yiddish – via American (American being a medium in which a word is on probation before aspiring to full membership of the English language).

However, English, though rich in most other respects, is fairly poor in dismissive expressions. This may be due to the basic civility of the English people. As a result, it has adopted, or is in the course of adopting, a great many expressions from Yiddish – which are almost custom-made for the purpose – such as *shmerel, shmendrik, shlemiel, shlemazel, shmok, shvantz, shloch, shlepper, shlumper* and, of course, *shnorrer*.

Splendid words all of them – and you don't even have to know what they mean. Their sounds speak for themselves, and they are not so much spoken as spat.

At which point, I must add that I myself have added a word to the Queen's English. It, too, begins with *sh* but, as befits my innocent ways, it is totally innocent in character. It is *shtieble* (sometimes rendered *shtibl*) and, although I have yet to hear Her Majesty use it in person, you will find it in the Oxford English dictionary, with the source duly acknowledged, though, sadly, the particular *shtiebl* (or *shtibl*) I referred to is no more.

All of which may show that Yiddish is not dead. But not being dead is not quite the same as being alive and if it is not, as yet, on a life-support machine, one has to admit that it is merely ticking over.

A living language not only lends but borrows and, since the war, Yiddish, which used to borrow and steal from everyone, everywhere, has hardly grown at all and has failed to adapt to the changing circumstances of Jewish life.

I have, for example, always felt that Yiddish was gravely deficient in terms of merriment. There are, as far as I know, only two Yiddish words for laughter – *gelechter* (laugh), and *shmeichel* (smirk), whereas in English we have laugh, smile, smirk, grin, chortle, chuckle, cackle, titter, giggle, snigger, snicker and guffaw, to say nothing of horse-laughs and belly-laughs.

This all suggests that, while Jews had a lot to quarrel about, they had little to laugh about, which was indeed the case. But if Yiddish had been living, rather than merely non-dead, it would have echoed the fact that we have arrived upon happier times.

Its failure to do so, I believe, arises out of the fact that, where Yiddish was the language of the street and the market-place, it is now almost exclusively the language of the *beis hamedresh* (prayer and study house) and the *yeshivah*, both of which tend to be changeless, and both of which regard laughter as subversive and un-*kosher*.

The God-fearing Jew, sadly, is not only straight-laced but also straight-faced.

12 December 1997

2
The Way We
Live Now . . .
Great Britain

'Thou shalt not be judgemental' has replaced
'Thou shalt not commit adultery' in the Ten
Commandments.

Miss Muffet and the C.R.E.

WHENEVER I CONTEMPLATE the work of the Commission for Racial Equality, I marvel that Britain has not been torn apart by race riots.

The CRE was formed under the 1976 Race Relations Act and its name speaks for itself, but it sometimes uses what powers it has, and even what powers it hasn't, to exacerbate race relations rather than improve them and, as one can see from the Carney case, it is pushing minority rights to the point where the rights of the majority could be impaired.

Middlesbrough, like many northern towns, has a large and hard-working Asian community, and although immigration has virtually stopped, the community has grown in size through natural increase. As a result, white children in some of the schools are now in a minority, for instance at the Abingdon Road Infants' School.

Katrice Carney, who is now nine, went to the school for two years. At first, she was one of only four white girls in her class. Then the number dropped to two.

'In the playground,' said Jenny Carney, her mother, 'the Asian girls all stuck together, playing their own games and speaking their own language. Katrice was left on her own.'

One day the child came home singing an old English nursery rhyme – in Hindi, which was the last straw, and her mother wrote to the local education authority to say that she wanted her daughter 'to go to a school where there will be a majority of white children, not Pakistani.'

The letter could have been more happily phrased, but it was the sort of reasonable step which any reasonable parent would have taken. It was, however, not reasonable enough for the Commission for Racial Equality, which last week took Jenny Carney to court on the grounds that she was in breach of the Race Relations Act.

If it was illegal for an English mother to want her daughter to have an English education in an English school among English children then there is something wrong with the law. The law, however, is not at fault, for the court upheld her aims. The CRE, however, was very much at fault for dragging her to court in the first place.

But wait. Would I have felt the same if the large majority at the Abingdon Road school had been Jewish and Katrice Carney had come home singing English nursery rhymes in Yiddish? I find it difficult to imagine such a possibility, but yes, I would.

In the early days of this century, during the years of mass Jewish immigration, most of the local authority schools in the East End of London had such a large majority of Jewish pupils that they closed early on Fridays and did not open at all on Jewish holidays. Even church schools were affected, and, for example, about 70 per cent of the pupils at St Stephen's, Spitalfields, were Jewish.

Jewish children did receive lessons in Judaism during the periods set aside for religious instruction, but there was otherwise no thought of inculcating anyone with a knowledge of Yiddish, or Hebrew, or Jewish history or folklore. If there had, Jewish parents would have been among the first to complain.

Jewish studies were pursued in *cheder* or Talmud Torah or *yeshivah*, but Jewish children were sent to school to learn English and to adapt to the ways of the host society. The six Jewish day schools in the East End which between them had 6,000 pupils (the Jews' Free School alone had 3,500), were devoted to the same purpose. Even adults spent what little spare time they had attending evening classes to make themselves into Englishmen of sorts.

One is reminded of the occasion when the late and beloved Barnet Janner, MP, found himself before a large Jewish East End audience and asked whether he should speak in Yiddish or English. 'English,' they replied in one voice. '*Yiddish kennen mir allein reiden.*' (Yiddish we can speak ourselves.)

To be sure, the England in which the Jewish newcomers made their home was not the England in which we live now. If it has deteriorated in some respects, it has improved in others and is certainly a more tolerant place. It seems to me, however, that the CRE is pushing its tolerance to intolerable lengths, for it is acting on the presumption that while it is natural and even desirable for newcomers to preserve their own identity and culture, it is somehow racist for any member of the host society to do the same.

Its attitude in fact is helping to make racism respectable and I sometimes feel it would be better for all concerned if the Race Relations Act and the CRE were abolished.

25 October 1991

Inertia and the Board of Deputies

THE BOARD OF Deputies of British Jews came into being in 1760 as a joint committee of Sephardim and Ashkenazim for the presentation of a loyal address on the accession of George III.

As there wasn't a further accession until 1820, it was not kept very busy, until, with the passage of years, it threw itself into the struggle for Jewish emancipation.

Then, as British Jewry grew in size, and Britain itself grew in importance, it became increasingly involved in protecting the interests of Jews in other parts of the globe. Its success was such that, when South African and Australian Jews eventually formed their own boards, they were based largely on the British model and, when the latter celebrated its bicentenary in 1960, it could look back on two centuries of solid achievement.

But then a few years later little Israel became larger Israel or, as some would have it, 'Greater Israel', and she found herself controlling the destinies of over one million Arabs who had no wish to live under Jewish rule.

The Board of Deputies, which for more than 200 years had been concerned with the Jew as victim, could not adapt itself to the phenomenon of the Jew as oppressor and it therefore resorted to a policy of undignified silence.

Well, that silence has now been broken by no less a person than Mrs June Jacobs, chairman of the Board's foreign affairs committee, who has declared publicly that what is happening in the occupied territories is 'quite appalling and absolutely horrific'.

She was rapped on the knuckles by the president, Dr Lionel

25

Kopelowitz, who told her that she cannot make public statements inconsistent with the Board's policy. Dr Kopelowitz is, I am told, a good physician. If so, the time he devotes to his office is a loss to medicine which is not matched by any gain to the community, for what, after all, is the Board's policy on this vexatious issue?

It was summed up by Mr Michael Fidler, a former Tory MP and an elder statesman of the Board, who declared ponderously: 'At this time of grave anxiety in Israel, it behoves Anglo-Jewry to be united.'

It does indeed, but united behind whom and for what? To deny what everyone knows to be true?

What he meant, I think, was inertia. Know nothing, do nothing and, above all, say nothing. But people who say nothing also say something, for silence in the face of injustice is a form of condonation.

I have to use my words carefully, for anything I may say in praise of Mrs Jacobs (and I could say a great deal) is unlikely to endear her to her colleagues – and could be used in evidence against her. But it is generally accepted, even by some of her severest critics, that she is the most intelligent, most articulate and most far-seeing member of the Board. She is its saving grace.

Could anyone seriously challenge her views on the events in the occupied territories? In fact, no one did, and what occasioned the displeasure of the Board was not so much what she said, as where she said it – in public, on the BBC. *Gevalt!* (Help!)

Her crime, if I may sum it up, is that she knowingly and wilfully displayed to the outside world that there are still Jews around with a Jewish conscience.

One does not expect the Board to be courageous, but what is unforgivable is its determination to stifle courage in others. Mrs Jacobs is not the only victim. The chief rabbi was also attacked when he suggested that the Israeli invasion of Lebanon (in the summer of 1982) did not carry all the hallmarks of benevolence and wisdom.

The Board's policy of inertia is, in fact, not one of inertia, but of tacit support for a *status quo* which is challenged by a large body of Israelis – including its foreign minister – and which, in my opinion, should be challenged by every Jew concerned with the future of Israel and the well-being of her people.

If Mr Peres can differ from Mr Shamir, Mrs Jacobs can, I think, be forgiven for differing from Dr Kopelowitz.

There are still occasions when the Board has to intercede with the government on behalf of Jews in Soviet Russia or in Muslim lands; but what moral weight can it have if it has resigned all moral responsibility?

29 January 1988

Be fruitful and multiply

THANK GOD OUR rabbis don't have to be celibate – they are trouble enough being married.

My thoughts are inspired by the story of the Rev Eamonn Casey, former Bishop of Galway, who recently abandoned his see after allegations – subsequently admitted to – that he had fathered a child some 17 years ago. There is, apparently, no statute of limitations in such things for men of the cloth and I gather the poor chap has left Ireland to become a missionary in Peru.

Rabbis in such ethical quandaries tend to have it easier in that respect. If they are forced to move at all, they are either re-employed locally or go to America, which may suggest that we take a more charitable view of human frailties.

I don't know how copulation came to be a sin among Christians when it has always been a duty among Jews. And if Catholic clergymen cannot marry, Jewish clergymen are virtually debarred from being single.

'Be fruitful and multiply,' is the first of the commandments. Jewish law states emphatically that every man is obliged to fulfil the duty of procreation and that he who fails to do so is virtually guilty of bloodshed.

The ruling was laid down by the great second-century sage, Ben Azai, who, however, failed to marry, which shows that whichever way one approaches the subject, it offers infinite scope for casuistry.

27

Ben Azai's excuse was that he was too devoted to the Torah to have a mind for anything else. 'Let the earth be peopled by others,' he said, which is but another way of saying: 'Let all the others do the dirty work.'

(All these rules, I may add, applied, and apply, only to men, the presumption being that where men do their duties, women can be relied upon to do theirs.)

The one Jewish sect which not only condoned celibacy, but prescribed it, were the Essenes and they, not surprisingly, died out.

The obligation to procreate was taken so seriously that at one time the Beth Din had the power to compel men over the age of 20 to marry, though this practice was eventually abandoned, presumably on the principle that you can take a horse to the water, but can't make him drink (or whatever).

The attitude of our sages to sex has been consistently brilliant. They knew their fellows Jews. Say 'Thou Shalt Not,' and there is every likelihood that they will. Say 'Thou Shalt,' and there is more than a chance that they won't. And by proclaiming sex to be a duty, rather than a pleasure, they have been able to keep it under reasonable control.

Which does not mean that Judaism ever sanctioned debauchery, or anything like it. The Seventh Commandment (or 'the tricky one', as it is sometimes called) still stands. The rule is abstinence outside marriage and continence within it, which is demanding enough and, as Maimonides observed: 'No prohibition in the Torah is as arduous as that of forbidden unions and illicit sexual relations.' (I suspect he wrote it in his youth, or he may have had an exceedingly attractive aunt.)

Which brings me back to the clergy. When the news about the bishop first broke, Ireland was stunned. But then one man after another came to his defence with the plea that he was only human. Well, certainly, siring a child is one way of proving one's humanity.

Any creed which demands a vow of celibacy from its clergy is asking for trouble. Judaism itself demands no more of the rabbi than it does of the laymen, but we – the laymen – expect him to live up to those demands, for in setting up as a rabbi, he claims to be holier than us, and we have to take him at his word.

We accord him a trust and a social standing we rarely accord others, plus a fairly enviable level of economic security, and we give him an access to our homes and our lives which we do not give others.

In return, we feel entitled to regard virtue as part of his stock in trade and expect him to be good on our behalf, to perform duties we may neglect and to abstain from prohibitions in which we may indulge.

In most cases rabbis live up to these expectations, which is why we are so shocked when they don't. And in recent years we have had more than our share of shocks.

The normal duties a rabbi has to perform are, in a way, secondary. Almost anyone can marry the living, bury the dead, conduct a service, give a sermon and even aspire to a bit of learning, but not everyone can be a *mensh* (decent human being).

And where a rabbi, no matter how brilliant he may be in other respects, fails to be a *mensh* he not only betrays his Maker, but his fellow men.

15 May 1992

Lesbian marriages

THE ANNOUNCEMENT BY Rabbi Elizabeth Sarah that she was proposing to officiate at a lesbian 'marriage' – albeit in a 'private capacity' – has caused a public furore.

I daresay the Catholic Bishop of Argyll was also acting in a private – very private – capacity when he ran off with one woman after siring a son with another. But nothing an ordained minister of religion says or does is strictly private, for his, or her, actions and utterances are taken to be expressions of, or a reflection on, his or her religion.

Rabbi Sarah seems to have been unaware of this fact, and was apparently so convinced of her own rectitude that she was not even remotely aware of the feelings of the congregations she was addressing.

She was well meaning and perfectly sincere, but one can be sincere and well meaning and still be utterly wrong. And, as she has never made any secret of her views, one can only wonder why she was asked to preach.

Where does the Reform synagogue movement find such people? Do they volunteer their services or is there a special committee to seek out men – or, more usually, women – who are likely to make a laughing stock out of the whole movement?

I used to think that Julia Neuberger was the best living argument against women rabbis, but Mrs Neuberger is almost the embodiment of Orthodoxy compared to Ms Sarah. And, if the former has set back the cause of women rabbis by a century, the latter, given half the chance, could set it back by a millennium.

The Reform movement has since distanced itself from Ms Sarah and has ordered her not to proceed with the marriage ceremony, but it has not quite made up its mind about the issue she raised. It merely said she was untimely; it did not say she was wrong. It is too inhibited by faddish dogmas to say any such thing.

'The subject of same-sex ceremonies is a complex and difficult one,' said Neville Sassienie, chairman of the Reform Synagogues of Great Britain. 'Until this year, it has not been widely discussed in RSGB circles, and no policy on the matter exists.'

The subject is, on the contrary, an extremely simple one. People of the same sex cannot marry for the simple reason that they are of the same sex. If they wish to cohabit permanently, for better for worse, for richer for poorer, in sickness and in health, to love and to cherish till death do them part, that is their business.

But I cannot understand why people should want the blessing of a faith which regards their way of life with abhorrence, and why a synagogal body which claims, however tenuously, to adhere to Jewish tradition should find itself in a moral dilemma over the issue.

The essential difference between Orthodoxy and Reform is that, among the former, the laymen are more progressive than their rabbis, while among the latter, the rabbis are more progressive than the laymen – and, it seems to me, they tend to progress in the wrong direction.

We are told that the Assembly of (Reform) Rabbis is, even now, contemplating the issue of same-sex commitment ceremonies. The fact that they should even be giving serious thought to the matter shows how far they have moved from the known views of their own congregants, or even the simple dictates of common sense.

The Reform movement has always claimed to temper faith with reason, and the claim, on the whole, has been amply justified. It is now, however, being pulled into the murky waters of unreason and, where people are faced with the choice between the old unreason – as preached in Orthodox synagogues – and the new – as preached by Reform – they will opt for the old. They will do so if only because it *is* old, tried, familiar and, not infrequently, benign.

Let me, therefore, pose some straight questions.

Does the Reform movement still believe in marriage as a sacrament to be celebrated exclusively between man and woman?

Does it still believe in the family – with all its faults – as the very basis of Jewish life?

Does it take tradition to mean an adherence to usage, or to mean what the Assembly of Rabbis takes it to mean?

Does it still embrace anything which might be vaguely described as a stable creed?

Or, on the other hand, is it merely a friendly society with fluid perceptions which lets out platforms to anyone with a bee in his bonnet or a bat in her belfry?

11 October 1996

Homosexuality and Rabbi Lawrence Kushner

TWO WEEKS AGO, I made the not unreasonable proposition that two people of the same sex cannot marry because they are of the same sex.

I did not question their right to live together. I did not even suggest that such a relationship was less than wholesome, but I was nevertheless assailed from all sides, or, as they used to put it in Yiddish, *Oy af mir, goy af mir, und kleiniker sheigetzel eich af mir.*

None of which worried me, but when I was actually praised by the *rebbe* of our local *shtiebl* in the course of his sermon, my conviction faltered. I might even have come round to the possibility that I had it wrong, but for an article by a Rabbi Lawrence Kushner, in the latest issue of *Manna*, the publication of the Manor House Society.

The article is in defence of homosexuality, for which there may, or may not be an argument, but Rabbi Kushner – who, perhaps needless to say, is American – tries to show that it is entirely compatible with Judaism and, as always when one has an impossible case to propound, he begins by debasing the very language of debate.

Thus, for example, he dismisses the thought that homosexuality is abnormal, unnatural or perverse and concludes: 'Ultimately the "unnatural" argument turns out to be merely a thin disguise for saying, "I don't like homosexuals." ' He then goes on to cite this or that rabbi or psychiatrist to dismiss any suggestion that the homosexual lifestyle is in any way unwholesome, unseemly, or unhealthy, and gives Aids only a passing mention as if it were but a passing irrelevance.

If one selects one's authorities with sufficient care, no matter how unauthoritative or unrepresentative they may be, one can, of course, prove or disprove any case.

It is only when Rabbi Kushner tries to show that homosexuality is not in conflict with Jewish teaching that he casts around with something like desperation. There are parts of scripture which are so vague and ambiguous that they lend themselves to every imaginable interpretation, and not a few unimaginable ones.

The same cannot be said of strictures on homosexuality, which are clear. Rabbi Kushner, nevertheless, comes up with 'cultic prostitution' – 'widespread throughout the ancient Near East, with both genders servicing male worshippers.'

Which is to say homosexuality was forbidden because it was associated with idol worship, but then so were the cultic sacrifices which fill Leviticus and, as if aware this argument does not hold water, he goes on to quote somebody called Bradley Shavit Artson:

'There is not a single case in the [Hebrew Bible], or in any rabbinic legal literature until the middle of the twentieth century, that deals with the homosexual act in the context of homosexual love. Every Biblical case deals with heterosexuals who engage in homosexual acts.'

In other words, if you don't have it both ways it's perfectly *kosher*. But wait, there is more:

'Our sages did not speak of the constitutional homosexual because they were unaware that such a person could exist. The idea of two men or two women loving each other, living together, nurturing each other and – in that context – making love has gained recognition only in modern times. The Torah did not prohibit what it did not know.'

If Bradley Shavit Artson and Rabbi Kushner can believe that, they'll believe anything.

I'm familiar with the casuistry of the Orthodox *pilpul* (hair splitting) but it is the epitome of honesty and reason compared to the Reform variety.

Rabbi Lawrence Kushner – could he have been named after D H Lawrence? – ends with a heart-warming account of how he consecrated the marriage of two lesbians in his own synagogue:

'They looked radiant, joyous, in love. Out of the corner of my eye I even caught sight of one of the brides' mothers. She was beaming with pride . . .'

I can imagine the scene with people crowding round her after the ceremony to wish her *mazeltov*, and she replying: 'Please God by you . . .'

There is a dénouement. Rabbi Kushner describes a naming ceremony in his synagogue for a baby born to a lesbian couple by artificial insemination. There could be no doubt about the Jewishness of the child, he adds, 'who, after all, had not one, but two, Jewish mothers.'

As Lady Bracknell might have said: 'To have one Jewish mother may be a joy, but two are a misfortune.'

Rabbi Kushner may have done me out of a job. I shall have no further need to attack the idea of homosexual marriage while he is around to defend it.

25 October 1996

Politically incorrect!

I WAS RECENTLY invited to address the fiftieth-anniversary meeting of the Leeds Council of Christians and Jews. It will be another 50 years before I'm asked back again, if indeed I should be asked back at all, because half the audience couldn't understand a word I said. What was worse, the other half could.

In the past, Christians and Jews have made common cause against religious bigotry and intolerance, and I argued that, while the battle on that front has not – and never will be – won, we had new, more serious enemies to contend with in the form of secular bigotry and the forces of dissolution and decay. As if to confirm my point, the very day I addressed the CCJ, the Church of England published a report giving its blessing to couples living in sin. The report, believe it or not, was called 'Something to celebrate,' and I used it as a prime example of dissolution. As there was a large sprinkling of clergymen in the audience, with a rabbi on one side of me and a monsignor on the other, I thought my remarks would be greeted with cheers and amens and loud cries of 'Hallelujah'. Instead, I noticed that those people who were not adjusting their deaf-aids were exchanging looks of dismay. The Jews were unhappy that I was attacking the Christians. The Christians were unhappy to be attacked. But, as the lions in ancient Rome may have said, if you can't maul a Christian, whom can you maul?

I had misjudged the occasion. As Solomon said, there is a time for everything. I was addressing a golden jubilee which, as its very name might suggest, is a time for jubilation, celebration and congratulation.

It is, of course, a *chutzpah* for someone like me, a Jew who wasn't even born in this country, to attack the established Church. But precisely because it is established, we are all affected by its ethos – or lack of one.

It is difficult for Jews to remain Jewish among Christians who are ceasing to be Christian. Or, to use a familiar Yiddish expression, *vi es Christelt zech, azei Yiddelt zech.*

(As Christians go, so do the Jews – meaning, essentially, that they are all going to the devil.)

A woman in the audience reminded me that fornication was not the only sin, nor the worst one. She was, of course, right, but the family is the particular province of the church – by which term I include the synagogue – and if the church should abandon all efforts to preserve its integrity, which it appears to be doing, then the whole of civil society is at risk.

A young Anglican canon, who addressed me more in sorrow than anger, recalled the words of Jesus: 'Judge not, that ye be not judged.' Our rabbis have said the same thing, albeit in different words, and they are both wrong. We should judge, and should be judged.

Which brings me to one of the ugliest and most fashionable words of our time, 'judgemental,' and its close cousin, 'confrontational'. The first means that, if we see something wrong, we shouldn't say outright that it is wrong. The second means we should not confront a wrongdoer with the results of his wrongdoing.

Both are among the silliest ideas ever to have acquired common currency, yet Thou Shalt Not Be Judgemental has replaced Thou Shalt Not Commit Adultery in the Ten Commandments.

The language of censure and reproof has been banished from religious debate, and being judgemental is about the only sin still recognised as sinful by the Church of England. Even if we should hesitate to judge and condemn, we are under no obligation to condone, and even less to bless.

Clergymen are the linesmen of morality. The least they can do is to indicate where people have gone wrong. It now seems that they are abandoning even that minimal function.

Forgive them, O Father, for they know not that they have sinned – but how can they know if even the church won't tell them?

Where the church used to condemn the sin and love the sinner, it has come round to sanctifying the sin. And gratuitously so, for those people who choose to live together as man and wife outside marriage are perfectly content to do so without the benefit of clergy. The news that it is all *kosher* and that they are no longer living in sin may possibly even spoil their pleasure.

There was a time when one could look forward to a whiff of fire and brimstone from the pulpit. Now all one gets is placebos.

Come back, Amos! Rise again, Savonarola! The world hath need of thee.

16 June 1995

The walled garden

ABOUT A YEAR ago, I suggested that the one certain way of avoiding the problems that can arise out of Jewish divorce law was to live in sin. My advice was no sooner given than taken, or perhaps it was merely anticipated. For a new survey conducted by the Institute of Jewish Affairs shows that nearly 40 per cent of Jewish men have non-Jewish partners, and by partners I do not necessarily mean wives.

A connubial partnership, as distinct from a commercial one, is an association involving limited liability, and if it goes bankrupt, one can assume a new one the next day without suffering any particular pains or penalties, hence its present popularity.

As my mother tongue was Yiddish, the term 'partner' immediately evokes the word *shutef*, which has purely commercial connotations, and not always happy ones. A *shutef* was someone you worked with, but did not always trust – which, I suppose, could also apply to a spouse, except that the word 'partner', as currently used, has sexual undertones, or rather, overtones, which *shutef* plainly doesn't – or didn't – and I would prefer to revive an ancient expression made famous by our patriarchs, namely, concubine.

The term 'concubine', as used in the Bible, is a quasi-wife, but it can apply equally to quasi-husbands, and it does clearly imply living openly together without the benefit of clergy or of lawyers, or even of caterers. (I suspect that the cost of a catered affair may be the cause of not a few uncatered ones.) And come to think of it, it's a way of having something like a wife, without having anything like a mother-in-law.

36

Where, however, does this leave Jewish women? On the shelf, I'm afraid, for as the IJA survey shows, most of them prefer to stay in the fold, which means that many of them will remain single. There is nothing new in this. Jewish women have always been more conservative, and more loyal to their faith, than their menfolk – and this in spite of the handicaps imposed upon them by tradition.

Indeed, one can almost regard the handicaps as a measure of their steadfastness, for had they been a bit less loyal, they would have shrugged off their handicaps long ago.

The irony of it all is that where men marry out of the faith, they constitute a net loss, while women who do so can constitute a net gain, for in *halachic* terms their children – unless they are actually raised as Christians – will always be Jewish and, where they have daughters, so will their grandchildren.

Yet the very expressions, 'marrying out' or 'intermarriage' or 'out-marriage', or call it what you will, are becoming anachronisms, for the main threat to Jewish continuity lies not so much in intermarriage as in non-marriage and the decline of family life.

The family can have its drawbacks, and its virtues are, sometimes, overestimated. Samuel Butler, to give but one example, condemned the efforts 'to prolong family connections unduly and to make people hang together artificially.'

Among Jews, especially, family life can become so close as to stifle all energy and form a breeding ground for neurosis. Yet with all its imperfections, it is the prime source of all social stability and cohesion and has yet to be replaced by anything better.

The family is a walled garden in which the young flourish and the old decline, and functions as a lasting source of mutual support. Remove it, and one is left to the caring professions, who can, within limits, be useful enough as a prop to the family, but are no substitute for it.

Judaism, in particular, presumes a family so that the Sabbath, for example – perhaps the most sublime of all Jewish institutions – is a bleak affair if spent in isolation.

No faith is so sustained by the family, and none so sustains it. Many of our celebrations and usages are built round the family, and yet even people who have abandoned all vestiges of Jewish belief and discarded all traditions somehow retain something of their Jewishness through staying together as a family. Judaism

37

cannot flourish, or even survive, where the family is in terminal decline.

One can only draw comfort from the thought that social excesses often correct themselves, and in another generation or two people may discover that families, with all their drawbacks, are a greater source of happiness than concubinage with all its joys.

16 February 1996

Depravity – the cause of our ills?

IN VICTORIAN TIMES, men were held responsible for everything that befell them, and although it was accepted that some had more than their fair share of misfortune, and others of luck, it was generally agreed that their fate lay in their own hands.

We have now moved to the other extreme and are asked to believe that man is responsible for nothing and society for everything. There has of late been something of a counter-reaction and the word is beginning to spread that it is possible for people to help themselves, that hard work can carry its own rewards and idleness its own penalties.

Yet no political leader has dared to utter the thought that there is also something to be said for moral conduct and that many of our ills are due less to deprivation than to depravity. The chief constable of Manchester has done so and the skies have fallen in upon him, but then the police are expected to deal with the consequences of moral decay and not their causes. He was speaking of Aids and said, in plain and forceful terms, that if ever a calamity was self-inflicted, this was it. Can anyone seriously deny it?

There can, of course, be innocent victims, the most obvious being haemophiliacs and others who may have picked up the infection in the course of a blood transfusion, but the overwhelming majority of cases are due not to any chance factor, but to drug abuse, promiscuity and, above all, sodomy, and the sympathy one feels for the victims and their families should not blind us to this fact.

There are laws against drug abuse which, however ineffective, at least suggest public disapproval. There are no laws against promiscuity or sodomy – nor should there be – but there isn't even an attempt to suggest that either one or the other could be wrong. Stick to one partner if you can, says the Health Ministry, lamely; use a condom if you can't.

One does not expect the government to buy air time to broadcast the Seventh Commandment, or to quote Leviticus to the effect that 'Thou shalt not lie with mankind as with womankind,' but there is not even a concerted effort to counter inducements to depravity.

A few months ago I switched on the television and, a little incredulously, I found myself watching what was virtually a party political broadcast on behalf of gay liberation.

Every university now has its gay society, which attracts no more comment or disapproval than the tiddlywinks society – one university union recently held a 'Lesbian, Gay and Bisexual Week' and in some of our schools religion is being phased out and homosexuality as an alternative life style phased in.

Aids is by far the deadliest venereal disease, but syphilis was deadly enough in its time. In its tertiary stages it was worse than death, and if promiscuity had been as rife in earlier centuries as it is now, it could have decimated the population of Europe.

I will no doubt be reminded that people in earlier centuries were not always saintly, and that the Victorians in particular, who are so often held up as exemplars of public morality, could also indulge in private vice; that we in our time are at least open, honest and frank about our habits, and that whatever we are, by God, we're not hypocrites, as if men who have no standards at all are somehow superior to those who have, but fail to live up to them.

One also reads frequent references to the 'guilt-ridden lives' of the Victorians, which almost suggests that one is better off without a sense of guilt at all.

Guilt is to the soul what pain is to the body. It is a signal that one is doing something harmful, the only difference being that what is harmful to the body hurts instantly, while what is harmful to the soul can initially be rather pleasant.

The guilt comes later, sometimes much later, not infrequently in old age. A sense of guilt or, if you prefer, a sense of shame, may not always stop people doing things they shouldn't, but there is every chance that they will do them less often.

Morals, or at least sexual morals, have in recent years been consigned to philosophers, theologians and biblical exegists. They have become a matter of life and death and may suggest the truth of Goethe's saying: *Alle Schuld rächt sich auf Erden* – all guilt is punished on earth.

26 December 1986

The killing of Jamie Bulgar

IT IS IMPOSSIBLE these days to read the papers or watch the news without a shudder.

A snake will strike when it is threatened, a jackal will pounce when it is hungry, but men can murder and maim for no reason at all. And it is infinitely worse when children do the same, for we all like to think of children as innocent, but how can children remain innocent when the society around them is depraved?

David Sheppard, the Anglican Bishop of Liverpool, has argued that we are all to blame, and in a sense he is right. Yet in a deeper, less obvious sense he is wrong, and dangerously wrong, for where we are all to blame then nobody is to blame.

The churches have always hesitated to condemn sinners, but they have reached the point where they are reluctant even to condemn sin. They have tended to ascribe every form of evil to social deprivation, so that censure and reproof have all but vanished from their vocabulary.

The Labour Party, which used to argue in the same terms, has finally come to recognise evil as evil and that serious crimes call for severe punishment.

There is no sign of the churches coming to their senses. 'Faith in the Cities,' published by the Church of England in 1985, though rich in compassion, was poor in sense. For it tended to blame the government for most of the ills of society and looked principally to the government for a cure.

The only senior religious figure I can recall finding fault with the document was the then chief rabbi, Sir Immanuel Jakobovits. In his critique, Sir Immanuel, as he then was, drew on Jewish teaching and, even more, on Jewish experience, to suggest that there was such a thing as personal responsibility. He was reviled for it, but he was right then, and he is even more right now.

Yet one can hardly blame religious institutions when we live in what is substantially a godless society and, if the churches have lost their authority, nothing has taken their place.

There is no discipline in the schools, not because it is impossible to enforce, but because they have abandoned the means of enforcement.

The family, which is at the core of every stable society, is not only in decline but under attack. No stigma attaches to illegitimate children and the single-parent family is not only becoming the norm but, to some eyes, the ideal.

Any young girl who wants a home of her own need only get pregnant and she will acquire one, more or less instantly, out of public funds. What sort of children can such a child bring up? Lord Rees-Mogg has argued in *The Times* that 'if we want children to know right from wrong, we should first teach them to pray.'

I have much sympathy with his argument but it is a little like saying if we want children to behave, we should first teach them to be good. How does one go about it?

The prime medium of instruction – if one may call it that – in most Western countries is television. In Britain, the average family watches 35 hours of television a week. As there are now little more than 35 hours to the working week, and as most people work under 48 weeks in the year, it means that the average Briton spends more time in front of the screen than he does at work.

There are some superb programmes on television, but not every night, and certainly not every hour of the night.

During a recent illness, I spent an evening switching from channel to channel – we are a deprived household and have only four – and soon lost count of the incidence of murder, mayhem, rape, sodomy and common-or-garden fornication. Even the news bulletins displayed a good deal more mutilation and gore than was strictly necessary.

The worst transmitted by the networks, however, does not compare to the worst obtainable from the video shops.

One can also, of course, see a great many dreadful things in the newspapers, but they, at least, imply the ability to read and call for the effort of reading. The chronic television viewer is passive, a mere receptacle, like a terminal patient on a saline drip.

After a time, the shadows on the screen, with all the evils they purvey, become more real than the actual world outside. We have allowed television to become the teacher, the preacher, the exemplar, the guide.

In that sense, and in that sense only, we are, as the Rev David Sheppard has said, 'all to blame'.

26 February 1993

Political correctness

THE FACT THAT the Jewish Socialist Group (the JSG) has received a grant of £56,000 (the LSD) from the Greater London Council (the GLC) has caused a great deal of agitation in the Anglo-Jewish Establishment (the AJE). Dr Jacob Gewirtz, defence spokesman of the Board of Deputies (the BoD), has described the grant as 'a slap in the face' (oh me, oh my!), and others have denounced it in even more vehement terms.

Three principal schools seem to have emerged on the matter.

The first insists that the JSG shouldn't have asked for the LSD.

The second, that it shouldn't have taken it.

The third, that it should give it back.

I represent a fourth school of thought, which feels that it should have asked for more. In other words, if the LSD is indeed 'a slap in the face', we should turn the other cheek.

The GLC has been scattering largesse as if there were no

42

tomorrow (which, in the case of the GLC, there won't be), everybody's been rushing for its share of the goodies, and the JSG can hardly be blamed for doing the same.

The LSD, I should perhaps add, is allocated by the Ethnic Minorities Committee (the EMC) of the GLC. I don't know how ethnic the JSG is, but as far as minority status goes it is un-impeachable, and given its size I would say that the grant of £56,000 should work out at just over £1,000 per member, which might pay for a lunch or two, but which isn't much compared to the fortunes allocated to, say, the Black Lesbian Single Parent Collective.

A Jewish *Women's* Socialist Group, one feels, would have done better, Jewish *gay* women would have done better still; *black* Jewish gay women would have hit the jackpot. The JSG should change their sex, or their membership, or their disposition (or preferably all three) and try again.

I believe that the JSG is the only Jewish organisation to have received a direct grant, which is surprising, for I am told that the GLC employs special agents who lie in wait for the unwary and stuff large cheques into their startled hands; and that anyone who is, or looks as if he might be, or who may be construed as being a member of a minority, or who is engaged in an endeavour which can only have a minority appeal (such as teaching Yiddish to Bangladeshis) will automatically receive a grant of many thousands of pounds, unless he informs the GLC, in writing, that he doesn't want one.

What is more surprising, even sinister, is the fact that one of the smallest – indeed, minuscule minorities going has been overlooked altogether. I refer to the Glum (as opposed to Gay), Bearded Jewish-Scottish Columnists of Lithuanian Extraction (GBJSCLE), which, for all its impeccable credentials, has not received a penny of public – or private – money, and I feel so strongly on the matter that I have addressed the following letter to the EMC of the GLC.

Dear Comrades,
I write on behalf of the GBJSCLE collective, of which, no doubt, you will not have heard and which may in itself be a proof of how minor we are, or rather I am, for were I to be more minor than I am, I would cease to be altogether.
My wife, I'm afraid is but a common-or-garden woman (as

distinct from the Greenham Common sort), but a woman she undoubtedly is, and a Jewish one to boot. She stems from Stamford Hill in the blessed borough of Hackney, home of ethnicity at its most ethnic, where even whites have claims to a blackness of sorts. My children are likewise Jewish, two of them female, and three of them minors in their own right, and we are all of us, whether as individuals or as a family, prepared to combat fascism, racism, sexism and any other ism you may care to name.

I am also a founder and life-member of the Royal Society for the Prevention of Cruelty to Columnists (the RSPCC), which seeks to defend Jewish columnists against calumny. It is not generally known, but until recently whole pages of the Jewish press have been given over to attacks on columnists, especially of the bearded Scottish-Lithuanian variety, for no better reason than that they gave voice to opinions which not infrequently left them in a minority of one, a matter which in itself should be worthy of commendation, commiseration and, above all, compensation.

It has even been rumoured that he/they are in the pay of the PLO, whereas, in fact, he/they are not even in the pay of the GLC, which is in itself a claim to minority status; and I would therefore be grateful if you would be good enough to let me have, under plain cover, a large quantity of pound notes (marks, Swiss francs and dollars will also do nicely, but not shekels).

Up the Revolution,
Comrade Chaim Bermant,
pp the GBJSCLE Collective.

11 November 1983

The Singer not the song

THE SINGER'S PRAYER Book, or 'Old Faithful', as I tend to think of it, will be celebrating its centenary next year, but there is a danger that it may not last long into its second century.

When I first came across it as a child, it struck me as being not quite kosher. It lacked the black covers, the large format, the yellowing pages and the mouldering edges of the devotional books I had become familiar with.

Everything associated with the sort of Judaism into which I was raised had a used, careworn look to it, whereas Singer's, with its crisp, clean, rosy-edged pages, verged on the smart. It was also neat and compact, with navy-blue covers, but what made it seem veritably goyish was the English translation.

I couldn't at the time quite understand the point of the English. The prayers were, after all, addressed to God, who presumably spoke Hebrew, and I came to appreciate the quality of the translation only when I was able to understand the original Hebrew. Thereafter, I became devoted to the book, as I still am.

The Rev Simeon Singer, who gave his name to the work, was obviously a master of both Hebrew and English, but when it came to the Psalms – which are the glory of our liturgy – he had the good sense to resort to the translation available in the King James Bible.

The first edition of Singer's was produced under the imprimatur of Chief Rabbi Nathan Marcus Adler and was styled the 'Authorised Prayer Book of the United Hebrew Congregations of the British Empire'.

Some of the passages became archaic and small revisions were introduced under the authority of Chief Rabbi Hertz, and again under Chief Rabbi Brodie. An entirely new centenary edition, with a new format, is now being prepared under the authority of Lord Jakobovits.

And not before time, for the supremacy of Old Faithful is being threatened even in London synagogues by the intrusion of an American interloper called the *ArtScroll Siddur*, which appeared in 1984 and has already gone into numerous editions.

It is a handsome publication with a rather gaudy exterior, and beautifully laid out, and may be readily recommended to anyone who can see but cannot read. Others may find it disappointing, for like many American products, it is a triumph of packaging over content.

The first edition of Singer's acknowledges 'the generosity and public spirit of Mrs Nathaniel Montefiore by whom the entire cost of production has been defrayed.' The acknowledgements in the ArtScroll Siddur (or ASS for short) extend to over two pages in terms that strike one as fulsome even by American standards:

'He came to a new world, but maintained his eternal loyalties. *Mitzvos* (good deeds) were his love, kindness was his passion. Integrity was the foundation of his dealings, Torah was the soul that infused his every activity.'

And that is only the half of it. It gets worse as it goes on.

But they, so to speak, are merely the plaques on the outside wall. It is the interior that troubles me.

The *siddur* contains an 'overview' and commentary, both of which are a good idea; but neither contains a single original thought, as if anything new were in itself un*kosher*, and where the editor does attempt to make his own contribution, his sentiments are banal and his language is fatuous. But worst of all is the translation. Not that it is inaccurate, for considerable scholarship has obviously been brought to bear on it, but it is almost wholly devoid of imagination or poetry.

First read this: 'The Lord is my shepherd, I shall not want. He maketh me to lie down in green pastures, he leadeth me beside the still waters. He restoreth my soul, he guideth me in the paths of righteousness for his name's sake. Yea, though I walk through the valley of the shadow of death, I fear no evil . . .'

And then this: 'Hashem is my Shepherd. I shall not lack. In lush meadows He lays me down, beside tranquil waters He leads me. He restores my soul. He leads me on paths of justice for His Name's sake. Though I walk in the valley overshadowed by death, I will fear no evil . . .'

If you prefer the latter version then the ASS is your – *glatt kosher* – meat.

The more discriminating worshipper will cleave unto Singer, but the chief rabbi had better be quick with his new edition.

24 November 1989

3
The Way We
Live Now . . .
Israel

*We have prayed for two thousand years for the
restoration of Zion . . . without preparing for the
possibility that our prayers may be answered.*

Could you take a letter?

'HELLO, YANKEL? HOW are you? I hear you're going to Israel.'

'You want me to take a letter.'

'How did you guess? But you can also do me a favour while you're at it. You know my married daughter – the one with the bad back?'

'You want me to take an orthopaedic bed.'

'No, but you're getting warm, which is to say, she's been suffering from the cold. Winters in Jerusalem can be worse than in London. I want you to take a duvet.'

'You expect me to take a *duvet*!'

'Yankel, it's as light as a feather and I'll pack it so it won't be bigger than a *matzah* box . . .'

'Yankel?'

'Who told you?'

'Told me what?'

'That I'm going to Israel?'

'You going to Israel? I didn't know, but if you are going, there's something you can do for me. You know my son in Kfar Saba? He's forgotten what his mother's jam tastes like —'

'Do you expect me to *shlep* jam to Israel?'

'Yankel, he's been *three* years in the army – one of them in Lebanon.'

'I'll take one small jar.'

'A biggish small jar.'

'No.'

'All right then, we'll compromise. A smallish big jar . . .'

'Yankel, did you hear about my father? I don't suppose you did, because we don't talk about it.'

'Didn't he settle in Israel last year?'

'That was the good news. The bad news is that the old joker is getting married again – at 86.'

'So what's wrong with that?'

'To a dolly bird of 35, if you don't mind – with seven children.'

'So please God she'll have an eighth, perhaps even a ninth. You're going to the wedding, I suppose?'

'How can I? My business would collapse if I was away for five minutes. But I'd like to send him a wedding present —'

'I'm over —'

'Nothing big. You know these new compact videos they make – it would fit into a *tallis*-bag . . .'

'Yankel? I bet everyone you know's been pestering you to take a little something to Israel, which is why I don't want to bother you—'

'Then why are you bothering me?'

'Yankel, I promise you this is something special, an emergency. You know my son, the one in the Israeli Army? He's just phoned to say he's lost his rifle.'

'So you want me to take out another.'

'How did you guess? But, listen, I'll wrap it up nicely to make it look like a *lulav* (palm branch) . . .'

'Yankel, my friend? How are you doing?'

'I can tell you how I'm not doing. I'm not taking anything to Israel.'

'For the grandchildren.'

'Grandchildren? You haven't got grandchildren.'

'Didn't you know? My daughter's just had twins, bless 'em. My wife's flying out today, but she's overloaded as it is – she's taking a pram in her hand luggage – and she thought you might be kind enough to take a few toys, that sort of thing . . .'

'Yankel —?'

'The answer is no.'

'You haven't heard what I'm going to say.'

'I know what you're going to say, and the answer is still no, because, firstly, I like to travel lightly. Secondly, I'm already overloaded. And thirdly, I'm not going.'

'You're not going to Israel?'

'No.'

'But you always go about this time of the year.'

'Well, I'm not going again, ever.'

'But you've got such a lovely house there.'
'I'm selling it.'
'It's a bad time to sell.'
'I'm giving it away . . .'

'Yankel, you know my *shmerel* of a son who went on *aliyah* (emigration to Israel) last week? Well, he took only one wellington boot out. Do you think you could take the other . . .'
'Yankel, a small jar of Marmite . . .'
'Yankel, a box of Sugar Puffs – a small one.'
'Yankel —'
'Ya —'

11 October 1985

Thriving on the wrong side

AH FOR A Shabbat in Jerusalem!

First, the morning service with its mellow tunes. Then home to a *kiddush* followed eventually by a substantial lunch, and then to a *shloff* (sleep), and finally – towards the cool of the evening – a riot along the Bar-Ilan highway.

Charedim (ultra-Orthodox Jews) long ago established the right to close off any street to Shabbat traffic in most areas where they form a clear majority and, over the past 40 years, something like 300 roads have been sealed off.

Bar-Ilan, however, is not just another street, but a major, four-lane trunk route linking the new suburbs of North-East Jerusalem to the outside world.

But it is flanked by *charedi* neighbourhoods whose inhabitants are not particularly interested in being linked to the outside world – even on weekdays. They resent the disturbance of their Shabbat peace by the roar of traffic and they want the road closed.

A few weeks ago, the Left-wing Meretz Party applied to the

police for permission to hold a demonstration against demands for the closure of Bar-Ilan.

When the police said no, Meretz turned to the high court, which said yes, and the *charedim* promptly threatened to hold a counter-demonstration. At which point, President Ezer Weizman asked Meretz to cancel their demonstration. Out of deference to the president, Meretz complied.

This was not enough for the *charedim* and, without seeking permission from the police, the courts, or anyone else, they went ahead with their counter-demonstration and attacked any passing vehicle they saw, as well as the police who tried to keep the road clear.

The following Shabbat, Meretz decided to hold its demonstration and a motorcade of about 50 cars drove up and down Bar-Ilan for about two hours. They were greeted by about 10,000 *charedim* and further riots ensued.

By last Shabbat, a new custom had been established, or rather an old one revived, known as the *minhag Yerushalmi* (Jerusalem custom), and the *charedim* demonstrated a third time. Meretz held its own counter-demonstration.

In the olden days, *charedi* demonstrators used to attack drivers and police with stones. Nowadays, they generally weigh in with soiled nappies, which shows that even *charedim* are sometimes prepared to accept the benefits of progress.

A compromise has been suggested whereby the road would be closed during the hours of prayer. But as no two synagogues begin or end their services at the same time, it would mean that the road would be closed for some three hours from dusk on Friday, and about five on Shabbat – added to which the times of service vary with the times of the year. In other words, the road would become virtually unusable, and the compromise would be not so much a compromise as a surrender.

Cars are the bane of Israeli life, not only because of their vast numbers, but on account of the aggressive way in which they are used, and the thoughtless way in which they are parked. It would therefore be refreshing if there were one major city which would be free of their intrusions for at least one day a week and, in simple terms, my sympathies are with the *charedim*.

The issue, however, is not simple. First of all, as I have observed, the *charedim* made no attempt to obtain permission either from the police or the courts for their demonstration, suggesting that they would like to think they are above the law. They also assume, once religious sensibilities are invoked, all others are of no account and they claim as of right what others would regard as a privilege. But, in a free society, *chilonim* – the secular – also have rights, even where they are in a minority.

The struggle, however, is not so much about the roads as about the character of the capital itself. The neighbourhoods along Bar-Ilan are, as I said, *charedi*. They weren't always so but there is a Gresham's Law at work and as *charedim* move in, others move out.

It is not that *charedim* make themselves unpleasant. On the contrary, they are often kindly and helpful neighbours. But they quickly transform the appearance and character of a neighbourhood, overlaying all sense of conviviality with a uniform drabness.

Jerusalem is unique. No Jew would like it to become yet another metropolis with the sleazy joys one normally associates with major cities. But the *charedim* would like to transform it into another Bnei Brak and, as matters go, they are likely to have their way.

26 July 1996

Bone-head

THIS IS A tale of two holes, one in the Musrara quarter of Jerusalem, the other in Sinai.

I have often observed that one can't dig a hole in Israel without uncovering some bones. In Musrara they have uncovered a whole graveyard, which may be good news for archaeologists (though not all that good, as it turned out), but was bad news for an enterprise called Prazot & Co, who are not archaeologists, but builders. They were innocently engaged in preparing the ground for a *mikva* when the bones came to light and at once bells started ringing in the office of Chief Rabbi Shlomo 'Bones' Goren.

Now, Rabbi Goren, in case you haven't heard, is hot on bones and is, for that matter, not all that lukewarm on *mikvehs*, and he rushed to the site by helicopter to examine the situation in person.

Two problems faced him. The *mikveh* is, of course, a ritual bath. Baths have to be wet, and ritual baths have to be pure, and bones are notoriously deficient in both properties – I mean, one hears of mud-baths and even blood-baths, but has anyone ever heard of a bone-bath? – and he immediately ordered work to stop.

The second problem was the identity of the bones. A spokesman for the antiquities division of the Ministry of Education said they dated back only to Byzantine and Persian times and as such were of 'no archaeological interest' (what, after all, is 2,000 years to us Jews?), but Rabbi Goren said that he felt it in his bones that they were Jewish and, if so, they should be given a state funeral.

To make sure that they are Jewish, however, he has asked archaeologists to visit the site and examine the bones; but they have so far refused to do anything of the sort, for they still have a bone to pick with the chief rabbi over his intervention in the excavations by the Old City Wall.

In the meantime, back at Musrara, Prazot & Co have ignored Rabbi Goren's order and have continued with their work. They have been engaged to build a *mikveh*, and a *mikveh* they will build, and they have received permission to do so – bones or no bones – from no less an eminence than the chief rabbi of Jerusalem, a peppery figure who goes by the name of Rabbi Bezalel Zolti.

Which does not mean, however, that the good matrons of Musrara are to wade thigh-deep in bones. Rabbi Zolti has ruled that a concrete 'hat' be built over the graves with a four-inch pipe connecting the air below the 'hat' with the air above it, and that a layer of air be left between the 'hat' and the floor of the *mikveh*.

I am not sure what principle is behind this (or rather beneath it), and it may only be the principle of obfuscation. Alternatively, it may be a safety measure to assure that when the dead eventually rise, they should suffer no difficulty with the ventilation.

Whatever the reasoning, however, it has gravely displeased Rabbi Goren. 'This is unthinkable, unbelievable,' said he. 'How can we allow a bath for purification to be built atop a place of uncleanliness?'

How, indeed? One sometimes hears of people dancing on other

people's graves, but to dunk on them does verge on the indelicate, and I would suggest that they resort to the Netivot compromise.

Netivot, a development town in the northern Negev, was the scene of conflict some years ago when they decided to build a swimming pool (though not over anybody's grave). It can get very hot in summer and the townspeople were all for it, but the local *yeshivah* opposed it because once one had a pool, men and women might go swimming together, and people who swim together, sin together (or so they argued, which shows that *yeshivah* people don't go in much for swimming).

The conflict continued for some time, and eventually they compromised (at least for a time) by building the pool, but not letting in water. They could do the same in Musrara. They could even let in water, as long as they didn't use it. They could call it the *mei meribah*, the waters of conflict, to commemorate the strife between the two chief rabbis. It could become a tourist attraction.

The situation in Sinai is rather less complicated, though more dramatic. A detachment of police based on Rafiah have come upon the greatest treasure trove since Lord Carnarvon opened the tomb of Tutankhamen. They have uncovered a collection of Volvos, Peugeots, Citroëns, Renaults and even Mercedes-Benz numbering some 57 in all, some of them in mint condition, in an area of Sinai known as the Valley of the Cars. The police, one must add, were not engaged in building a *mikveh*, but their find was no less remarkable for all that.

Some archaeologists believe that the cars are the property of an Egyptian sect among whom it was customary to be buried with one's most precious possessions, like Tutankhamen himself. Others believe that they are of no archaeological interest whatever, for they date back only to Mr Begin's first administration, when the rate of inflation made it impossible for people to buy a really good car, and they had to steal them instead.

Rabbinical opinion is divided on whether the cars can be used. Rabbi Zolti believes they can be used as long as they are encased in concrete, with a layer of air between the outer shell and the inner one. Rabbi Goren, who was rushed to the scene in a helicopter, believes that they should not be touched. He is convinced that they are Jewish and will demand that they be given a State burial.

11 December 1981

The wisdom of Solomon

I HAVE ALWAYS thought that being a judge was about the most sublime occupation open to man, and it is one of the few which is divinely ordained: 'Judges and officers shalt thou make thee in all thy gates, which the Lord thy God giveth thee, throughout thy tribes, and they shall judge the people with just judgements.'

And, with the occasional lapse, it is generally accepted that they do. Their standing is high, their expenses are low (no overheads except wigs, and they're paid for), their perks are many, their duties are few, their burdens are light, their recompense is heavy, and they have a security of tenure second only to that of Orthodox rabbis. No wonder most of them live for ever – or as near for ever as counts.

But all that, it would seem, applies only to England, for I was startled to hear that an entire bench of Tel Aviv judges, six in number, and all good men and true, are demanding compensation for the 'tension-filled atmosphere' in which they have to work and which, they say, has given them all heart ailments.

They claim that, before being raised to the bench, they were bursting with health, sound of limb and fleet of foot, that they would do 40 press-ups and jog round the city's perimeter before breakfast, and the same again after lunch, without as much as pausing for breath; but that ten years on they were doddery old men, hardly able to get about, broken in body and maimed in spirit (though, if their claim is anything to go by, the judges are still fairly agile in mind).

Asked to furnish further and better particulars, one judge said he had had a bypass operation, another spoke of a flyover, a third an underpass, and a fourth (if I understood him rightly, which I probably didn't) said he had been filled with cones for an arterial counter-flow system, all of which reminded me a little of our motorways, which, I will admit, are in a fairly parlous state.

The National Insurance Institute, from whom they are making their claim, has, however, regarded their case with scant sympathy. Or rather, it has given them a great deal of sympathy, but no money. I dare say that if one judge had sought compensation for his ailments, it would have been one thing, but when an entire bench of judges all succumb to the same ailment, and flash their X-rays to prove it, it begins to look like an epidemic, if not a conspiracy, which may explain the negative attitude of the N.I.I.

The trouble with all insurance institutions is that, while they are fairly prompt in paying for the fully dead, they are disinclined to compensate the half-dead. The Tel Aviv six, however, feel that the N.I.I. should, on the grounds that they half-killed themselves in the course of their work.

In other words, they believe that their ailments arise wholly, solely and exclusively from their occupation and that they would like to put judges' hearts on a par with housemaids' knees, clergymen's sore throats and journalists' livers, and to that end they have taken the N.I.I. to court.

'Judge not lest ye be judged,' sayeth the Good Book. I would not like to be the judge who will have to preside over the hearing, for he will need the wisdom of Solomon and the stamina of Samson.

Can a judge hearing the claims of fellow judges be impartial in his judgement? I fear that long before the hearing is over, he will himself fall prey to a heart ailment and sue the N.I.I. for compensation.

Whatever the outcome, I shall be following the case with more than academic interest, for before I became a scribe and a Pharisee and embarked on this column, my head was a cascade of golden curls and my beard a russet brown, so that men turned in the street and each said to the other, 'Verily, a god walketh among us'; but now, alas, my head is bare and my beard is white and I, too, feel entitled to compensation from someone.

It may be argued that no one has died of a bald head or a white beard, but the Tel Aviv judges, for all their complaints, are also alive (may they live to be 120), which, as I have suggested, is the root of the trouble.

Perhaps they should have compounded their disorders, and instead of filing six individual claims for ill health, they should have put in for three fatalities and shared out the proceeds among each other. But whatever the outcome of the hearing, they deserve full marks for trying.

10 October 1986

Banning breaded water

I SHALL HAVE to watch myself.

There is a Hebrew adage, *al tiftach peh lesatan,* 'Do not·open your mouth to the devil.' I am not worried about the devil, and I don't suppose he is too worried about me, but I am worried about the rabbis. No matter how light-hearted my intentions or bizarre my ideas, they pounce on almost everything I utter as if it were holy writ – and before I know what has happened, it is part of the *halachah.*

There is in existence a Secret Society for the Prohibition of Just About Everything (and the Banning of Almost Everything Else). A few years ago, while commenting on the work of the society, I mentioned that a growing number of Jews were becoming vegetarians and were thus escaping rabbinical scrutiny – and, of course, rabbinical levies.

I asked whether the rabbis were quite sure that lettuce was kosher. Hardly had my question appeared in print when I learned that a kibbutz was marketing 'kosher' lettuces grown in sealed plastic bags under rabbinical supervision. (This struck me as entirely appropriate, because most rabbis these days are grown in sealed bags, or are bottled, under strict supervision.)

More recently – in fact, only last month – I raised the question whether tap water was kosher for Pesach. I now have the answer. It is not – or, at least, not if it comes from Lake Kinneret (also known as the Sea of Galilee).

Rabbi Moshe Aryeh Freund, who is head of the strictly Orthodox Eda Charedit Beth Din in Jerusalem – and who, as such, could lay claim to being vicar-general of the Secret Society – has discovered that fishermen on the lake use bread as bait and has therefore forbidden its water for the purposes of drinking on Pesach. This may explain the expression, 'Cast thy bread upon the waters,' but it does not quite explain Rabbi Freund's attitude.

The amount of bread used is minuscule, while Lake Kinneret is fairly large. On a rough estimate, I would say that the proportion of bread to water would be in the region of

1:613,000,000,000,000,000,000,000,000,000,000,000,000,000 (give or take a trillion).

Rabbi Freund, however, has no sense of proportion – or rather, he claims that the *halachah* has none. 'Even a single crumb makes the entire Kinneret unfit for drinking,' he has said. (Henceforth, no doubt, the Sea of Galilee will be known as the Bread Sea, *yam halechem*, to distinguish it from the Dead Sea, *yam hamelach*.)

I suspect that Rabbi Freund may have read the parable of the loaves and the fishes, wherein, according to St Matthew and St Mark, five small loaves were enough to feed 5,000 men (so were two fishes, but they could have been leviathans). A loaf in the Galilee clearly went a long way, and possibly still does, so that Rabbi Freund may have a point. And as the Kinneret feeds the national water carrier, it means that tap water in Israel cannot be used over Pesach. (I should perhaps add that, given the meagre toilet facilities around the Kinneret, there are worse things than bread that may be cast upon the waters, but I understand that they pose no problem as far as *kashrut* is concerned.)

No one has raised the possibility of using *matzah*, or even *shemurah* (specially supervised) *matzah*, as bait, but Rabbi Ovadiah Yosef, the former Sephardi Chief Rabbi, who is a corresponding member of the Secret Society, has adopted a less stringent attitude and has ruled that, while tap water may be used, it should be filtered before being drunk.

The fact that the water is already filtered by the Mekorot water company is apparently neither here nor there, possibly because the water engineers may eat their sandwiches over the water (and perhaps even in the water). Water bottlers should do well in Israel, and filter makers even better.

In case those of you who live in the London area think that you are all right, I should add that I have seen a whole line of anglers using bread as bait while fishing at a reservoir which feeds the Thames Water Company – and the same could apply to almost everywhere else. No wonder Moses struck a rock to arrange his own water supply.

But what about the fish who actually swallow the bait? Perhaps I shouldn't ask, because if I do, the Secret Society may move into action, and you can be sure that a month hence – and certainly a year hence – you will be told from the pulpit that you cannot eat fish either, even if they have fins and scales and cloven hooves and chew the cat (though, from my understanding of wild life, it is usually the cat who chews the fish).

14 May 1993

Rock of Israel

I HAVE TO confess that I have trouble with names.

For many years I couldn't tell Madonna from Maradona. I knew one was a footballer and the other a singer, and that the footballer was the better looking of the two, but I wasn't always sure which was which. My difficulties were, however, resolved when Madonna (she's the singer, by the way) published her famous photograph album. I now know who she is and, indeed, am fairly certain of what she is.

I had the same trouble with Elton John and Ben Elton. I was aware that one was a comedian and the other a singer but, again, I wasn't sure who was what, especially as both wore glasses and the one was about as comical as the other was musical.

Now I know. Elton John is the one who can take Israel only in small – very small – doses and he was hardly in the country before he was out. I can't recall a more striking example of instant *yeridah* (emigration from Israel).

His manager complained that EJ had not been accorded any special treatment at Ben-Gurion airport, and that he had to queue at passport control along with everybody else. Bob Dylan apparently suffered the same indignity the previous day and was even importuned for autographs. Israel is clearly no respecter of pop stars, which is entirely to its credit.

If EJ was incensed at his treatment, Israelis were incensed at his flight and the inference in the international press that they had behaved in a less than civilised manner. An international incident was created. Everything that matters – and everything that doesn't

– is a matter of state in Israel and I understand the issue was raised at Cabinet level. Angry faxes flew back and forth between London and Jerusalem, and there were even reports – which I can't confirm – that the ambassador to London was about to be recalled.

The issue was eventually resolved by Her Majesty's ambassador to Israel, Andrew Burns, who prevailed upon the aggrieved singer to return and sing. And he returned and sang. I don't know if Mr Burns will get a knighthood for his intervention, but he certainly deserves one. Disraeli got an earldom for less.

Peace has been restored between EJ and Israel, and Mr Rabin and his colleagues are now free to resume their efforts to reach a peace settlement with the Arabs. Yet there are threatening clouds ahead. Heavy Metal is due to descend upon Israel shortly, followed by Light Metal (or something like it) and, for all one knows, by Non-Ferrous Metal, and then Any Old Iron.

The season will come to a climax with the advent of no less a person than Michael Jackson. All of which may explain why the Messiah has been slow in coming – he doesn't want to be upstaged. Jackson's visit is being sponsored by Pepsi-Cola, which used to have a kashrut licence. The licence has now been revoked. Perhaps the Beth Din regards Jackson as non-kosher. This may have something to do with his lyrics, though I have heard that it is felt that the adoration young Michael excites is a form of idol worship. I don't know what the ruling will do to Pepsi Cola, but it has left the sales of tickets for the Jackson concert totally unaffected. They were sold out four months in advance.

Now if Elton John can bring about an international incident, what on earth will happen when Jackson, a super-duper superstar, as opposed to a mere run-of-the-mill superstar, descends out of the skies? I think they should impound his passport as soon as he arrives, in case he should be tempted to do an Elton John.

I must say I do feel a trifle disappointed at the constant descent of rock stars. Israel in its early days was unashamedly élitist. When they built Afula, for example, they had plans for an opera house long before they had plans for a synagogue. Well, if there is still no opera in Afula, there is hardly a town in Israel so God-forsaken as not to have its own symphony orchestra and Israel has more instrumentalists and concert-goers per head of population than any other country in the world.

Yet if élitist Israel is self-sufficient, populist Israel is not. There was a time when Israel produced first-class pop music and first-class pop groups. No longer.

What has happened to the legendary Rock of Israel? 'Their rock,' as Moses said, 'is not as our rock.' Cannot Israel, which excels in so many other fields, produce its own rock idioms and its own rock stars and dispense with imports?

25 June 1993

Smoking

THEY'RE COMING DOWN heavily – cough! splutter! wheeze! – on us smokers in Israel, for the word has apparently gone round (one doesn't know on what authority) that smoking is not only unhygienic and unsocial, but is positively bad for one's – cough! splutter! wheeze! – health.

I find this negative attitude surprising, for there is clear evidence not only from such popular folk songs as 'Have a Nargila', but from actual Scripture, that Jews have always been a nation of smokers. I have heard it suggested that the 'pillar of cloud' we read about in Exodus was really a cloud of smoke sent up by the 600,000 Israelites (to say nothing of the 'mixed multitude') as they lit up after crossing the Red Sea. There is more direct evidence from Isaiah (14:31), who not only prophesied the habit, but indicated its provenance:

'Howl, O gate; cry O city; thou, whole Peleseth, art dissolved: for there shall come from the north a smoke . . .'

Yet, in spite of all that, the Knesset recently passed a bill restricting cigarette advertising, and attempts are being made to ban smoking in cinemas, concert halls, public offices, private offices, synagogues and kindergartens.

There are, of course, bans and bans. They have, for example, banned smoking in buses, but one can hardly see some buses for the billowing smoke within and without.

Smoking is also banned in supermarkets, but I recently had to ask a counter-hand to remove some ash from a smoked mackerel I was hoping to buy, and she retorted: 'It's all right, the ash doesn't add anything to the weight.'

There are, however, places where zealots take it upon themselves to enforce the law.

A few months ago, a young man was having a quiet smoke in a fairly public place, when an irate woman descended upon him and demanded that he stop. He wouldn't. She then asked him to leave the room, and when he refused again, she took him by the scruff of the neck and put him outside.

But before you marvel at the audacity of the woman, I must add that the young man in question was nine, that the room was a schoolroom, and that the woman was a school teacher. The incident tells one almost as much about school discipline in Israel as about the attitude to smoking.

First, as to smoking. Almost everything in Israel is expensive, except public transport, bread, milk, fats, fruit and vegetables in season, synagogue offerings and, above all (or rather, below all), tobacco. The best cigarettes here cost about a quarter of their English equivalent, and the cheapest (which, one gathers, are made out of old socks and are therefore referred to as *garbayim*) cost about 15 pence a packet. As a result, almost anyone here can afford to smoke himself to death, and not a few people do.

Sweets, on the other hand, are expensive, and I should imagine, therefore, that where a chap's pocket-money doesn't stretch to a bar of chocolate or a packet of liquorice allsorts, he settles for a packet of king-sized, filter-tipped *garbayim* (I should add that, though cigarettes are cheap, lighting them can be expensive, for they have developed a super-safety match here which hardly catches fire at all, and one can go through a whole packet before getting one to ignite.)

I don't know if children round here are allowed to eat in school, but they do – whole meals at a time. I don't know if they're allowed to chew, but they certainly do – and sometimes blow bubbles while they're at it, without let or hindrance. So I don't see why the teacher should have taken such violent exception to an innocent lad enjoying a quiet smoke over his six-times table, for tobacco – cough! splutter! wheeeeeeeeeze! – does concentrate the mind wonderfully and is an aid to study.

The trouble with schools, however, or at least elementary schools, is that they don't provide ash-trays, and boys are liable to mark the desks when stubbing out their cigarettes, and they could even set the school on fire (which is exactly what happened to the elementary school I went to in Glasgow). The solution, I suppose, is either to provide ash-trays or to insist that the boys smoke only pipes or nargilas.

I must add that Israeli parents are fairly understanding about the habits of their children, for when the nine-year-old I mentioned above ran home and complained, between coughs and splutters, that he had been ejected from his class for merely lighting up, the father descended upon the school, marched into the classroom and, without so much as a 'good morning' or 'how-d'you-do?', socked the teacher in the eye.

It all happened in Beer Yaakov, a small town in the centre of the country, and the local teachers went on strike as a result. Hence the saying: 'There's no smoke without ire.'

Incidentally, if you should like to be a school teacher in Israel, there are any number of vacancies – especially in the smaller towns.

25 February 1983

4
Israel and the Diaspora

I share the common belief that Israel is at the centre of Jewish life, but not its corollary, that the periphery is expendable.

Diaspora welfare

WE DO NOT need you, and if you were all to disappear, it would be better for us. We do not need you politically, and as for money, which is two or three per cent of the budget, it helps you more than it helps us. What you have done by remaining in the diaspora is to give an option to the Israeli who wants to move from Israel.

Thus A, B.Yehoshua, the Israeli writer. There is a lot in what he says, including a lot of nonsense, and it may be useful to dispose of the nonsense first.

Israelis who want to move from Israel need no options. They go abroad, and stay abroad, because it offers, or they think it offers, greater scope for advancement. Such Israelis, in the main, have little to do with the diaspora communities among whom they settle.

America, for obvious reasons, is the greatest attraction, but one also finds Israelis in places like Scandinavia or West Germany, in towns which are almost devoid of Jews. If Yehoshua's dream were to be fulfilled and the Jewish diaspora, as we know it, were to vanish, it would in time be replaced – as it is, to an extent, being replaced – by a diaspora of Israelis.

One readily agrees that Israel is at the centre of Jewish life, but Mr Yehoshua goes further and insists that the diaspora has legitimacy only in so far as it is useful to Israel. As far as he is concerned, there is no other consideration, and as he is convinced that it is not only useless, but positively harmful, to Israel (a point which we shall examine in a minute), he suggests that it can go to – and, indeed, should go to – perdition.

I think that the political influence of the diaspora has been exaggerated, especially by enemies of Israel. It does, however, exist, but in recent years it has been used merely as a claque to cheer on every turn and twist of Israeli policy and every caprice, no matter how unreasonable or extreme, and as such it has harmed both the Jewish State and the Jewish people.

I don't know if that is what Yehoshua meant by 'we don't need you politically,' but I would agree that, politically speaking, Israel might on balance be better off without us.

The same is true of the fund-raising drives, except that I wouldn't agree that they help us more than they help Israel. They are harmful to both. They harm Israel because they perpetuate the *chaluka* (hand out) mentality which Ben-Gurion used to denounce with such vehemence and which he was confident Zionism would change. Instead, it has merely broadened its scope.

The old *chaluka*, whatever its failings – and it had very serious ones – was at least concerned with genuine distress. It provided food, clothing, shelter and, when funds dried up (as they sometimes did) people starved. The new *chaluka* provides tennis courts. Given present trends, it will, in time, be providing yachting marinas.

Yehoshua, to do him credit, has been one of the very few Israelis to speak out against the dangers of the system, and to assess the cost in dignity and self-respect. But he is not really familiar with the diaspora and is not aware how far the endless Israel appeals have pushed our educational and welfare institutions to the brink of bankruptcy, how far they have made fund-raising the be-all and end-all of communal life, and fund-raisers the arbiters of communal priorities.

I am, however, concerned mainly with Yehoshua's central thesis that the diaspora has no legitimacy in its own right. I am not quite sure how such legitimacy is acquired, but time is surely one factor, and contribution to the well-being of the host society is another, so that one would have thought that the diaspora has earned a right to self-perpetuation on both grounds.

I would agree that it is easier to be a Jew in a Jewish State, and that it forms a more natural environment in which to raise one's child as a Jew, but I do not think that one is living in sin, or exposing one's progeny to unimaginable moral hazards, by choosing to remain outside it.

Indeed, given the direction of Israel's policies on the West Bank and in Gaza, it would not be too difficult to make out a convincing moral case for *not* going on *aliyah*, and if Sharon should succeed Begin, there may even be a moral case for leaving Israel.

Most Jews – including most Israelis – have never accepted, and will never accept, the harsh doctrine that their Jewishness requires them to be eternally tied to one place, even if that place is Israel. Anyone anxious to encourage *aliyah* should accept – if only as a working hypothesis – that the diaspora is here to stay. If it isn't, then I wouldn't give much hope for the future of Israel, either.

There is only one effective argument for *aliyah* – the hedonistic one, by which I do not mean the materialistic one. Most Western immigrants would probably be less well-off in Israel, and would have to work harder for less, but they might be infinitely happier with it.

Israel is a sunny, colourful, exciting place, full of zest and vigour, and it gives a keener edge to one's senses. I am not at all sure whether it offers a more wholesome life, or a greater sense of fulfilment, because such things cannot be easily measured, but it obviously offers a *different* life, and I know a great many individuals who, in spite of the frustration, hardships and heartaches they may have suffered, would unhesitatingly proclaim: *vive la différence!*

18 December 1981

Zionist Federations

THERE WAS SUPPOSED to have been a merger conference between the Zionist and Mizrachi Federations last Sunday, but they failed to agree on terms, or rather, they had agreed on terms, but failed to agree on their implementation, or rather they had agreed on their implementation, but failed to agree on their execution, and instead, therefore, they had a non-conference, or what they called a 'symbolic' conference, which is to say there was nothing to confer on, but as the conference season was at hand, and as they had prepared their speeches and booked the hall they thought they might as well have a conference as not. And who says they were wrong?

You may have noticed, and perhaps even read, the letters on the subject which have been darkening the correspondence columns of this paper, and as they have but obfuscated what is a sufficiently complex subject, I feel I should offer a simple guide.

There is first of all the Zionist Federation, which, however, should not be confused with the General Zionist Federation, or the Federation of General Zionists, or the United Zionist Federation, or the Confederation of United Zionists, or the Union of Zionist Federalists, or the Federation of Zionist Unionists, or the Union of Zionist Generals, or the Federation of Synagogues, or the Union of Orthodox Hebrew Congregations, or the Amalgamated Confederation of Dyers, Bleachers and Laundry Operatives, or the National Union of Public Employees, though if you should happen to confuse them, no great harm will be done.

The important thing to remember, however, is that the Zionist Federation is the oldest of them all and includes such bodies as Poale Zion (Zionist workers), Mapam (Zionist thinkers), Herut (Zionist non-thinkers), and the Federation of Synagogues (Zionist undertakers), all of whom (to judge from their letters) want to get down 'to the grass roots', except for the Federation of Synagogues, which, for a fee, will cheerfully take you under them.

To these must be added the aforementioned United Zionists, which is, or purports to be, a non-party party, and the GZF, a party-party affiliated to the old Israeli General Zionist Party (which, however, no longer exists), and which brings us finally to the party of the first part, namely the Mizrachi Federation.

Are you still with me? (Anyone who replies: 'No, I'm with the Woolwich,' must go to the bottom of the class.) The Mizrachi has always been slightly apart from other Zionist groups, if for no better reason than that it has always stayed apart, but it has of late been finding its isolation irksome and a few years ago it entered into negotiations with the Zionist Federation to form yet another Zionist Federation to be known as the United Federation of Zionists, which should however, not be confused with the . . . Sorry, we've been there before.

The talks were painful and protracted and no effort was spared to reach a successful conclusion. They kept their ears to the grindstone, their backs to the wall, their nose to the ground, put their shoulders to the wheel and left no stone unturned to reach the grass roots, but when it came to the crunch, and they reached the nitty-gritty, they found a spanner in the woodpile and a fly in the works, to say nothing of an Indian in the ointment, and it has left them with a flea in their ear and not altogether up to scratch, hence last Sunday's symbolic conference.

And therein lies the value of the Zionist movements, even 34 years after the Jewish State came into being; it is the ultimate refuge of the cliché.

I have for long felt that the so-called Zionist movement and its subsidiaries, appendages and outcrops, are not worthy of honest rage, but that they were eminently worthy of ridicule. After last year's fiasco of a conference, however, I felt that it was not even worthy of that, but the agitation of recent weeks, the re-criminations, the threat of writs and counter-writs, charges and counter-charges, have been too good to miss, especially in a thin week in which not a bone has been uncovered and in which even Rabbi Goren has stayed silent.

What is it that makes fully grown men whom one knows to be otherwise sane, and even intelligent, busy themselves in this frantic round of nothingness? Is it a means of getting away from their wives? If so, let them take up jogging, or join the boards of management of their synagogues.

This paper is partly to blame, for it encourages them. I cannot understand why it devotes a whole column to the ZF, when it gives only half a par to a comparatively significant event like a coffee morning in Ebbw Vale, or a bring-and-buy sale in West Hartlepool. The worst culprit, however, is the Jewish Agency, for it pays generous subsidies to the ZF, and it is the fact that they are spending real money which gives the Zionist groups the illusion that they are doing real work. They certainly keep themselves busy but would not all their problems be instantly solved by the simple expedient of going into liquidation? None of us would be poorer for it, and Israel would be the richer.

19 March 1982

Spiritual wealth of diaspora communities

THE PLAN TO hold a public inquiry into communal finances and financing is both timely and necessary, but I feel compelled to quibble with one sentence in the letter in which the plan was announced, and it is this: 'We are convinced that one of the most important services that we can render Israel is to have a virile community with a knowledgeable and committed youth.'

I find it unduly apologetic, even a trifle unctuous, for it suggests that the existence of the community is justified only in so far as it can be useful to Israel. If that is the case, I would urge that the inquiry be abandoned, that our communal institutions be wound up and that we apply all our energies and resources to emigration, for no money we could raise for Israel, and no influence which we could exercise on her behalf, would equal the value of 400,000 – or even 40,000 – *olim* (immigrants to Israel) with professional and entrepreneurial skills, and the urbane attitudes which usually go with a Western upbringing.

I share the common belief that Israel is at the centre of Jewish life, but not the corollary that the periphery is expendable. I feel that even small diaspora communities like our own have a life and a character of their own, and have a right to a future of their own. They seem less troubled by such questions in America, but then they have the numbers and wealth to feel fairly confident in their own future.

We, with our shrinking numbers, and shrunk resources, are rather more ambivalent. We needn't be. Certainly we shouldn't be. Three centuries of history also count for something, for they have seen the evolution of traditions, qualities and institutions which, I believe, are worth preserving.

I believe that British Jewry has a contribution to make to the well-being of both Jewish society and the society around it, and this is true not only of our community, but of the French community, the South African community and even the tiny Dutch community.

72

But that is only the positive side of the story. There is also, unfortunately, a negative one. Israel has made immense strides in science, technology, agriculture, even – though one wouldn't think it – economics. In military terms it is by far the strongest power in the Middle East.

Nor has it been backward in the arts. It has a lively theatre, with inspired directors and gifted artists. In music it has an embarrassment of talents – too plentiful, in fact, to be supported by a country of four million. It has an immense array of literary talent. Its press is independent, outspoken and colourful and I have sometimes felt that one should have two days Shabbat if only to enable one to get through the wealth of reading matter offered by the Friday editions of the Israeli papers.

The one area from which one expected most is the one in which Israel is – for the time being at least – the most deficient, and that is the spirit.

People will no doubt remind me that Israel is in the throes of a religious revival if a *kipa* (skull cap) count is anything to go by, this is certainly true, but there is more to religion than covered heads, dangling tassels and the accumulation of *mitzvot*. It implies charity (in the broadest sense of the word), understanding, a higher level of conduct and an intolerance of injustice.

What one has instead is arrogance, bigotry and a rapacity which, at times, has not stopped short of theft; and as for the intolerance of injustice, the religious establishment has instead exerted all its energies to enlarge and perpetuate it, and the religious parties have, in the main, been concerned to benefit their followers at the expense of everyone else.

But also, instead of attempting to spread their beliefs by example, they have resorted to coercion, with the result that there has evolved within Israel a hatred of religion and the religious to which anyone living in Mea Shearim or Bnei Brak may be oblivious, but which is palpable to any observant Jew who intrudes into an area inhabited by the non-observant.

There is no religious leadership to speak of in Israel, no religious guidance, only religious pressure groups, and I would invite any fair-minded individual to pick up and read any of the papers published by these groups and see if he would not feel compelled to wash his hands after the experience. They do not represent the sort of Judaism in which most of us here were brought up, or the sort which we would wish to transmit to our children.

All this may be a temporary phenomenon, but whatever has been coming forth out of Zion, it is not the law, and I feel the diaspora communities must perpetuate themselves if only because they may be nearer the spirit of their faith than its traditional heartland.

23 September 1983

Commercial break

ONE OF THE dangers of having guests hanging around for too long is that, if they settle in comfortably, they never want to leave; and worse, they begin to tell their host how to run his establishment. This has happened in our own community with the Joint Israel Appeal and the United Synagogue.

There was a time when the Kol Nidre service was given over to supplication and prayer. Then, nearly 40 years ago – as 'an emergency measure' – a commercial break was introduced on behalf of the Keren Hayesod (forerunner of the JIA).

That emergency has now continued for more than a generation and, if we are to wait until Israel is solvent, it will be continuing to the time of the Messiah or beyond.

To the right, the Adath (or Union of Orthodox Hebrew Congregations) has never allowed the principal service of the year to be disturbed by the shuffling of cards and the tramp of collectors. To the left, the Reform synagogues still persist with their appeal, but they divide the proceeds between Israeli and local causes.

It is in the United Synagogue, and only in the United Synagogue, that the JIA is able to make off with the lot. Now Mr Manny Carter, co-treasurer of the US (they have more treasurers than treasure), has come cap – or, if you prefer, top-hat – in hand to Messrs Kalms, Levy and Millet (otherwise known as KLM, the flying troika of the JIA) to ask if they might possibly see their way to leaving something under their plate, if only by way of commission, for Jewish education.

Mr K said no.

Mr L said the proposal was inappropriate.

Mr M felt the appropriation was not proposable.

But just who is running the shop (by which I mean the US) in the first place?

I have yet to be convinced that the most sacred service of the year should be disrupted for any cause, no matter how urgent; but if it must be disrupted, then local causes (and not only educational ones) should have a share – and, I would hasten to add, a very large share – of the proceeds.

In America, where there is rather more money about, they do not have a Joint Israel Appeal, but a United *Jewish* Appeal, which is precisely what its name implies, and through which funds are divided between Israeli and local causes by local leaders. In South Africa, where they are also not short of a bob or two, they alternate between local causes and Israeli ones.

It is only in our small and semi-bankrupt community that the JIA is allowed to cream off most of the available funds, while the United Synagogue, our welfare institutions, and the London Board of Jewish Religious Education – and, yes, even Jews' College, Mr K – have to scratch around the bottom of the barrel for any petty cash which may be left.

The Jewish Agency, said Mr K, already gives considerable sums to Jewish education in this country, which it does, but whose money is it in the first place? Money is sticky, and every time it changes hands, it loses something in value. If we raise money here which is passed on to Jerusalem, and part of which is then, after due deliberation, passed back here, we may be certain that every pound we receive will have cost us nearly two.

But the cost – and the waste – is the least of it. The fact that we have to look to Jerusalem for money to run our own educational institutions means that we are no longer in control of our own destinies. In effect, we are reduced to schnorring from the schnorrers.

I know of businessmen who sometimes contrive to buy over a company with its own money, and while I am not suggesting that Messrs K, L and M are among them, the JIA has done substantially the same with the Anglo-Jewish community.

I am aware that Israel is in dire economic straits, but, as the chief rabbi observed in Jerusalem last week, 'a few million may make precious little difference to the country's economy and the astronomical sums needed to maintain it, while the same amounts may make all the difference to the donor communities, to a Jewish school rising or collapsing . . . or to a Jewish old-age home opening or closing its doors to scores of old people who have nowhere else to live out their days in a Jewish environment.'

The United Synagogue should be a bit more brisk, and business-like in its approach and not negotiate with KLM as if it were seeking a favour, when it is, in point of fact, bestowing favours. It should state its terms clearly and the JIA will have no alternative but to comply. And when it does, a modest step will have been taken towards the creation of a UJA along American lines, and the recovery of local autonomy.

12 July 1985

Goodnight, ladies.
It's time to come home

DR YOSSI BEILIN, Israel's deputy foreign minister, has told a plenary session of the Wizo executive, that Israel is no longer the needy, pioneering society it was when Wizo and other inter-national Jewish charities were founded.

'If our economic situation is better than in many of your countries,' he said, 'how can we go on asking for your charity?'

No one fell into a dead faint as he uttered those dread words, but there were gasps of outrage, and shrieks of dismay. It was, in short, one of the darkest days in the history of Wizo.

Government ministers are normally invited to such occasions to boost the egos of the participants, praise their hard work, applaud their outstanding qualities of leadership, thank them for their generosity, spur them on to even greater efforts, and, in general, to anoint them with flattery.

Dr Beilin did none of these things. Instead he more or less undermined their very status as Ladies Bountiful, and Wizo president Raya Jaglom immediately sent off an angry letter to Prime Minister Rabin.

'It is unthinkable that a member of the government that you head should express himself in a manner that enraged all the members of the plenum,' she protested.

Unthinkable? Well, yes it is unthinkable but only because they haven't thought about it, and it's about time they did.

For the past 45 years, and indeed before, while the Zionist movement as a whole was busy with words, Wizo was busy with deeds. It has created a whole network of welfare institutions for young and old and has helped with the absorption of immigrants. It is one of the most admirable and admired Jewish institutions we have – energetic, thrusting, tireless – and a word of appreciation would certainly not have been out of place. But then, neither was Beilin's candour. And his remarks applied not only to Wizo.

Israel is no longer a developing society, but – as I never tire of repeating – a fully developed one. It is now actually one of the 13 richest countries in the world, and if it does not, as yet, have a higher standard of living than Britain, it soon will have.

There are, to be sure, still serious gaps in its welfare structure but, when it comes to welfare, no society, however prosperous, can ever meet all the claims upon it because the levels of expectation rise with the level of prosperity.

Mrs Brenda Katten, an honorary president of Wizo, has pointed out that the Israeli government does not provide crèches for working mothers, but how many of the world's governments do so?

Indeed, how many such crèches are there in Britain? I have not made a detailed study of the matter but I suspect that in many ways, the working mother in Israel is better off than her counterpart in this country.

When the Likud was in office, the government asserted its national pride with expansionism and a determination to impose its rule over others. Dr Beilin and his colleagues are asserting theirs with simple self-respect. It is an entirely welcome development, and if the Wizo ladies had been less inflated with their self-importance, and more aware of what was happening in Israel, they would have cheered Dr Beilin to the echo. Instead, the response was Mrs Jaglom's letter to Mr Rabin. A classical instance of wounded *amour propre*.

Israelis do not like to think of themselves as poor relatives dependent on hand-outs from rich uncles in America – or even rich aunts in Britain – especially as they now happen to be fairly rich themselves. Beneficiaries are rarely grateful to their benefactors once they are able to stand on their own feet.

What Dr Beilin has done is to give notice that the *shnorrerei* (begging, scrounging) industry, and its wholly owned subsidiary, the flattery industry (for which there is a coarser but more appropriate Yiddish expression which I dare not use in a family newspaper) are about to be wound up. And the sooner Wizo ladies become aware of the fact the better.

Wizo has been in existence now since 1918 which, in itself, is no reason why it should continue to exist, but it has some very intelligent and energetic members and a wealth of experience which could be, and should be, harnessed for local needs.

It will, however, call for a revolution in attitudes. It may even entail a change of name but, if Wizo is to have a future at all, it will lie in any work it may plan to undertake in the diaspora.

28 January 1994

The Bedouin

THE JOINT ISRAEL Appeal has recently seemed to be fading into oblivion, and not before time. It did a valuable job well – perhaps too well, for it raised so much money for Israel as to starve local causes of badly needed funds.

It was never completely an *Israel* fund because its money went only to Jews. Thus, for example, when the Jewish Agency – the ultimate repository of JIA funds – builds a housing estate for poor Israeli families, Arabs, who comprise the poorest families, are excluded. This is even where the houses are built on public land leased on favourable terms from the government.

Such discrimination, which would be unthinkable in any other democracy, has led a number of people who used to subscribe to the JIA to send their money to the New Israel Fund. This seeks to help *all* Israelis in need; to advance social justice for *all* Israelis; and to integrate Arabs more fully into the life of Israel.

A worthy cause indeed, and I was delighted to read that it is to receive a grant of £280,000 from the National Lottery. I have been an occasional subscriber to the the NIF, and a regular investor in the National Lottery, without winning as much as a tenner, and I am glad to see that my money was not entirely wasted. I am half hoping that the NIF will now declare a dividend.

But, given the urgent cause which NIF has taken under its wing, and the fact that the grant is to be spread over five years, £280,000 isn't all that much. By JIA standards it is petty cash. The NIF plans to use the money on pre-school education for Bedouin children, and the training of Bedouin teachers.

If the Arabs are the poorest Israelis, the Bedouin are the poorest Arabs. Not that they were ever anything else; their traditional, nomadic way of life never called for more than humble sufficiency, and sometimes not even that. But they were hardy and resilient and were content with the little they had – or hadn't.

The emergence of Israel changed everything. They were no longer free to roam across borders, and their movements were restricted within Israel itself. They were cherished in that they – and their black tents and their camels – lent a splash of colour to the drab stretches of the northern Negev, and were good for the tourist trade. They were also useful as trackers in the army, but were otherwise regarded as a nuisance and, since there are about 100,000 of them, a fairly large nuisance.

Once Israel began to develop the northern Negev for agricultural settlement, the Bedouin began to complain that they were being cut off from their traditional grazing grounds which, of course, they were. The trouble with any claims, however far they may go back in antiquity, is that they have to be backed up by documents, especially in Israel. And the trouble with the Bedouin is that they never went in much for documentation of any sort.

They could not back up their claims in the courts and, as a result, the government has confiscated their lands and they have been shifted, shunted and decanted, now to this area of the Negev, now to that, and finally into Bedouin towns.

It would be wrong to ascribe these politics entirely to the Jewish hunger for land, for there was a belief that, if the Bedouin were more concentrated, it would be easier to provide them with decent housing, education and welfare.

The Bedouin themselves were rarely consulted and the schemes were thrust upon them. When the towns were finally built and regional councils appointed, all the councils were headed by Jews, usually from one of the religious parties, which assured a minimum of competence, with a maximum of indifference.

The towns have not been a success, partly because successive governments have allocated funds to the different communities in opposite ratio to their needs. The Bedouin, being the poorest of all, got the least of all.

The towns became instant slums and were never provided even with proper sewage systems. But that is perhaps the lesser part of the problem. Their main drawback has been social, for the Bedouin have not adapted readily to their new environment and they have been distanced from their old ways without being integrated into the new Israel.

The NIF is now trying to ameliorate some of the wrongs they have suffered. It can do so only in a minor way because – even with the help of the National Lottery – it has only meagre resources, but the very fact that it is drawing attention to the plight of the Bedouin is, in itself, an important contribution to their welfare.

13 June 1997

Charitable priorities

THE UNITED JEWISH Israel Appeal – hereinafter the UJIA – is in essence a confluence of two organisations, the JIA and Jewish Continuity, the one old, the other new, but both having passed through troubled times.

Jewish Continuity represents a belated determination by British Jewry to stay alive. At its unveiling, everybody agreed that it was a good thing and a timely thing. But, as it was launched under the auspices of the Chief Rabbi, religious disputations promptly and inevitably ensued which threatened to kill it, and which very nearly did.

The Joint Israel Appeal is our principal taxmaster, and, given the fact that it has no strong-arm men to enforce its levies, it has been phenomenally successful. Never, one might say, in the field of Jewish philanthropy, has so much been extracted for so many from so few.

The JIA was born out of a succession of emergencies, and thrived on them. Once there were no actual emergencies in sight, however, it tried to invent them. Thus, a few years ago, after helping to arrange flights out of Azerbaijan, it ran a full-page ad suggesting the possibility that it might have to arrange rescue flights out of Golders Green. I can't imagine that either Saatchi & Saatchi, which was the agency involved in the wheeze, or the JIA leaders who paid for it, could possibly have believed it, but they obviously thought that their subscribers would – which shows what they thought of their subscribers.

Had the JIA been a democratically elected body, answerable to anyone but itself, everyone responsible for that campaign would surely have been fired. In fact, it might not have been such a bad thing if the JIA itself had been wound up there and then. There are, however, some good reasons why it should still be kept going. Firstly, because it has over the years built up an excellent, professional machine, which should be kept ticking over in case a real crisis should arise, and which can be adapted to serve the community as a whole. Secondly, the JIA, as was, has been one of the few major organisations in the community which has somehow managed to transcend religious factionalism. This – given the temper of our times – is no mean feat. Finally – and this, I would say, is the most important of the three – there is the link with Jewish Continuity.

The JIA raised over £13 million in its last year, while the UJIA has undertaken to allocate at least £3 million to local causes in its first one. This is a good start, but not good enough and I, for one, am less than truly thankful for what we are about to receive.

In America, where the United Jewish Appeal raises something like £500 million a year, they retain about 60 per cent for local needs. This is not a new development, but then American Jews have always believed in themselves not only as a lasting phenomenon but as a desirable one.

We, on the other hand, have somehow been brainwashed into thinking that we are so few, so weak and so poor, as to be transitory and expendable, and that the best we could do was to transfer our meagre resources to Israel before fading finally into extinction.

Jewish Continuity came as a necessary, if belated, corrective but, because it was belated, it needs rather more than the promised £3 million, and needs it urgently.

Unless there should be a complete collapse of the Russian economy, the days of mass immigration to Israel are over. I am not even sure that Israel still needs immigrants; the Israeli public has made it clear for some time that it doesn't really want them.

The UJIA still likes to talk in terms of 'rescue' as if there were communities in immediate danger. Such dangers, for the time being at least, are a thing of the past and we are talking about the routine transfer of Jewish families from, say, Uzbekistan and Kazakhstan, who think they may be better off in Israel.

Their absorption may be costly but, if they are liabilities in the short run, they are assets in the long term. Israel has been immensely enriched by the Russian immigration of the past few decades and is now perfectly capable of absorbing newcomers out of its own resources.

Which does not mean that we are not under some obligation to share in the costs; but it does suggest that we should adopt the American scale of priorities and should reconcile ourselves to the fact that charity begins at home.

17 October 1997

Redefining our relationship

EZER WEIZMAN IS the most popular president Israel has had.

This is not only because of his record as a soldier and statesman, but because of his colourful and vigorous personality, and a capacity for plain speaking which is rare in any politician and almost unknown in a head of state.

Some of his utterances, however, have not only been plain, but wrong-headed. This is particularly true of his frequent references to the diaspora.

'I just don't understand it,' he said. 'I have no illusions that the whole of the diaspora will come one day to Israel, but don't ask me to justify it.'

No one has, but neither should he feel obliged to denounce it – which he does at every opportunity, and in barrack-room terms. He tends to confront Jewish visitors with the same question: 'What the hell are you doing out there, when you should be living right here?' – or words to that effect. And, in the main, they are too polite to answer in kind, or to answer at all.

When Israel is in peril, there is an obvious duty for Jews everywhere to rally to its side, but the idea that there is a moral imperative obliging anyone to live in one place rather than another is absurd.

In spite of the loaded terms we apply to the process, not every *oleh* (immigrant) is a hero, and not everyone who chooses to remain in the diaspora is a fool or a villain. The diaspora, after all, is not a new phenomenon. Most Jews taken in captivity to Babylon after the fall of the first Temple chose to remain there after they were free to return. And, as early as the second century BCE, there were more Jews in Egypt than in Judea.

Our liturgy is full of reminders that 'because of our sins we were exiled from our homeland' but, for most of our history, our exile has been voluntary, so that the term hardly applies.

We remain in place, not necessarily because life in the diaspora is easier but because we happen to like it and perhaps even love it. We are attached to our homelands even where we do not think of them as home. We are drawn to their sights and sounds, their traditions and culture, their way of life. Our sense of adhesion can be profound even where our roots are shallow.

I speak as a newcomer to a very old and very conservative society. Most Jews now in the diaspora, however, live in comparatively new societies – whose history, cultures and attitudes they have helped to shape. They are not accretions but are, so to speak, founder members. They may have a powerful sense of kinship with Israel but this has not impaired their loyalty to their own countries. They do not think of themselves as exiles, and could in no sense be described as such.

Even Jewish communities in Europe feel secure enough to remain in place. British Jewry, for example, may have declined by about 40 per cent in size in the past 50 years, but it has become more intensely Jewish, with a larger and better system of Jewish day schools and a richness of cultural life it has never had before.

Last summer, Weizman summoned diaspora leaders to a conference in Jerusalem on ways of deepening ties between Israel and the diaspora. It was less than a success. It was followed by a further conference on the same subject this March which was a fiasco and broke up in acrimony.

Delegates complained that it was badly prepared, but that was only part of the problem. President Weizman had hoped that they would come up with plans for the liquidation of their various communities, and they failed to comply.

Ties between Israel and the diaspora are about as deep as they reasonably can be. Perhaps they are deeper than they should be, not only in the sense that Israel attracts most of our money, but because it remains at the centre of our preoccupations.

We have let Jerusalem dictate our agenda and list our priorities. Our communal leaders may be assertive enough in defending our interests in the face of local politicians, but not in the face of Israeli ones.

What we need is a conference which would redefine the relationship between Israel and the diaspora. This would have to recognise that the diaspora has its own life, its own legitimacy, its own past, and its own future, and that we can flourish beyond the Jewish state.

We do, however, need a clearly pronounced will to continue. If we allow ourselves to be browbeaten into believing that we have no future, then assuredly we shall have none.

19 May 1995

5
Dress that Maketh Man

Nor moreover, do our rabbis have anything to say regarding culottes, which are a sort of cross between trousers and skirts, but which are neither one nor the other, and which should be banned on the simple grounds of misrepresentation.

Patent nonsense

NOW FOR SOME light relief – though, on reflection, I am not sure whether the issue I'm about to raise is a laughing matter.

We have a growing number of Jewish day schools in Britain, some of which are more Jewish than others. This does not mean, however, that they are necessarily better, merely that they are under tighter rabbinical control. In some instances, the control has grown so tight that they are in danger of asphyxiation.

The school I particularly have in mind is the Hasmonean High School, which, given the quality of its staff, could be one of the best in London. But their efforts are being constantly undermined by ecclesiastical overseers who know nothing about education and have no sense of proportion, or even of the ridiculous.

The Hasmonean comprises a boys' and a girls' school, but on two different sites, with the former in Hendon and the latter about half a mile away in Mill Hill.

The boys' school recently planned to stage a performance of *Macbeth* by a touring company, until word got out that Macbeth, Macduff, Banquo *et al* were to be played by male actors, while Lady Macbeth and the witches were to be played by females.

A rabbi thereupon intervened to say that this was not kosher. He may also have had misgivings about the 'liver of a blaspheming Jew', but, at all events, the performance was cancelled – and this in a school which purports to give its pupils a clearer under-standing of English literature.

We must, however, turn to the girls' school for a ruling so bizarre that it has stretched even my fairly extended sense of credulity. The rabbis have declared that the girls may not wear patent-leather shoes either in school or out of it.

Now, while I'm aware of the untiring efforts of the Sacred Society for the Prohibition of Just About Everything, this was new to me and I racked my brains for its origins, until a parent put me wise. Girls may not wear patent leather because, if their feet are large enough and the leather is gleaming enough, it could reflect their unmentionables. Chelm was not a patch on Chendon.

87

The rabbis obviously have a livelier imagination than I have – or better eyesight, for since hearing of their prohibition, I have kept my eyes firmly on the ground, without, however, coming upon one interesting reflection. I have ordered a new pair of glasses.

I offer these titbits as a measure of the intelligence which the rabbis bring to their work and which has been accepted without protest as one of the penalties one has to pay these days for a Jewish education. But a major issue has now arisen which has finally brought on a revolt by teachers and parents alike.

The boys' school is a rickety slum and the governors, after searching around for other sites, came up with two options. One is to erect a new building beside the girls' school in Mill Hill, the other is (was?) to move five miles away to the former Orange Hill School in Edgware.

The former option has everything to commend it. The parents are for it, the teachers are for it, but a body called the 'elector rabbonim' are against it.

The boys and girls would be in separate classes, in separate buildings, and use separate playgrounds, and never the twain would meet; but they would be within sight of each other – and that, even without the benefit of patent-leather shoes, is, apparently, contrary to the *halachah*.

It so happens that I was once a teacher in a sister school of the Hasmonean, and the boys and girls were not only on the same site, but in the same buildings, and even used the same dining-room, without, to my knowledge, showing any outward signs of moral degeneration, and without a word of objection from the rabbis.

We are often told that the *halachah* is changeless, unchanging and eternal. I almost wish it were, but – as we can see – it can be changed, and is changing, all the time, and almost invariably for the worse.

I blame the laymen rather than the rabbis, for there is no limit to the nonsense they will swallow. The Hasmonean parent-teacher association has, however, not accepted the rabbis' ruling as the last word. If it persists in its attitude, it may discover that the *halachah* can be more reasonable than it has been led to believe.

26 February 1988

Knitted *kipot* required

I DON'T KNOW if it has anything to do with the atmosphere of this place, but residents of the Holy Land have always had the tendency to segregate themselves either along religious lines, or according to their country of origin.

This is especially true of Jerusalem. In the Old City, for example, one has Jewish, Arab, Christian and Armenian quarters, as well as smaller areas occupied exclusively by Ethiopians, Copts and others. Outside, one has (or had) the Hungarian quarter and the Bokharan quarter, the Russian compound, the German colony and the Greek colony.

Rehavia was largely an English quarter and is now, with Talbieh, an Anglo-Saxon one. Mishkenot Sha'ananim is for very rich cosmopolitans, Bayit Vegan for prosperous Orthodox Americans, and the Katamonim for penniless Moroccans.

But now I note the beginnings of a new tendency – segregation along *sartorial* lines – and in case you should think that this is a figment of my over-worked and over-heated imagination, let me quote from a recent advert in the *Jerusalem Post.*

'For religious, *knitted kipot* (skull caps), Har Nof site, selected areas, 3, 4, 5 rooms and penthouses, register quickly (my italics) . . .'

I hurried along to see the flats. They are still in the course of construction (in Israel one is expected to pay for a property while it's still a hole in the ground, or even before), but they seem nicely planned and reasonably priced. They are certainly beautifully situated, and I might have been tempted to buy one, but for the matter of headgear (or lack of it).

I do not wish to shock readers with my iniquities, but I must confess that, although I am not irredeemably profane, I normally go about my day with a naked head, which does not mean, however, that I am devoid of all forms of covering. I have straw hats, stetsons, sombreros, a trilby, homburg, porkpie hat, steel helmet, *kova tembel* (floppy cotton sun hat), balaclava, biretta, *shtreimel* (round fur hat worn on the Sabbath by Chasidin), astrakan, fez, glengarry, dundreary, beret, cloth cap, solar topee and sou'wester.

I also have velvet *kipot* (picked up at various barmitzvahs and weddings), a white satin *kipah*, blue and white *kipot* embroidered with silver thread, silk *kipot* with biblical scenes, a huge Russian dome of a *kipah* made out of carpeting and bought in Tiflis, an embossed *kipah* picked up in Damascus, and even tartan *kipot*. But as fate would have it (or rather, as it wouldn't), I do not have a knitted *kipah*, nor is there any prospect that I might acquire one.

My wife and daughters don't knit, and when I put it to them that they should, they told me to get knotted.

So there we are. No matter how quickly I may register, or how much I might pay, I cannot qualify for a flat or a penthouse among the 'religious knitted *kipot*' of Har Nof.

But the developers have started something, and in the coming months and years I can anticipate new neighbourhoods springing up with similarly emphatic ideas as to what type of residents they want to attract. And I can already imagine their adverts:

'For religious, velvet *kipot* . . .'
'Ultra-religious, white socks . . .'
'Secular, off-the-shoulder gowns . . .'
'Ultra-secular, see-through blouses . . .'
'Penitents, sack cloth and ashes . . .'
'Bohemians, bare feet . . .'
'Hippy, flowers in their ears . . .'
'Back to nature, hand-made dhotis . . .'
'Right back to nature, nudists . . .'
'Valetudinarians, thermal underwear . . .'
'Very rich, Yves Saint-Laurent . . .'
'Ex-Mossad, dark glasses . . .'
'Americans, Bermuda shorts . . .'
'French, naughty nighties . . .'
'English, bowler hats . . .'
'Ramblers, wellington boots . . .'
'Highlanders, kilts . . .'
'Gays, kaftan and earrings . . .'
'German, *lederhosen* . . .'
'Orientals, jellebas . . .'

But, of course, it needn't stop at dress. One can imagine new neighbourhoods based on social habits, or combining habits and places of origin, such as: 'For gum-chewing Americans . . . Pipe-smoking Englishmen . . . Beer-swilling Irishmen . . . Garlic-eating

Italians . . . Quat-chewing Yemenites . . . Wife-beating Welshmen
. . . Stone-throwing zealots . . . Snuff-sniffing Lithuanians . . . Pot-
smoking Californians . . .'

To each his own.

24 December 1982

Farewell to the topper

I DO NOT wish to sound unduly alarmist, and even less to spread
gloom and despondency, but I think people should be warned that
the top hat is in danger.

When I came to this country shortly before the war and first set
foot in a synagogue, I felt as if I had come among giants.

I had heard of the top hat – or *tzylinderhut*, as it was known in
Yiddish – even in Latvia. I had seen pictures of it, as I had seen
pictures of the king and queen of England in their coronation
robes, and I thought of the topper as part of the same regalia.
When, therefore, I came upon not one top hat, or even two, but
whole ranks of them in the synagogue, it seemed as if we Jews had
already inherited the Kingdom of Heaven.

That the clergy, and even the para-clergy (such as beadles),
should have worn them was, of course, understandable, for they
were, after all, in holy office and the toppers could have been
regarded as the badge of their sanctity. The same could be said for
the toppers worn by the synagogue wardens, for if not holy in
themselves (and some were distinctly unholy), they worked closely
with the clergy and therefore could aspire to a passing holiness by
contagion.

But the *neiben on* pews – which is to say, those nearest the ark
– were likewise packed with top-hatted figures who were neither
holy nor even honorary officers. They were men of substance who
had made their mark not in the world-on-high, but in this one.

In those days, the garb not only proclaimed the man, it

proclaimed his income, and a prosperous draper who appeared in synagogue in a cloth cap, or even a bowler, would have been deemed guilty of deceit.

And the topper was only the beginning, or the end (as the case may be), for it went with striped trousers and a frock-coat, and a waistcoat, and spats, and a boiled shirt and wing collar, and cravat with a pearl pin. A man thus arrayed was not only displaying his substance, but proclaiming the fact that he was the object of divine beneficence. Thus shall it be done to the man whom the King of kings delighteth to honour.

All that died with the war and the years of Crippsian austerity and the tide of egalitarianism which followed. I don't know if anyone actually believed in equality, but almost everyone believed that they should appear equal, and top hats were consigned to the attic along with the Pesach cutlery and crockery, except that the latter were at least taken down for an airing one week in the year, while the toppers remained hidden away for ever – or almost for ever.

They are taken down once or twice in a lifetime (depending on the duration of one's life) for the induction of a chief rabbi, very much as the nobility bring down their coronets and tiaras (or take them out of pawn) for the coronation of their sovereign.

The last time I saw a mass array of toppers was at the induction of Dr Jakobovits in April, 1967. It was a marvellous sight, for there was hardly a soul in mufti, and when the congregation rose, standing shoulder to shoulder, they formed a smooth surface large enough to take a jumbo jet. The glory had returned to Israel, if only for an evening.

Since then there has been a process of constant decline which reached its climax, or rather its nadir, last week when a warden of the Hampstead Garden Suburb Synagogue, of all places, reserved the right to sit in the *warden*'s box sans topper! It was as if Her Majesty had reserved the right to preside at the state opening of Parliament in her famous pearly cap. At which point I must confess to having helped the rot set in, if only unwittingly.

Every member of the United Synagogue is called upon to be king for a day by wearing a topper at his son's barmitzvah. When my turn approached, I went to Moss Bros, but they had nothing in my size. (I don't know the size of my head, but I wear size 12½ shoes, and I can't imagine that my head is much smaller.)

I went to Lock's of St James's, who offered to make me a bespoke topper, but at a price which left me speechless (it would have cost almost as much as the barmitzvah). The biggest local bighead then offered to lend me his topper, but it sat on my skull like an apple, and I finally wore a *kipah* – not, may I add, one of those minuscule knitted affairs popular in certain circles, but a velvet skull-cap of rabbinical blackness and rabbinical size.

Indeed, it was almost a floppy topper, but a topper proper it wasn't, and I established an unhappy precedent which has been all too faithfully followed. But who would have dreamed that it would spread so soon to the hallowed precincts of the wardens' box?

A warden without a topper is like a high priest without his holy vestments. It deprives him of all authority and standing and reduces him to the rank of mere mortal. And people who wish to remain mortal should not aspire to a place in the wardens' box.

25 May 1984

Dress sense in Manchester

A NUMBER OF rabbis in Manchester have circulated a letter urging greater modesty in dress on their womenfolk.

Skirts, they stress, should be at least ten centimetres below the knee. Tights should be thick and opaque, and sleeves should be long and not so wide as inadvertently to expose the arm. Lace should not be worn at all because it is really a network of holes. Indeed, perforations of any sort and anything transparent should be avoided.

They have also stipulated that skirts of whatever length, even when worn over thick tights, should be without slits; that clothes in general should not be tight-fitting, that collars should go up to the neck – by which I think they mean up to the jaw – and that colours should be 'refined and quiet', which presumably means that lurex, for long the uniform of the devout matron, is no longer admissible.

Who says our rabbis are behind the times? They have not only kept abreast of fashion, but have gone metric! On the other hand, they do not seem to know what's afoot and are completely oblivious to the possibilities of the big toe (known in some media quarters as the Mellor), or even the little ones (known as Fergies), and they make no reference whatever to open sandals.

Nor, more surprisingly, do they have anything to say about culottes, which are a sort of cross between trousers and skirts, but which are neither one nor the other and which should be banned on the simple grounds of misrepresentation.

No Manchester-style encyclical has, as far as I know, been circulated in the London area, which might suggest any or all of three things: that London women are more modest; that Manchester women are more stylish; or that Manchester rabbis are more observant, or at least more conscientious, for they must have scrutinised their womenfolk at great length and with great care to come up with all those details about hemlines and necklines and slits. One wonders – given the height of the typical Manchester screen – how they went about it. Perhaps they used periscopes.

One is reminded of the lady who complained to Dr Johnson about the naughty words in his dictionary, to which he replied: 'Madam, you must have had great fun looking them up' (or words to that effect).

One would not, of course, suggest that rabbis in Manchester or anywhere else could be guilty of such prurience, but it does show the range of expertise which our spiritual leaders are expected to display. In the olden days a man was regarded as a sage if he was but a *boki b'shass*, meaning that he was an authority on the Talmud. Today he also has to be a *boki b'skirts*.

I can't recall ever seeing rabbinical advice on how men should dress, though a woman even in the gaudiest gear would look drab next to a Chasid in buckled shoes, white stockings, velvet knee breeches, silken *capote* (long coat) and mink *shtreimel* (round fur hat). It used to be said (by Lloyd George, I think) that it cost more to equip a full-blown duke than a battleship. The equipage of a full-blown Chasid must be almost as expensive, but Chasidim dress to impress their Maker, while women dress to impress their menfolk – or rather their womenfolk.

More to the point, men have less to hide, and are more easily distracted, which brings me to the crux of the matter. Mrs Rita Rosemarine, president of the Manchester Jewish Representative Council, has said: 'There must be better ways of persuading women in our community to lead an Orthodox life than by issuing such rigid edicts,' but the rabbis are less concerned with the proclivities of women than with the weaknesses of men.

There are passages in the Talmud and Midrashic literature suggesting Jewish women can be light-headed and vain, but they are outnumbered and outweighed by the many references to their intelligence, modesty and virtue. There is a general belief that, even where they are prone to temptation, they have the strength of character to rise above it.

No such claims are made for Jewish men, which is why, presumably, women may listen to men singing, but not vice versa; why women, but not men, are carefully instructed to cover their hair; and why our rabbis go to such lengths to define what women may, or may not wear, but are totally silent on masculine gear. A brightly clad woman will divert a man from his prayers, but nothing a man can wear will divert a woman from hers.

The Manchester encyclical, for all its prohibitions, is thus a tribute to Jewish womanhood, and a fine example of subtle – perhaps too subtle – gallantry.

2 October 1992

6
Freedom . . .
and the press

*The liberty to cause offence, even outrage, is
precisely what freedom of speech is about. It
presumes the right to be wrong.*

Harold Pinter

HAROLD PINTER IS a man of few words, most of them silly.

Yet he is one of the foremost playwrights of our time – which does not mean he is a Shakespeare or even an Ibsen, but he does have a deep insight into the quirks of human nature, and a unique ear for the ambiguities and gaps of human speech.

He eavesdrops on silence. Where others are generally concerned with people who have too much to say and say it too vehemently, he is concerned with people who have little to say and don't know how to say it at all and his audience gets caught up in trying to extrapolate meaning from what may seem to be meaningless. He is the poet laureate of the inarticulate.

I can't claim to have seen all of his plays, but the only one of his characters I found unconvincing was the professor in *The Homecoming*, for professors seem a little outside his range. He is far happier with characters of limited intelligence and, if his public utterances are anything to go by, he shares their limitations.

Yet there seems to be a general belief that anyone who displays a talent or genius in one area of life must have something worthwhile to say on every other, and when a week or two ago the *Observer* invited about a dozen well-known figures to comment on the rights and wrongs of the Gulf War, Pinter was inevitably among them.

There has been much debate in recent months on the concept of a just war. Wars are murderous and messy, for if one knows how they begin, there is no telling how they will finish and if the world was full of Pinters (who was a conscientious objector even in peacetime) one could probably get by without any wars (though it would become an insufferable place in other respects).

The world, however, is rather more complicated than that and there can come a time when war with all its hazards carries fewer dangers than appeasement and that time came when Saddam Hussein devoured Kuwait on 2 August.

If ever there was a single instance of unprovoked aggression, this was it and one might have thought that it would not be impossible for even the most peace-loving of men to muster a good word for America, or at least a bad one against Iraq.

Not Pinter.

Pinter's thinking, if one may call it that, goes back to the Vietnam war, when all good men and true – not a few of them Jewish – seemed to think that the Viet Cong were the innocent victims of American aggression. America in fact had good grounds for its intervention. I'm only sorry it failed, and given the subsequent history of the area, the people of Vietnam must be even sorrier.

In this particular instance, however, Pinter invoked America's intervention in Grenada, Panama, and Nicaragua, as if they could be spoken of in the same breath as Iraq's invasion of Kuwait.

America was welcomed as a liberator by the overwhelming majority of the population in all three countries, and, in each instance, it withdrew the moment it established a stable and representative government, whereas Kuwait has actually been incorporated as a province of Iraq.

Pinter laughs at the suggestions that the Americans 'were inspired by a determination to keep the world clean for democracy,' but in fact they were doing just that.

They are unlikely to make Kuwait clean for democracy because there is no such thing as a democratic Arab state (and precious few Muslim ones). But the fact that Kuwait happened to have been, and is likely to remain, a feudal oligarchy, is no reason why it should be left to the mercy of a Saddam Hussein. And, of course, if he had been allowed to keep Kuwait, he wouldn't have stopped there.

Nor does Pinter spare a thought for the unprovoked attacks on Israel, the threat of gas warfare or the actual use of poison gas against the Kurds. He sees the world in simple terms and reacts to events like the product of a third-rate poly who has been brought up on a diet of pre-packed political slogans and presumes that any country or cause actively supported by America must be in the wrong.

America has not always been inspired in its presentation of policies, and it has occasionally been clumsy in their execution, but, with all its faults, no great power in history has been so mindful of its responsibilities, and none has been less assertive, and it can be seen at its best in the present crisis.

15 February 1991

Sunday shopping bill

THE TIMES COMPLAINED recently of the motley packs who had ganged up in an improbable coalition against the government's Sunday shopping bill, including socialists, capitalists, corporatists, 'friends of small business accumulation', Ulster Unionists, policy irrationalists, Conservative sabbatarians, 'Christians who put formality of observance before all', and – most improbable of all – 'Jews, brought up in households which managed with full rigour to observe their holy day on a conventional Christian work day, suddenly turned apologists for the misshapen puritan Sunday'.

I plead guilty to being one of those Jews, for although I am not an MP, I did write a strong, if good-humoured, polemic against the bill in the *Guardian* on the day of the debate, which I like to think (on meagre evidence I'm afraid) swayed sufficient votes to kill it.

Another of those Jews, undoubtedly, was the shadow home secretary, Gerald Kaufman, MP, who spoke of his own upbringing in an Orthodox household, and described how his father suffered poverty and hardship in his efforts to remember the Sabbath day and keep it holy, and preserved it as 'a tranquil island in the stormy sea of the week'. It was all nicely put and rather touching, but Mr Kaufman did not suggest that he followed his father's example and a Jew who does not observe his own Sabbath is not well placed to urge Christians to observe theirs.

On the other hand, as I followed the debate, and noted the strong feelings in various parts of the House on the issue, I was glad that Mr Leon Brittan was no longer home secretary, for though it may seem incongruous for Jews to be apologists for 'the misshapen puritan Sunday', it would have been indelicate for a Jew to take the lead in undermining it.

As a Tory speaker observed, the Sabbath was perhaps the greatest of all Jewish contributions to the well-being of man. It is certainly basic to the well-being of the Jew, and Jews who owe so much to its benefits can, I think, be forgiven for recommending them to their neighbours.

Moreover, no matter how enclosed their own world may be,

Jews are never wholly immune to the influences of the world about them, or, as they used to say in *der heim* (the old country), '*vi es Christelt zech, azei Yiddelt zech,*' which in rough translation means, as Christians go, so do the Jews. Judaism cannot flourish in a pagan environment. One of the reasons why there is so little Jewish life in Sweden and Denmark, for example, is that they are largely devoid of Christian life, while the small Jewish community in Ireland has a disproportionate vibrancy because it is part of a deeply religious society.

Of course, things can be pushed to extremes, and in religion they often are. Many of the hardships and hazards faced by East European Jewry derived from the religious fanaticism of the surrounding population, and the open season for pogroms generally coincided with Easter. In our own time, no one would suggest that Iranian Jewry has benefited from the revival of Muslim fundamentalism and, indeed, Jewish fundamentalists, if given their head, would make Jewish life unviable. In particular, they are trying and, to an extent are succeeding, in changing Shabbat from a day of joy, into a day of mortification. There is, however, no danger of a revival of English Christian fundamentalism (as distinct from the Anglo-Jewish variety). Most of the discernible trends are the other way, and if the English Sunday (what there is left of it) should vanish completely, it would be that much more difficult to maintain the Jewish Sabbath.

Early Christians, who were nearly all Jews, were not quite sure which day they were meant to observe, the seventh or the first, and to be on the safe side they kept both. It could be argued that some Jews are now reverting to this practice.

I spend many of my Sundays touring English villages, country towns and cathedral cities, or walking in the Chilterns or Cotswolds, and I return refreshed, for there is a tranquil charm to the day which would vanish if it were to become a day like any other. It adds immeasurably to the unhurried, pensive quality of English life, its passing moments of serenity, and I, for one, do not feel in the least apologetic for being an apologist for the English Sunday, no matter how misshapen it may seem.

2 May 1986

Holocaust denial

THE FOLLOWING SHOULD be reprinted in large letters and circulated among all the members of the Board of Deputies, and every other organisation anxious to defend Jewish interests under whatever name it may function and in whatever place it may operate.

It is from a recent article in *The Times*, written by Matthew Parris:

> What made the heart sink at Tony Blair's promise to consider a new crime of 'Holocaust-denial' was not that it opens up any prospect that such an offence will be created in Britain. The idea is un-English; simply to entertain it is to dismiss it as impossible.
>
> Mr Blair's pledge, made without thought, to please his immediate audience, can easily be reneged upon, and will be.
>
> No, what is unsettling is the realisation that, after 3,000 years of European civilisation, after Socrates and Galileo, Erasmus and Voltaire, after Mill, Shaw, Russell and Orwell, it should be the case that, within three years of the end of the twentieth century, a man of Mr Blair's evident decency could suppose it even arguable that the expression of an opinion should be made punishable by law.

I have said as much, and more, on many occasions, if in less elegant terms, and have no hesitation in saying it again: the whole campaign to make Holocaust-denial a punishable offence is abominable in principle and unattainable in practice.

It is almost unbelievable that Jews, of all people, who owe their very survival to the fact that they live in a free society, should be ready and even anxious, to undermine such freedom.

In a recent television programme, Professor David Cesarani waved several publications to show that there was already a burgeoning Holocaust-denial library. Clearly, some feel that the law should be tightened before such an unsavoury collection grows any larger.

I am amazed that an historian of his standing should lend his weight, however implicitly or even perhaps unintentionally, to such a campaign, for his whole craft is based on a continuing re-evaluation and reinterpretation of given information and accepted ideas. No body of knowledge in a free society can be frozen by law.

In the same programme, Greville Janner, MP, pointed out that Germany, France and several other European countries had laws against Holocaust-denial. That is true, but I have never regarded Germany, or France for that matter, as exemplars of freedom, and I am surprised that he does.

What is more pertinent is that America has no such laws, because its constitution would not allow it, and Britain has none because its traditions would not permit it.

The arguments in favour of laws against the dissemination of what has become known as 'revisionist literature' are basically two. The suggestion that there was no organised campaign to destroy the Jewish people would outrage thousands of individuals whose families were the immediate victims of the campaign and who are themselves scarred by memories of it.

Secondly, it would suggest that Jews were guilty of a vast international conspiracy to extort billions in compensation from innocent people for injuries they had never suffered and property they had never lost.

The first point is undeniable, but the liberty to cause offence, even outrage, is precisely what freedom of speech is about. It presumes the right to be wrong. The only effective answer to lies is not a ban on their dissemination, but the truth. Even if the truth is not always readily discernible, it has a capacity to emerge in the face of all attempts to pervert it.

The second point is more debatable. But even if such a view were to spread, it would not be half as harmful as the growing belief that Jews are engaged in an international conspiracy to limit freedom of speech.

In other words, no danger which has arisen, or might arise, from the dissemination of revisionist literature, is half as dangerous as the attempt to stop it. Further, every such attempt gives rise to the suspicion that there is something to hide.

I have read some of the publications flourished by Professor Cesarani. Their arguments are as flimsy as their format, and the idea they could in any way undermine the vast corpus of serious histories by serious historians, the innumerable newspaper articles, biographies and diaries, the films and plays, the videos and Holocaust museums all giving testimony to the truth, is laughable.

The very attempt to ban the revisionist books merely draws attention to their existence and gives a passing credence to their case.

14 February 1997

7
Personalities

Primo Levi – Best antidote to Jewish paranoia that I've come across.

Yehudi Menuhin

AGE SEEMS TO be regarded as an attainment in its own right, and not only among Jews, but the one old man who deserves all the praise which has been heaped upon him – and not only by music-lovers – is Yehudi Menuhin, who has just turned 80.

He, of course, doesn't look it – who does these days? But he has always retained the boyishness which first brought him to prominence as a child prodigy, except that boyishness is usually combined with mischief while his most obvious quality is innocence.

About 20 years ago he was kind enough to compliment me on something I had written. I wrote back to thank him and he invited me to meet him.

Legends can be something of a disappointment when encountered in the flesh. Menuhin was not. He lived at the time in a large Georgian mansion in Highgate with lofty ceilings. He is not a tall man and his surroundings made him seem even smaller and slighter. He also had that glow about him which made him look beatific.

One's idea of sanctity is coloured by childhood memories. The sort of saints who peopled my childhood were figures like Abraham, Moses and Elijah, all of them bearded and stern. Menuhin did not quite fit the picture because he was clean-shaven and affable. He did his best to make me at ease but I was so overwhelmed by his presence as to be almost tongue-tied. We talked about the Middle East, or rather, he talked and I listened.

Great talent is rarely accompanied by great wisdom, or even a gift for self-expression. Menuhin is both articulate and wise, but extremely unworldly. His view of life was and is based on a belief in the perfection, or at least the perfectibility, of human nature. He likes to think that, if one approaches a problem with sufficient charity and goodwill, one must inevitably bring out the charity and goodwill in others.

It did not tally with my view of mankind, certainly as applied to the Middle East. It was difficult to believe that a man who had lived through the greater part of the twentieth century could regard his fellow creatures with such benevolence. Although it was refreshing to listen to him, it seemed to me that he had either been sheltered from reality, or that he embraced a faith which transcended all human experience.

A few years later, a publisher invited me to write Menuhin's biography. I felt flattered but explained that I knew little about music.

'Everybody knows about Menuhin the musician,' he said. 'I want a book about Menuhin the man. And you're just the chap to write it.'

He also mentioned a very large sum.

I, of course, accepted and what followed reminded me of a famous Jewish joke:

There was this wealthy gown merchant who had a lovely and gifted daughter. No one she met was good enough for him, or her, and finally the *shadchan* came up with a proposal which he was convinced neither of them could reject.

'He's good-looking, of good family – the best, with lots of money, and a good education, Eton and Cambridge. He's also gifted.'

'So where's the catch?' demanded the father. The *shadchan*, caught off guard, admitted that there was indeed a catch, the boy wasn't Jewish. 'But, for your daughter,' he added quickly, 'he'll convert.'

'So who is he?'

'Prince Edward.'

'Hasn't he got a girlfriend?'

'Yes, but, for your daughter, he'll leave her.'

The father puffed at his cigar for a while, and said, 'It's okay by me.'

'Excellent, excellent,' said the *shadchan*, rubbing his hands, 'now for a word with Her Majesty.'

Her Majesty in this case turned out to be Lady Menuhin, a tall, elegant woman, attractive and formidable, a former ballet dancer who had made it her life's work to shield her husband from the harsher intrusions of this world. She had taken the trouble to read two or three of my books. The first thing she said was:

'You do have an irreverential attitude to people.' I said that I took them as I found them.

'But you do look for the worst in them.'

'I don't look for it, but where I find it, I don't ignore it.'

'Indeed.'

Which was her way of letting me know I was not the man for the job.

I was disappointed in some ways, relieved in others. It takes a saint – which I'm not – to understand a saint and I doubt whether I would have been able to do justice to the man. But then, neither did the chap who actually wrote the book.

26 April 1996

Teddy Kollek

NOT MANY CITY bosses acquire international stature, but then Jerusalem is no ordinary city and Teddy Kollek was no ordinary boss. And the fact that he is universally known by his first name is in itself a measure of the affection and esteem he enjoys.

Teddy first became mayor in 1965 when Jerusalem was still a small, messy and divided city, the capital of Israel in name, but very much a small, provincial backwater. Most government offices were still in Tel Aviv.

Two years later came what was called 'the miracle' of re-unification, though perhaps the most important part of that miracle was the fact that Teddy happened to be mayor. The area of the city was more than trebled, and the population was doubled, to include more than 100,000 Arabs.

Where there would have been strife and chaos, he brought reconciliation and order. He made sure that Arabs were treated as full citizens and took urgent steps to convert Jerusalem into a city worthy of its name and give it capital status.

He cleared the rubble and barbed wire which divided the new

111

city from the old, and planted gardens in their place. He built theatres and concert halls, laid out parks, extended museums, and erected a new stadium.

His very name was sufficient to help attract generous overseas benefactions, the most recent of which is the magnificent Supreme Court building erected by the Rothschild Foundation. He gave Jerusalem self-assurance, vitality, colour.

As a man seeking peace, he suffered a serious setback with the election of a Likud government in 1977. The Likud may not have sought conflict, but it eventually provoked it with its efforts – some of them open, most of them devious – to edge Arabs out of the Old City. (The intifada – an inevitable by-product of Likud misrule – also had its melancholy effects.)

In the main, however, his plans and hopes were undermined by inexorable demographic trends. The *charedi* elements in the city were growing at an unprecedented rate through natural increase. As they moved into one area after another, non-*charedim* moved out and, in spite of massive Russian immigration, Jerusalem is the only city in Israel whose population has fallen in recent years. When I spoke to Teddy last year he was quite adamant that he would not be running for re-election, or, as he put it, 'no one can go on for ever.'

Well he had a jolly good try, and he failed, as he was bound to fail, not because of his age, but because of his party. Labour in Jerusalem has a built-in majority against it, which will grow with every election, and the tragedy for Jerusalem is not merely that Teddy has ceased to be mayor, but that he has been replaced by a mere opportunist like Ehud Olmert.

Few political campaigns in Israel are clean, and some are downright squalid, but I can recall nothing quite as squalid as an advertisement published on behalf of Mr Olmert which warned that, if Teddy were re-elected, there would be 'thousands of Arabs roaming the city, raping, drug-trafficking and thieving'.

Olmert later disowned the ad. However, he also told a gathering: 'One of the greatest myths of Jerusalem is that Teddy did something for the Arabs and therefore they were quiet . . . They are not quiet. Whenever they can stab someone in the back they will do so . . .'

As if all Arabs were assassins, and all Jews lovers of peace. I cannot imagine any other politician in a free society talking about

112

his fellow citizens in the same terms.

But worse than the things said will be the price Olmert will have to pay to the Orthodox and ultra-Orthodox parties for their support. He has vowed that 'the nature of the city is not going to change one iota'. The coming months and years will show how far the promise will be kept.

I can foresee only growing strife, not only between Jews and Arabs, but between the religious and the secular, and a growing exodus of the more enlightened, progressive and moderate elements in the city.

Teddy has warned that 'the Orthodox would turn Jerusalem into a sterile city, with no museums, no theatres, no libraries – no fun.'

A fun city, Jerusalem never was and never could be. However, it did have a certain aesthetic quality which will now be lost. Teddy sought to direct it towards the twenty-first century: it will now slide back towards the Middle Ages. Where it could have become a cultural metropolis, it now threatens to become a larger Bnei Brak.

12 November 1993

Hugo Gryn

HUGO GRYN WAS more than a great rabbi, he was a symbol of Jewish resilience, and one could see, in the way he went about his work through the last days of his dreadful illness, the sheer grit which sustained him through Auschwitz. About a week before he died, weak, white-faced and in pain, he gave a public lecture in a clear and spirited voice, to a large audience.

Hugo did not care to dabble in theology. When asked where was God in Auschwitz, he replied: 'Where was man?' And yet his personal experience of evil did not temper his love for mankind.

In a way he was to Britain what Elie Wiesel is to America,

though, as if nervous of becoming a cult figure, he rarely missed an opportunity to laugh at himself. He brought many qualities to his calling: energy, resourcefulness, learning, eloquence, sympathy, patience, insight, but outstanding among them was one which can be expressed only in Hebrew: *chasidut*, a loving kindness and sense of concern which he combined with an understanding of human frailty.

As rabbi of the largest Jewish congregation in Europe and as a public figure, there were endless demands on his time, yet he always found time for the anguished or distressed. And people didn't even have to importune him with their problems. If he saw an anxious face or a troubled look, he would want to know what the trouble was about.

Though a Reform rabbi with an American training and an American accent, he retained many of the attitudes and mannerisms of the *shtetl* from which he stemmed.

Faced with some complex issue, he would often illuminate it with an anecdote drawn from Jewish lore. He had something of the style of the wandering *maggid* (preacher), which he used to good effect as a broadcaster, but what made him a household name, was not so much his sagacity or wit, as his warmth, and when his voice was finally stilled, thousands of people throughout the country felt as if they had lost a personal friend. No one did more to enhance the standing of Jews and Judaism in the eyes of the general public.

He was a man with a mission and saw in the elimination of factionalism, disunity and distrust the one hope for the survival of mankind, and he devoted his life to searching out common ground between Jew and Christian, Jew and Hindu, Jew and Muslim, and usually found it. He was less successful when it came to Jew and Jew, but never made a public issue out of it because he hated acrimony and dissension.

No rabbi in Britain was more loved or esteemed, as was evident from the vast congregation which packed the West London Synagogue for his funeral service. All sections of the community were represented together: bishops and archbishops, ambassadors and high commissioners, and eminent figures from all walks of life, *but there wasn't a single Orthodox rabbi among them* (to which I should add that Rabbi Abraham Levy, spiritual head of the Spanish and Portuguese Congregation, was present at the funeral itself).

.One didn't expect anyone from the extreme right because, though they make forays into the wider community to collect money for their institutions, they otherwise scorn it. Where, however, was the United Synagogue, which still likes to think of itself as embodying the mainstream of Anglo-Jewry?

The chief rabbi, Dr Jonathan Sacks, was otherwise engaged but sent a representative in the person of the Rev Alan Greenbat, who is not a rabbi, and Mrs Sacks was present at the funeral in Hoop Lane, but where were all his colleagues? There are scores of them; could they all have been otherwise engaged? Could not one of them have snatched an hour to pay tribute to the memory of a remarkable man? To be sure he was a Reform rabbi, but if that is a defect, was it not outweighed by his virtues?

The lay leaders of the United Synagogue were likewise absent, presumably on rabbinical advice, or perhaps they were so house-trained as to anticipate the advice. Hugo would have understood their attitude and would have forgiven them.

I don't.

I have been a member of the United Synagogue for more than 30 years and though not unfamiliar with its faults, I had a lingering affection for it, not so much for what it is, as what it was. This particular incident has, however, highlighted the mean minds, the mean souls and the mean principles which govern it.

There have been prolonged debates in recent years on whether it could be saved. I am now beginning to wonder if it is worth saving.

30 August 1996

Andrei Sakharov

I WAS HAVING supper with Professor Benjamin Levitch in Moscow one evening when he suggested that there was someone I might like to meet.

115

We drove to a nondescript flat in a nondescript suburb and he introduced me to a white-haired figure with a slight stoop. The man was only 52 then, but looked much older. I recognised the famous features at once. It was Andrei Sakharov.

'My rebbe,' said Levitch.

The refusenik movement had thrown up many great figures and Levitch was among the greatest. A physicist and academician of international standing he was among the country's élite, but once he applied to go to Israel he was shorn of all his privileges and shunned by most of his colleagues.

I found him at a low point in his fortunes. He saw no prospect of leaving Russia. He was not allowed to get on with his work. His wife was ailing. One of his sons was a prisoner in an Arctic labour camp, but a meeting with Sakharov could save him from despair.

Sakharov had a similar effect on other refuseniks, for even if they did not know him personally, they knew of him. He was an inspiration to all those with a yearning to be free.

The Soviet Union was, and still largely is, a bleak wasteland brightened by occasional centres of excellence. Where a child showed serious promise as an athlete, musician or scientist, he was treated like a precious plant in a carefully tended hot-bed; and where he fulfilled his promise, he was showered with privileges.

One lived in a different world from the mass of people and one could lead a good life, provided one kept the rules and did not ask awkward questions.

It was difficult for a Solzhenitsyn to work with the system, for all great literature demands a commitment to the truth.

Scientists, and notably physicists, have it much easier in that respect, for they can thrive even in a world of lies, particularly where it gives every priority to their special needs, and they can become so engrossed in their work as to lose sight of the world about them.

Sakharov was an exception in this respect, as in every other, and if he devoted the first half of his working life to science, he devoted the second to human rights. He made his mark as a physicist even as a student at Moscow University. At 30 he was virtually supreme in his field. Two years later, he was a full member of the Soviet Academy of Sciences, the youngest person to be so honoured in the history of the academy. By then he had assumed a leading role in producing the H-bomb and was showered with every honour, including the Stalin Prize and three Orders of Socialist Labour.

He was still in his thirties, however, and at the height of his power and influence, when he began asking awkward questions and coming up with even more awkward answers. The authorities became alarmed and, as he grew more voluble and outspoken, they withdrew his privileges.

But he could not be silenced. He became the champion of every oppressed minority in Russia and was particularly concerned with the fate of Soviet Jewry, not because his wife Yelena was Jewish, but because he was all too familiar with their history.

In 1968 he drew attention to the anti-Semitism prevalent in the Soviet Union and demanded that people be given the freedom to emigrate. In 1970 he founded the Committee for Human Rights.

The authorities then tried to terrorise him into silence, and he and Solzhenitsyn were implicated in a widely publicised treason trial. Solzhenitsyn was expelled, but they could not expel Sakharov because he knew too much; his international standing was such that they could not kill him, and in a final, if futile, attempt to isolate him, he was exiled to Gorky.

And it was in Gorky, almost exactly three years ago, that he received a personal phone call from Gorbachev inviting him to return to Moscow.

Sakharov was often called 'the father of the Russian H-bomb', a title he abhorred, but I regard him as the father of the peaceful revolution in Eastern Europe that has been unfolding before our eyes over the past few months.

I don't know if Gorbachev was directly influenced by him, but many of the ideas Sakharov propounded have since become Soviet policy.

He was the greatest man of our time, and among the greatest of all time. One feels privileged to have been his contemporary.

22 December 1989

Edwina Currie

I AM NOT in favour of intermarriage but the fact that former Tory MP Edwina Currie (née Cohen) has spoken out against it, suggests that there must be something to be said for it.

This is certainly a subject on which Mrs Currie can speak with authority, for she not only married out, but she married in church – which is to say she married inside out. She says that, in doing so, she did not convert to Christianity. This is rather like President Clinton's confession that though he smoked cannabis, he did not actually inhale.

Mrs Currie clearly feels that her failure to convert suggests a residual loyalty to Judaism, but does it?

She appears to have given considerable thought to the content of her marriage service, and asked for a reading from the book of Ruth.

'Whither thou goest, I will go' – 'If it was good enough for Ruth and Boaz,' she says, 'it was good enough for me.'

But she appears to have forgotten – or perhaps she never knew – that the passage in full reads – '. . . for whither thou goest, I will go, and where thou lodgest, I will lodge; thy people shall be my people and thy God my God.'

As enunciated by Ruth on the way to Judea, it represented an affirmation of Judaism. As enunciated by Edwina Cohen in church, it could only have meant an affirmation of Christianity, unless, perhaps, she kept her fingers crossed while she was saying it.

But whether she converted to Christianity or not, the fact remains that once Mrs Currie was elected an MP and became a health minister in Mrs Thatcher's administration, she seemingly preferred to be thought of as non-Jewish.

She never featured in the list of Jewish MPs published annually by the *Jewish Year Book*. And she never mentioned her maiden name in *Who's Who*. She doesn't even mention her parents, which is about as far as one can go in denying one's past. It would have been easier for Mike Tyson to deny he was black.

There is no such thing as an ex-Jew in Jewish law, or in Gentile eyes, and had Mrs Currie been baptised, taken holy orders and become the Mother Superior of a Carmelite convent, she would still have been thought of as a loud, pushy and assertive Jewess.

She now claims to be 'appalled at the statistics that said that half of the generation is marrying out and is lost,' and at the prospect that 'the community is in danger of disappearing altogether in a couple of generations.' Which, coming from someone who has done her best to get lost in her own generation, is a bit much. Whatever deficiencies Mrs Currie may have, she is not short of effrontery.

The more I contemplate her career, the more I recall the last years of another Jewish politician, Robert Maxwell.

Maxwell also married in church and, once he entered politics and became a public figure, he also tried to give the impression that he wasn't Jewish. But when he reconciled himself to the fact that, with all his millions (in so far as they were his), he would never be fully accepted among *goyim*, he recast himself as a super Jew.

He was accepted as such in Israel and was accorded a state funeral on the Mount of Olives (thereby desecrating the entire mount).

The parallels should not be carried too far because Maxwell was a crook and a megalomaniac. Mrs Currie is neither. Nor can I see her ending up on the Mount of Olives, because, apart from anything else, I doubt if she could afford the freehold. She has, however, taken the Maxwell route in other respects, for she began to rediscover her Jewish roots only when her political career was over and once her marriage had broken down.

If one may quote a verse from the Bible which Mrs Currie presumably did not use in her marriage service: 'There is more joy in heaven over the sinner that repenteth, than over 99 just persons who have no need to repent,' and one might have welcomed the return of the prodigal daughter, had it not coincided with a new phase in her career.

Where Mrs Currie was a struggling politician, she is now a struggling scribe. And scribes depend on publicity even more than politicians.

She chose her book launch as the occasion to announce the end of her marriage and one can, I think, be forgiven for suspecting that the rediscovery of her Jewishness and her aversion to intermarriage may be linked to the same event.

119

Perhaps I'm being too cynical. For we are not only at the height of the publishing season, but of the atonement season, too. For all we know, her change of heart could be perfectly sincere.

10 October 1997

Primo Levi

I WAS SORRY to read of the tragic death of Primo Levi. I had been among his devotees for many years, but I only got to know him personally last summer and had hoped to see very much more of him in the future.

Writers can be a disappointment when encountered in the flesh, for no matter how lofty the characters they create, they can sometimes be petty, peevish, self-centred and tedious in themselves, but Levi could have stepped out of his own pages. He was a slight, silvery-haired figure with a neat little beard, donnish, soft spoken, diffident, kindly, smiling eyes behind large glasses, and the bearing of a natural aristocrat.

I had to interview him for a radio broadcast and I came with a list of prepared questions: 'You've been through hell,' I began, at which he immediately raised a hand to stop me.

'I suppose you mean Auschwitz,' he said. 'Auschwitz was hell, but I was only there for about a year, you know. I was also a chemist so the Germans found it useful to keep me alive.'

Which almost suggests that he had it easy. His books show otherwise, for he did go through hell, yet they are singularly free of self-pity or even rancour. He doesn't preach forgiveness or forgetfulness, but he does suggest a need to transcend experience and avoid bitterness so that his main characters emerge from their torments not only with their souls and their sanity intact, but even with their sense of humour. To be embittered, he seems to say, to harp on the past, is to give Hitler a posthumous victory.

Most of his books are concerned with the Holocaust and its aftermath, but he never became obsessed with it and warned his readers of the dangers of obsession, or as one of his characters put it: 'These aren't thoughts for every day. They're all right every now and again, but if you live with them, you just poison yourself.'

Levi was born in Turin and when the Germans occupied northern Italy after the fall of Mussolini in 1943 he joined the partisans, but he was betrayed and transported to Auschwitz. Yet the betrayal never rankled in his memory. There were, he said, a few Italian Nazis and a great many Italians who were afraid of the Nazis, but for every Italian who betrayed a Jew, there were countless others who risked their lives to save Jews (which, incidentally, is a point also made by another Italian, Professor Dan Segre, in his recently published, *Memoirs of a Fortunate Jew*) and he went out of the way to show that we are not, and never were, constantly surrounded by enemies, and that the world is, on the whole, a rather benign and attractive place. (To which I would add that even if it isn't I can't offhand think of a better one.)

His books are about the best antidote to Jewish paranoia that I've come across. They have an oddly uplifting effect: one not only feels a better man for reading them, one feels a better Jew.

His most telling work was perhaps *If Not Now, When?* which has just appeared in paperback. Everyone should read it, for apart from being a particularly gripping and heartening story, it is also, in a way, his final testament.

The title, of course, comes from a famous Talmudic passage: 'If I'm for myself, who will be for me? But if I am only for myself, what am I? And if not now, when?'

The first point which Levi makes, the need for Jews to assert themselves, is obvious. The second is rather less so, for he suggests that Jews who are too assertive and are concerned exclusively with their own survival are being untrue to themselves.

The Jew in his stories comes to stand for the universal victim, and, as one of his characters says: 'Everybody is everybody else's Jew. The Poles are the Jews of the Russians and Germans,' to which he himself once added, 'and the Palestinians are the Jews of the Israelis.'

I have heard him described as the greatest Jewish writer of our age, which I think is something of an exaggeration, for some of his characters are too good to be true and would not be out of place

121

in the novels of Walter Scott, but he had more than talent, or even genius, he had grace.

His untimely death is a loss to literature and a great loss to the Jewish people, but one can draw some comfort from the thought that his teachings will continue to survive through his books.

24 April 1987

Rav Joseph Soloveitchik

IT IS NOW a month since Rav (Rabbi) Joseph Soloveitchik died, but it will take much longer than that to assess his impact on Jewish life and his influence on Jewish thought.

He was one of the few men who could be genuinely described as a *godol hador*, a giant of his generation, though he would not have allowed himself to be described in any such terms. Only small men glory in grand titles.

He stemmed from a dynasty of great scholars dating back to the eighteenth century, of whom the best known was possibly his grandfather, who became rabbi of Brisk and was generally referred to as Reb Chaim Brisker.

There were close links between the family and Volozhin Yeshivah, a centre of excellence to which only the most gifted students were admitted. Its very renown brought it to the attention of the Russian authorities, who called for the introduction of secular studies to its curriculum. The *yeshivah* refused to comply and it was closed in 1892. Reb Chaim, who had been one of the glories of the *yeshivah*, became rabbi of Brisk. (It was later reopened, but never regained its old pre-eminence.)

Joseph Soloveitchik was educated by his own father in the tradition of Reb Chaim. He also received his secular education from private tutors. He went on to the University of Berlin, where he received a doctorate in philosophy in 1931.

His thesis was on the epistemology and metaphysics of Hermann Cohen, one of the leading German philosophers of his day, who died in 1918 and left an ambiguous legacy.

There were in essence two Cohens. The younger, drawing heavily on the ideas of Kant, argued that God was a remote entity about whose being no definite statement could be made.

The older Cohen – he was in his seventies by then, and possibly anxious to hedge his bets – began to feel that not everything could be explained by reason, and that there was a link between God and man.

God had, so to speak, set the ball rolling with the act of creation, and it was up to man to complete the job and bring about the millennium through self-sanctification (which, I hasten to add, is not the same as sanctimoniousness).

This philosophy was at the core of one of Soloveitchik's few published works, *Ish Ha-halachah* (man of Jewish law), but he carried the process further by suggesting that sanctity was a two-way process; that man not only sanctified himself through religious observance, but that he made the observances sacred through adhering to them.

In practical terms, this could have meant rigid conformity, but when, for example, there were mumurings about the idea of teaching women the Talmud at Yeshiva University, he silenced opposition by giving the opening lecture.

He allowed mainstream Orthodoxy to work together openly and unashamedly with Reform synagogues, which would not be tolerated in Britain. He also tempered legalism with compassion when dealing with vexed personal issues which were brought to his attention. Yet he never enunciated any broad general principles which would have made it easier for other rabbis to do the same.

Volozhin, in whose traditions he was brought up, was established virtually to combat *Chasidism*. But, although Soloveitchik was far and away the most respected rabbi of his day, he did nothing to check the wilder excesses of *Chasidism* or the spread of half-baked mysticism and crude superstition.

One must add that he suffered from Parkinson's Disease and that he was incapacitated for the last five or six years of his life, but he was the ultimate legatee of all that was enlightened and rational in Lithuanian scholasticism. Indeed, he represented it in his very person and I fear it may have died with him.

He was also the virtual godfather of religious Zionism in America, which was all right while religious Zionists were a benign force, but when they began to foam at the mouth and become chauvinistic xenophobes, he did not utter a public word to upbraid them. This was despite his own lack of belief in a greater Israel, and little patience for Greater Israelites. During his last years, Yeshiva University became a recruiting ground for Gush Emunim and I doubt whether the great prestige he brought to the university will survive his passing.

He was a teacher and philosopher and cherished the tranquillity of his study, which is why he turned down the invitation to be chief rabbi of Israel in 1959 and of Britain in 1966. But eminence carries obligations, and his fear of controversy was the nearest thing he had to a defect.

7 May 1993

Maimonides

THERE IS A Hebrew saying, 'From Moses till Moses there was none like Moses,' the other Moses being Rabbi Moshe ben Maimon, or the Rambam, one of the foremost figures of his time and the greatest Jewish scholar of all time, who was born 850 years ago this week in Córdoba, Spain.

The Rambam, or Maimonides as he was more generally known, was a polymath: philosopher, halachist, codifier, physician, mathematician and astronomer; the sort of figure who would today be described as a 'Renaissance man', except that he lived nearly 300 years before the Renaissance.

When a man as attained a lasting place in history, everyone likes to claim him as his own, and thus the Rambam has been described as a liberal by the Left, as a staunch defender of Orthodoxy by the Right, and – wait for it – as Moslem by the Arabs.

In 1148 when the Rambam was 13 Córdoba was conquered by

the Almohads, a fiercely intolerant Moslem sect who forced Christians and Jews – among them, it would seem the Rambam's own family – to convert to Islam at the point of the sword. He and his family were forced to flee Spain and he finally settled in Egypt, where he devoted himself to a life of scholarship.

He was already by then the pre-eminent figure in the large and influential Egyptian Jewish community, but when he was urged to consider the rabbinate as a livelihood, he retorted that it would be 'better to earn a drachma as a weaver, a tailor or a carpenter'.

He took up medicine instead and soon became supreme in his field. It is said that he was appointed court physician to Saladin, which is unlikely, and that he even treated Richard the Lionheart, which is impossible, but he was certainly court physician to al-Fadil, Saladin's viceroy in Egypt, and probably to al-Malik al-Afdal, Saladin's heir.

Maimonides died at the age of 69 (or 66, according to some authorities), so that how he managed to produce his vast body of written work is something of a mystery.

At the bottom of his genius was an infallible sense of order. He saw everything with great clarity and wished to share the vividness of his perception with the Jewish people, and it is this which lies behind the greatest of his works, the *Mishneh Torah* (*The Torah Reviewed*), which was no less than an attempt to put the Talmud (and the responsa which followed), with its repetitions, its apparent contradictions and its chaos, into systematic order.

It took him ten years to do so, and the *Mishneh Torah* runs to 14 volumes, but for the first time a body of work, which had hitherto been regarded as the private province of savants, was made accessible to the intelligent layman.

If the Rambam's conversion to Islam was nominal, his immersion in the Islamic culture was not. Much of his work, including the 'Guide for the Perplexed', was written in Arabic, and he sought to synthesise all that was most relevant in Jewish, Greek and Islamic thought. In *The Guide for the Perplexed* he discussed the sacraficial rites which darken so many pages of Scripture, and he argued that they were in fact of pagan origin, but were retained because Jews in the time of Moses could not be weaned from them.

He also dismissed the idea of a bodily resurrection, which troubled many of his contemporaries, but what they found

unacceptable was not so much his individual ideas as the broad
thrust of his reasoning and his readiness to invoke external
philosophers in his pursuit of eternal truths.

He was prepared to drop any usage, no matter how venerable,
if it made no sense. Thus, to give but a small example, he found
that congregations were restive and unruly during the repetition of
the *amida* (which they still are) and ruled that the repetition be
dispensed with.

The Rambam died in 1204 and was buried in Tiberias. A few
years later, his grave was desecrated with the inscription 'Here lies
Moses Maimuni, the Banished Heretic.'

For the Jew who is attached to tradition and would like to
believe, yet finds too many obstacles to such belief in holy writ, an
encounter with the Rambam can be an exhilerating experience.

In Jewish terms, however, he was in some respects, more than a
millennium ahead of his age and he touched nothing which he did
not illuminate.

5 April 1985

Menachem Mendel Schneerson
(Lubavitcher Rebbe)

MENACHEM MENDEL SCHNEERSON, the seventh Lubavitcher
rebbe, was the greatest Jewish leader of his age and among the
greatest of any age.

Many a flourishing centre of Jewish life would, without him,
have been a wilderness and, to students of Jewish history, the
second half of the twentieth century will be known as the
Schneerson era.

Like many great men, however, he made great mistakes, some of
them so serious as almost to undermine his own achievements.

Unlike other *Chasidic* leaders, the rebbe himself never set foot in

126

Israel. The merest considerations of delicacy should, therefore, have prompted him to keep out of Israeli politics. Instead, he intervened repeatedly and crudely on a number of issues, and failed on every one. Lubavitch may have been strong enough to make itself a nuisance, but was not strong enough to change anything.

A second mistake was more serious. We are repeatedly assured that the rebbe never claimed to be the Messiah, or even the Messiah-in-waiting. Yet the whole bizarre messianic campaign – with the incessant chants of: 'We want Moshiach now' – began more than ten years ago. He could have stopped it with a word, but the fact that he remained silent gave it extra momentum, until it got out of hand and he was widely acclaimed as 'the Messiah, the King'.

And still he was silent. It made Lubavitch something of a laughing stock, and was a source of embarrassment and grief to its more intelligent adherents. In fact, the entire campaign became so wild, preposterous and costly – fortunes were being spent on full-page advertisements in the Israeli and American press – that I began to wonder if Lubavitch, having tired of its own achievements, had embarked on a course of self-destruction, as if it had no wish to survive the rebbe.

Which brings me to his third and most serious mistake. The rebbe, though childless, has never designated a successor. The matter, whether on his orders or not, was never even openly discussed, which almost suggests that the rebbe himself had come to believe that he was the Messiah – either that or immortal.

But there is another, and more complex possibility. Seven, and the multiples thereof (as in 770 Eastern Parkway) have a particular place in Jewish lore. There is said to be a mystic belief that there would only be seven rebbes in the Lubavitch line. Thus, the rebbe may not have actually wanted a successor.

So what now? There were men who claimed to speak for the rebbe when he was dying, and who may continue to do so now that he is dead. And they will no doubt be readily believed by many believers. For those who thought that the rebbe had materialised as the Messiah the King in the course of his lifetime, it requires no great leap of faith to accept that he is still the Messiah even though he is dead. Not all Lubavitch followers, however, are that credulous.

There was a great deal of infighting among the American chieftains during the last sad months of the rebbe's life and it may be a long time before we see a puff of white smoke from the chimneys of Eastern Parkway to indicate that a successor has been elected.

Even if a successor should emerge, it is by no means certain that he will be universally accepted as the eighth rebbe, especially if he is not a Schneerson. I suspect the empire will break up and that power will be divided among the satraps of the different provinces.

The obvious leader in Britain will be Rabbi Faivish Vogel, an erudite man with vast energies who may find new scope for his talents once he has shrugged off Brooklyn rule. In Australia, it will be one or another of the Gutnicks – though they may choose to rule as a collective brotherhood and their followers may become known as the Gutnick Chasidim.

The belief that the rebbe was possibly the Lord's Anointed inspired his followers to heroic efforts and enabled them to revive Jewish life in areas where it would by now have been extinct.

Yet, at the same time, the very cult of the rebbe, added to the excesses of Brooklyn, were serious handicaps among Jews who had good reason for distrusting messianic fervour and claims to divinity. As a result, Lubavitch *Chasidim* were regarded with suspicion, and sometimes derision, and were never fully integrated into communities they served.

The death of the rebbe and the end of the Brooklyn connection may finally bring them down to earth and I would like to think that, for all their past achievements, the best years of Lubavitch are still ahead.

17 June 1994

8
The Old
Wild West

*Israel is supremely capable of defending itself
against external enemies, but rather less effective
in defending itself against the enemy within.*

Interview with Professor Leibowitz

THE SUMMER ISSUE of the *Jewish Quarterly* is a little late this year, as it is almost every year. In fact, it is so late that the summer and autumn issues are combined, but it has been worth waiting for and one piece in particular is well worth the price of a year's subscription – an interview by Lynne Reid Banks with Professor Yeshayah Leibowitz.

Leibowitz is a polymath. He has for the past 20 years been professor of neurophysiology at the Hebrew University. But he is also a philosopher, historian, Talmudic scholar and was for a time editor-in-chief of the *Encyclopedia Hebraica*. Tall, lean and choleric, he carries an almost constant air of despair which, given the state of the world about him, is richly justified. Moreover, he is not only a scholar, but a prophet. He has seen the dangers ahead and has warned of them, but his warnings have, in the past, been largely ignored, though time and time again he has been proved right by events.

A sincere and deeply religious man, he has always regarded the religious establishment in Israel as corrupt in itself and as a source of corruption in others, and Lynne asked him if he was therefore in favour of a separation of state and religion. His reply was characteristic: 'Not only in favour – it is absolutely necessary. The prostitution of religion as an executive arm of the state is something terrible. The state has no authority over anything spiritual, cultural, moral or religious. That is fascism.'

He was then asked how religious Jews could bring about the acceptance of religious observance without political power.

YL: They can't.

LRB: But shouldn't they try?

YL: Moses tried and didn't succeed! God himself tried and didn't succeed. *Man can only be changed by himself.*

Every enlightened person is now aware of the dangers to Israel inherent in the continued Jewish occupation of the West Bank and Gaza, but Leibowitz has consistently warned against it since 1967 and he fears the emergence of what he calls 'a Rhodesia-Zimbabwe

131

under Jewish domination', which is to say, a state with an Arab majority under Jewish control, and he is sustained by the hope that America 'will impose a settlement here, which will mean the partition of the country.'

LRB: Would you prefer it if we did it ourselves?

YL: Yes! But, no hope.

LRB: Why no hope?

YL: Because the majority of the people here have no other national concept than nationalism and patriotism. Which means: the Israel flag over Jericho.

Lynne then asked him if there was partition where he would draw the boundaries.

YL: The Green Line! It's absolutely clear. The Green Line was the consequence of our War of Independence. The world recognised it. We must go back to it. The situation of Israel today is not a consequence of '48, but of '67; '48 was a war of national independence. The other three wars don't make any sense. They were wars of political interest. Wars of domination. In '56 we were just mercenaries of the shareholders of the Suez Canal Company. The Six Day War was an opportunity we seized to conquer Palestine and the Sinai. And the opportunity was presented to us by this bloody fool Nasser.

I think Leibowitz is wrong about the '56 war. Israeli forces may have seemed like mercenaries of the Canal Company, but the scale of the fedayeen incursions before the war gave Israel every right to use the opportunity created by the Canal crisis to invade Sinai. The Yom Kippur War, too, was imposed upon her, but it came only after efforts by America to reach a peace settlement had proved futile.

Leibowitz has no illusions about the character or temper of the Arabs, even if he understands their aspirations. If they had won the Yom Kippur War in 1973, he says, 'they would have exterminated us,' but he sees greater dangers within than without.

'I want to get out of the territories, not for the sake of the Arabs, but for the sake of the Jews, just as de Gaulle got out of Algeria, not for the sake of the Algerians, but for the sake of the French. The state of Israel has to be liberated from the territories, as de Gaulle liberated France from Algeria.'

I sometimes have the feeling that Leibowitz is obsessed by the fear that he is only a voice in the wilderness. That may have been the case when he first assumed the thankless role of a prophet of woe, but he has been proved right too often to be completely overlooked and his disciples have grown in numbers and influence as the situation has continued to deteriorate.

When I read the long paranoiac bleat in the Rosh Hashanah issue of this paper by the president of Bar-Ilan University, Emanuel Rackman, who is often spoken of as a 'modern' and even 'enlightened' rabbi, I began to wonder whether the terms religion and enlightenment were not a contradiction in terms, for nowhere in the course of his lament over the isolation of Israel was there a single hint that Israel *might* have done something to bring her isolation upon herself. The Leibowitz interview settled the question. The two *can* be combined, but the combination calls for extraordinary powers of character and intellect.

19 September 1980

Attack on Arab mayors

ONE ARAB MAYOR has lost his foot, another his legs, and a gallant Jewish soldier has lost his sight.

Will the Israeli government now deport Ayatollah Levinger of Kiryat Arba (together, possibly, with Arik Sharon, Moshe Shamir and Geulah Cohen?) Will it dump the viragos squatting in the Hadassah building in Hebron (and who are in many ways at the source of the trouble) in an abandoned refugee camp in Jericho? Will it impose a curfew on Kiryat Arba (to save it from the wrath of Hebron) and allow Hebronites to tour its deserted streets?

The government is not sure exactly who perpetrated the outrages of 2 June, but then it wasn't sure who perpetrated the Hebron massacre, yet that did not prevent it from imposing collective punishment on the Arabs. Why not apply a similar policy to the Jews? Mr Begin, we all know, is a devout Jew (though

133

his black *kipa* has been less evident of late than it was in his first months of office) and he must be familiar with the biblical injunction: 'One law shall ye have for the stranger as well as yourself.' But Mr Begin is also a lawyer and may argue that the Arab isn't really a stranger – which is, indeed, the case – and may be treated like dirt.

The government has sown the wind and is reaping the whirlwind. Every nation has its lunatic fringe, but Israel is the one free country in the world where such a fringe – and I am referring, of course, to the Gush Emunim – enjoys not only tolerance, but state patronage. The government has put its full resources at the disposal of the movement, and has ordered the army not only to defend it, but to prepare its sites, move its homes, and generally act as its hewers of wood and drawers of water. And wherever there are protests against the spread of such settlements, one is answered with the word 'security.'

It is the new password. In the name of security papers are banned, movement is restricted, people are deported without due process of law, land is expropriated, families are made homeless, and whole communities are exploited and oppressed. There are circumstances when such measures – and worse – become necessary, but the Gush Emunim settlements have nothing to do with security. Moshe Dayan has said as much, the Gush itself has confessed as much, and far from reinforcing the defence perimeter of the country, it poses a security problem, and much of the unrest on the West Bank derives from its efforts. And, in any case, the idea of entrusting security outposts to the motley collection of cranks, fanatics, drop-outs (mostly American) and common-or-garden lunatics who form more than a small part of the Gush is laughable.

One might have thought that Mr Begin and his colleagues would have learned something from the experience of the Bourbons, the Hapsburgs, the British, the French, the Dutch, the Italians, the Belgians, the Portuguese and others, all of whom thought they could maintain their dominion over subject peoples until the end of time, but were forced eventually to withdraw. Israel, however, has defied so many other rules of history and economics that they, and their supporters abroad, think they will escape the fate which – with one exception – has overtaken all other empires. The exception is, of course, the Soviet Union, which is large enough, strong enough and brutal enough to get away with it (for the time being). Israel is not.

The classical cycle of unrest and oppression, oppression and unrest, has already begun and Mr Begin's ambition will be frustrated, not only because of the yearning for freedom common to all people – even Arabs – but because the Jewish conscience – within Israel and without – will not permit it. When the army dumped two Arab families in abandoned refugee camps, there was an international outcry, but nowhere was the outcry more vehement and sustained than in Israel itself, and the families were restored to their homes.

There are also reports that Israeli troops are becoming restive at the sort of policies they are having to enforce, and I have no doubt whatever that Israel will have to withdraw from the Gaza Strip and the greater part of the West Bank, including almost all of the areas now occupied by the Gush Emunim, and it is then that the trouble could start in earnest.

It is uncertain whether the terrorists responsible for the attacks on the Arab mayors stem directly from the Gush Emunim, but it is fairly clear that they have been fed on the same dark philosophy and nurtured on the same hatreds. Today they are attacking Arabs. Tomorrow – once the withdrawals begin – they could be attacking Jews.

Israel is supremely capable of defending itself against external enemies, but rather less effective and perhaps even less determined in defending itself against the enemy within. If extremists, and extremism, are allowed to flourish and are allowed to think that they are not only above the law, but above the expressed will of the people, Israel will find herself fighting the one war which she could lose – a war between Jews.

13 June 1980

Emil Grunzweig

I WAS AT the Peace Now march in Jerusalem which ended in the death of Emil Grunzweig.

It was scheduled to begin at five in the evening, and I arrived at five, both as a sympathiser and as observer. Within minutes the crowd had grown to over 1,000, among them several hundred thugs who were clearly there not as supporters of the demonstration, but with the intention of breaking it up, and who rent the air with harsh cries of 'Begin, king of Israel'; 'traitors'; 'terrorists'; and 'You should all be strung up with the Inquiry Commission.'

As the numbers multiplied, so their cries grew louder, harsher, more menacing, and they rushed the demonstrators in an attempt to tear down their placards. The police were too few to restrain them and seemed disinclined to make the effort to do so, and I found myself functioning as a sort of auxiliary policeman. One could stand up to the pushing and jostling and the name-calling fairly cheerfully, but there was a moment when I had to be restrained myself as I was spat at in the face.

And so it continued, from Zion Square, where the rally began, to the prime minister's office some two miles away. Darkness soon descended and, although police reinforcements were called, it was by then more difficult to separate marchers from assailants; and, again, it was not my impression that any serious effort was made to do so. There were no arrests, though the violence was continuous.

The scene was not altogether unfamiliar. I had seen and heard it all before in Israel during the 1981 elections, the same chants, the same slogans, the same frenzied mobs, the flailing of arms in a manner made famous by supporters of the Ayatollah Khomeini.

It seems to me that Mr Begin's commitment to democracy and the rule of law is taken too much for granted. He has never disowned the mobs who broke up, and continue to break up, the meetings of the Labour opposition, and he has himself declared that any Jew who supports the Reagan plan is a traitor, which is hardly the language of democracy, and not a little of the violence evident in Israel's political life has received its cue from his office. But few people were prepared for what actually happened – a Jewish grenade, thrown, presumably, by a Jewish assailant, at a Jewish gathering.

Bloodshed is not entirely new to Israel, or rather, 'Greater Israel'. More than one Arab has been killed by Jewish gunmen in East Jerusalem and the West Bank, and in the one case where the attacker was caught and sentenced, he was released from prison after a few weeks. It is not so long since an attempt was made on the lives of three West Bank mayors, and I thought at the time: they are attacking Arabs now, it won't be long before they are attacking Jews. It has all happened rather sooner than I expected.

Events in Israel have, I'm afraid, overflowed to poison the language of debate in the diaspora; and there are some, indeed, who would like to stifle debate altogether. There is, for example, the charming Mr Lionel Bloch, who is so pleased with his discovery that only 'a few hundred people – the vast majority of them men' – were butchered in Beirut (the actual figure was at least 700, though it was probably well over 1,000) that, having made the point in a preposterous article, he goes on to repeat it in an absurd letter.

But that is not his only enormity. While claiming to admire the work of the Kahan Commission (he does like to have it both ways, doesn't he?), he 'cannot help wondering if it foresaw the extent by which it exacerbated Israel's divisions and undermined the spirit of national unity.'

But who caused the divisions in the first place, the people whose criminal negligence (and I put it no higher) led to the massacre of 'a few hundred people – the vast majority of them men,' or Justice Kahan, Justice Barak and General Efrat, who made it their business to arrive at the truth and to publish it? I take it that somewhere in Mr Bloch's make up there is sufficient soul – and goodness knows, he has room for it – to know what the truth is; only it seems that he would rather it wasn't uttered.

Mr Bloch, at least, is still prepared to argue his case. Others, including not a few people who call themselves rabbis, being unable to answer argument with argument or perhaps having doubts about the consistency of their own case, have resorted to slogans, chants, denunciations and plain abuse.

Others still have gone beyond abuse, and last September there was a concerted effort by Herutniks to break up a Peace Now meeting in London's Hillel House.

If Israel has so far triumphed against overwhelming odds, it is not only because of the valour and ingenuity of its fighting men, but because it has had truth and justice on its side. Can the same be said now? If we are to resort to the ways of our enemies, we may yet share their fate.

4 March 1983

The West Bank

THE EVENTS OF the past few weeks on the West Bank have a terrible familiarity about them and remind one of the last days of the British Empire, of the last stand of the French in North Africa, the Belgians in the Congo, the Portuguese in Angola and Mozambique. Almost every stage of repression is being replayed, the banning of books, the closing of universities, the dismissal of political leaders, and the installation of puppets.

Other observers have made the same point, and all have suggested that the days of empire are finished. This is, unfortunately, not quite the case, for one of the biggest, and probably the most brutal, empires in history is still flourishing – I refer, of course, to the Soviet Union – and is keeping hundreds of millions in subjugation by the very same methods now being tried in Israel.

The most frequent reason given for the retention of the West Bank and Gaza is that they are vital to Israel's security. The idea of 'natural' or 'defensible' frontiers is an anachronism, and has been ever since the first bomber dropped the first bombs; but, as the Yom Kippur War showed, it is certainly useful to have space, if only to withstand a surprise attack.

Yet I believe that the Yom Kippur War could have been avoided if Mrs Meir had been more receptive to the peace overtures made by President Sadat, and the sort of security which Israel craves can

138

only be obtained, not through the retention of territory, but through a comprehensive settlement with her neighbours. Mr Begin himself is not unaware of this, hence his readiness to return vast tracts of territory to the one Arab power which Israel need fear – Egypt – and that for nothing more substantial than a promise of peace; but if he thinks that his treaty with Egypt will give him a free hand on the West Bank, he will soon discover his mistake.

Egypt wants peace as much as Israel, and is, for the present at least, in no position to make war, but it still thinks of itself as the leading Arab power, and would like to be thought of as such by others; and once it has recovered Sinai, it will not stand idly by while Israel tramples on the rights of the Palestinians. In other words, there is no such thing as a semi-peace, and unless Israel is prepared to make the sort of sacrifices in the West Bank and Gaza that she has already made in Sinai, her sacrifices in Sinai may prove to be in vain.

And there is no time to be lost. Israel can close all the schools on the West Bank, fire all the mayors, impose curfews on all the towns, find elderly Arab collaborators, and bring in sufficient troops and tanks to impose a semblance of peace, but for how long? There will be more confrontations, more riots and more deaths.

Israel is, for the time being, the most powerful state in the Middle East. In military terms, indeed, she has no peer between the Atlantic and the Indus. The Arabs know this better than anyone, and if Israel were to make real concessions now, she would be doing it, and would be seen to be doing it, from a position of strength. If, however, she waits while the hatreds simmer and the unrest grows, until they assume the gravity of a full-scale rebellion, and she is forced to make concessions out of weakness, she could be in danger.

At present, Palestinian leaders – by which I mean the elected West Bank mayors, as distinct from the bloated windbags of Beirut – would be content with an independent state on the West Bank, but if they sensed weakness, they could think that the whole of Israel was within their grasp, and any hopes which may still exist for a comprehensive settlement could vanish.

One can draw some comfort from the fact that the events on the West Bank have aroused strong opposition within Israel itself. The Peace Now movement has been revived, and last weekend there was a massive protest rally in Tel Aviv. We can do with a Peace

Now movement here, and I believe I can see the beginnings of one.

I am glad that June Jacobs, for example, spoke out against the closure of Bir Zeit at the recent meeting of the Board of Deputies, but the matter should be taken further. I would suggest that those students who have manned the front line in the fight against anti-Zionism in our universities call off their effort – and do so publicly – until academic freedom is restored in the West Bank.

Over a million Arabs live in the West Bank and Gaza. They cannot be thrown out, though I am ashamed to say that there are people who call themselves Jews who would be prepared to do just that. They are too numerous to be absorbed into the Jewish state, and they have the same hunger for freedom that people have everywhere. The longer we attempt to deny it, the more we are endangering the freedom we have won for ourselves.

2 April 1982

Reproach for Zionism

'EVEN IN MY worst dreams, I could never imagine such a thing,' said General Amram Mitzna, Israel's commander on the West Bank, when told that some of his men had buried four Arabs alive with a bulldozer.

Mitzna sounds like a decent chap charged with imposing an indecent policy and I sympathise with him. But then, who would have imagined that Israel's defence minister would launch a campaign of 'force, beatings and might,' which was virtually an invitation to every thug in the army (and there are thugs in every army, even – though this may come as a shock to some people – the Jewish Army) to put his boot in?

Or who could have imagined this scene, witnessed by Jewish travellers on a Jewish bus and reported in the *Jewish Chronicle* on 5 February:

In Bethlehem, soldiers in an Egged bus at which stones were hurled leaped out and seized a boy of about 14, whom they suspected of throwing stones. A soldier who hustled the boy to a command car was seen to punch the boy repeatedly in the face, butt his head and kick him while passengers watched.

The beatings continued although the boy offered no resistance. After his mouth had been reduced to a bloody pulp, he was pushed into a command car and driven into custody.

They used to talk in Israel of 'the nobility of the gun'. Will they now talk of 'the nobility of the club'? Or perhaps 'the nobility of the bulldozer'?

The concept of the nobility of the gun is not as bizarre as it sounds. It stems from the Arab uprising of 1936 when unarmed men, women and children were often attacked by Arab bands and there were demands that Jews should retaliate in kind.

Chaim Weizmann and his colleagues, on both ethical and political grounds, urged a policy of *havlaga*, restraint, with guns being used only in the face of immediate danger. We have moved a long way since then.

It is, in fact, easier to act justly when fighting for a just cause. It is rather more difficult to show restraint when defending a wrong one. What we are seeing now is the inevitable result of 20 years of occupation. Where Zionism was a source of pride, it has now become one of reproach.

The present situation, we are told, is not of Israel's making. If only the Arabs had accepted the UN 1947 partition plan, there would have been no 1948 war. If only they had adhered to the 1949 armistice agreements, there would have been no Suez war. If Nasser had not sent troops to Sinai and closed the Straits of Tiran, there would have been no Six Day War.

All of this is true – and in each instance the Arabs paid dearly for their intransigence and folly. Now, by hanging on to the West Bank and Gaza, Israel is paying for hers, and she is sagging under the moral weight of the occupation.

Some good, however, may come out of the present tragedy, if its lessons are quickly learned. The army has already recoiled from its own excesses. Soldiers have been arrested and charged with atrocities, and I think we shall hear less of 'force, beatings and might'. I also think that it has led to changes in political attitudes and that it may lead to a realignment in political forces.

Labour was interested in retaining the West Bank and Gaza as bargaining counters in an eventual peace settlement. It now recognises that they are not bargaining counters, but liabilities to be jettisoned at the first opportunity, and even members of the Likud are edging slowly towards reason.

The forthcoming general election may show a shift to the Right, but if it does, it will be a chastened Right, and I can foresee a shake-up of political forces with the moderate elements in the Likud, as represented by Lahat, joining forces with Labour in a new alignment for peace.

Until last December, the arguments about the West Bank and Gaza were almost academic. The hawks pressed for outright annexation on historical and security grounds; the doves opposed it on practical grounds. But both presumed that the decision was entirely Israel's, and neither paid much attention to the wishes of the actual inhabitants.

Well, the Arabs, even without the benefit of representative institutions, have now made their feelings known, and they will continue to do so for as long as the occupation lasts.

The choice is no longer between a so-called Greater Israel and a small one, but between an oppressive society and a free one.

19 February 1988

The West Bank and Ulster

DURING THE PAST two or three months, whenever British reporters questioned Israeli politicians about the conduct of troops in the West Bank and Gaza, they often got the retort, 'And what about Northern Ireland?'

That retort is unlikely to be heard again in a hurry because, as all the world has been able to see, Britain has, if anything, been acting with excessive restraint in the face of a remorseless, savage and intractable enemy.

The Palestinians, too, can be remorseless, savage and intractable, but the two situations are hardly comparable. The Republicans in Ulster have full political and civic rights, the Palestinians in the West Bank and Gaza have none.

Most people in Ulster have demonstrated in successive elections that they want to remain part of the United Kingdom; the overwhelming majority of Palestinians would – if given the chance – show that they have no wish to be part of a Greater Israel.

The Sinn Fein have resorted to the bullet because they have been rejected by the ballot; the Palestinians are turning to violence because they have no democratic process to resort to.

To put it more bluntly, the former are trying to force Ulster into a Greater Ireland at the point of a gun; the latter are being kept within a Greater Israel at the point of a gun.

Irish Republicans – as I shall show – have genuine grievances, but they go back to the past, whereas Palestinian grievances arise out of the immediate present.

There are, however, many lessons to be learned from the tragic events in Ulster, but they are not ones that would commend themselves readily to any Right-wing Israeli politician, and least of all to Prime Minister Yitzhak Shamir.

Between 1594 and 1601, there was a series of insurrections in Northern Ireland caused largely by the attempt to impose the English Reformation upon a staunchly Catholic population. The insurrections were brutally suppressed and Presbyterian settlers were brought over from Scotland to colonise the area, much as the Gush Emunim settlers have been colonising parts of Judea, Samaria and the Gaza Strip.

The results of that policy came home to roost 300 years later, when the British government resolved to give Ireland home rule, and the descendants of the settlers threatened to revolt against any scheme which might detach them from the United Kingdom.

The government prevaricated and, with the outbreak of the First World War, the matter was shelved. The Irish, however, were impatient for independence and rebelled.

The rebellion was followed by a drawn-out and bloody civil war and finally, in 1920, southern Ireland was given home rule while Ulster remained, and remains, part of the United Kingdom –

though not, as we can see, a particularly stable part.

And there is no practical solution in sight, though someone, in a fit of exasperation, has suggested that Ireland be towed out into the Atlantic and sunk.

The late Moshe Dayan used to refer to the Jewish settlements in the occupied territories as 'creating facts'; but the fact which they are creating is another Ulster, except that it took Ulster three centuries to erupt, while the West Bank and Gaza are erupting after 20 years.

The Jewish settlements used to be spoken of as defence bastions, whereas Yitzhak Rabin has now made it clear that they are a defence burden. The rampages of the settlers have exacerbated the problems of occupation and whole battalions are now employed to ensure their safety.

There has, in recent months, been no attempt to enlarge the settlements; they should now be allowed to atrophy.

One reads wild schemes in the Israeli press, including one put out by Rehavam Zeevi, a reserve general in the Israeli Army, to make life within the occupied territories 'unattractive' to the Arabs (how attractive is it now?) and to encourage their transfer to another country. And I have already referred to the plan of Minister without Portfolio (and without brains) Yoske Shapiro to bribe Arabs to leave.

Most Israelis, however, still wish to live in a humane and democratic society. Such a wish must inevitably involve a territorial compromise, and every settlement and every settler in the West Bank and Gaza is an impediment to such a compromise.

25 March 1988

Vicious follies

A FEW WEEKS ago, West Bank Jewish settlers ran berserk through the Arab village of Kifl Harith, firing guns, smashing cars and vandalising homes.

Such attacks are fairly commonplace nowadays and the authorities tend to ignore them. They are not even always reported in the press, if only because they are no longer news.

In this particular instance, however, an Arab child was killed, and when the police arraigned a number of settlers before the courts, their spiritual leader, Rabbi Yitzhak Ginsburg, rushed to their defence with the declaration that 'one must recognise the fact that Jewish blood and non-Jewish blood are not the same.'

And he went on: 'The people of Israel must rise and declare publicly that a Jew and a non-Jew are not equal, God forbid. Any trial based on the assumption that Jews and non-Jews are equal is based on a travesty of justice.'

There are, one must add, Jewish sources to support his view. Rabbi Meir Kahane, who would like to see Nuremberg-type legislation introduced into Israel, has never tired of quoting them, and one can find similar sentiments, if less blatantly stated, in the works of Rabbi Eliezer Waldman, a Techiyah member of the Knesset.

But then, there are Jewish sources which would support almost any view, and while a wise man will draw on wise sources, a fool will draw on foolish ones, and a vicious fool will come up with vicious folly.

Rabbi Ginsburg, it seems to me, would be an ideal chief rabbi of the West Bank settlement of Ariel, where they recently adopted the idea of requiring Arab workers who move around the town performing various menial tasks – one of the advantages of living in the West Bank is the abundance of cheap Arab labour – to wear special badges, not unlike the yellow star forced on the Jews by the Nazis.

It would not have been a star, or even a crescent, but it went too far for Israeli opinion and, after a loud public outcry, the scheme was quickly killed. That the thinking behind it is still alive, however, may be seen from Rabbi Ginsburg's remarks.

If he cannot move to Ariel, he may consider a place on the judicial bench alongside Judge Yitzhak Banai, of the Beersheba District Court, who refused to place on remand a Jew who had allegedly thrown a petrol bomb at an Arab car because, said Banai, a Jew attacking Arabs cannot be compared with an Arab attacking Jews – his argument being that, while the Arabs are engaged in a national insurrection, the Jews are merely settling local accounts.

Israel is blessed with a gifted humorist called Yossi Banai and when I first saw the report, I thought there had been a misprint and that I was reading a piece of satire; but nothing thought up by satirists can match the realities of Israeli life. This was no misprint and Judge Banai was in earnest.

A few years ago, a Russian Jewish immigrant in Kiryat Arba was given only a nominal sentence for attacking Arabs and Arab property because, said the judge, he had been harassed over many years by the Russian authorities.

And that's at the bottom of it. Jews are a harassed and persecuted race and they therefore have an inalienable right to harass and persecute Arabs.

Israeli rabbis, with a few notable exceptions, have never enjoyed an extravagantly high reputation, either within Israel or without. Their education is limited, their ignorance is limitless, and there are a great many of them, so that one is not particularly disturbed by the *obiter dicta* of this or that idiot, even though he may claim to be speaking in the name of God.

It is rather more serious when words of folly are uttered not from the pulpit, not from the witness box, but from the judicial bench, for Israel's judiciary is (or rather was) respected, nationally and internationally; and the fact that even a judge can come up with the sort of sentiments voiced by Banai shows how far demoralisation has spread within Israeli society.

Amos Keinan, a gifted if somewhat vituperative writer, drew attention to this fact in a forceful article in *Yediot Achronot* when he urged that Judge Banai should be 'vomited' out of office.

Keinan may be charged with contempt of court as a result, but if anyone has exposed the courts, the judiciary and the law to contempt, it is Banai himself.

16 June 1989

Hebron massacre

THE VICTIMS OF the Hebron massacre may, with their blood, have sealed the fate of the West Bank settlers.

There was a time when settlements and settlers represented all that was most heroic in the Zionist movement. Now the very words have almost become terms of abuse. The old settlers were a source of pride, the new ones are a source of shame. The old settlers built the Jewish state, the new ones could destroy it.

President Ezer Weizman has described the Hebron massacre as the biggest crime in Jewish history. His view will be shared by most sane Jews, but not all Jews are sane and the insane ones are well represented among the West Bank settlers, and particularly in Kiryat Arba.

The late Sir Israel Brodie once asked me to visit an Israeli *yeshivah* – of which he was patron – for born-again Jews. They were mostly Americans, young, earnest and zealous, and many of them seemed to be deranged.

A few years later, I visited Kiryat Arba. There, too, they had a large contingent of Americans, bulky, bearded, with God on their lips, guns in their hands and hatred in their hearts, not only for Arabs but for any Jews who questioned their attitudes and convictions.

Their womenfolk were in some ways even worse, for they had a wild light in their eyes and they seemed incapable of referring to the Arabs as human beings. I left the place with a shudder.

One should perhaps not read too much into the frenzies of one, lone, murderous lunatic, but to judge from the reactions of some of his fellow settlers, what Baruch Goldstein did was substantially what they would have liked to do, and they have hailed him as a hero.

Someone has even compared him to Samson. There are parallels, although Samson brought down the temple of the Philistines about his head, while Goldstein may have brought down the settler movement about his.

A young friend who was a student at Kiryat Arba *yeshivah* told me he was surprised that something like the Hebron massacre had not happened before, because it was entirely in keeping with the sort of teachings he received. The principal in his day was Rabbi Eliezer Waldman, whose opinions about Arabs were poisonous enough. The present principal is Rabbi Dov Lior, a poor man's Mengele who has advocated medical experiments on Arabs.

Kiryat Arba is a snake-pit and, as long as it stands, it will be a source of reproach both to the Jewish people and the Jewish state.

Some good may yet come out of the Hebron massacre. The peace talks have now been suspended, but they will no doubt resume with a new sense of urgency. I suspect that neither the Israeli government nor the Israeli public will be too concerned about the interests or opinions of the Jewish settlers. Goldstein has undermined their case.

Chief Rabbi Jonathan Sacks has denounced the massacre as a 'devastating criminal act . . . Such an act is an obscenity and a travesty of Jewish values. That it should have been perpetrated against worshippers in a house of prayer at a holy time makes it a blasphemy as well.'

The crime has also been denounced by leading Israeli rabbis but so far there has been silence from the American Orthodox establishment. There are several brands of Orthodoxy in America, stretching from the so-called modern Orthodoxy of Yeshiva University – Goldstein's *alma mater* – to the vociferous We-want-the-Moshiach-now brethren of Brooklyn. But they have one thing in common: they have all denounced the peace process, and senior Israeli peace negotiators have been spat upon and reviled when they visited Orthodox synagogues in New York.

Neo-Nazi groups like Kach (to which Goldstein belonged), and its offshoot, Kahane Chai, are American creations, financed by American money. In Israel, they are manned largely by American immigrants, products of the American gun culture, all the more lethal in the belief that they act in the name of God. They regard their situation in Cowboy-and-Indian terms, with the occupied territories as the old wild west, and Arabs as the last of the Mohicans, and they are allowed to run amok with guns in hand like so many Buffalo Bills.

A new law – the Brady Bill – has just been introduced making it necessary for Americans to wait five days before they can buy a gun. The measure will enable police to check if the buyer has a criminal record or known mental problems.

It would not be a bad thing if similar restrictions were imposed on American immigrants to Israel because in recent decades the country has become a dumping ground for American psychopaths.

In the meantime, Purim* will never seem the same again.

4 March 1994

Human rights

I READ A great many newspapers and journals, not all of them with pleasure, but there is one in particular which turns my stomach.

If I read it first thing in the morning, I find it difficult to get down to work, if I see it last thing at night, I can't sleep and I'm ashamed to say that there are times when I leave it unread.

It is called *B'Tselem* and takes its name from, and is published by, the Israel Information Centre for Human Rights in the Occupied Territories.

After the Six Day War, in 1967, Israel claimed that its occupation of the West Bank and Gaza was 'the most benign in history'. The claim was first made by the late Chaim Herzog, who was the first military governor of the West Bank. It may have been true in his time, but it did not remain true for long because it is not in the nature of occupiers to stay benign and, as the years passed, the occupation became arbitrary, oppressive and harsh.

The situation deteriorated further once Jewish settlers began to move into Hebron and other parts of the West Bank and Gaza. For they believed they were asserting a God-given right and tended to regard the Palestinians as hewers of wood and drawers of water.

*The Hebron massacre was perpertrated on the festival of Purim.

149

It was then that *B'Tselem* began monitoring events in the occupied territories and published regular reports, with sickening details of alleged thuggery – not only by the army and police but by settlers.

The authorities in each case promised a full inquiry and that, where the charges were proved, they would take action against those responsible. But, *B'Tselem* reports, 'nothing has been done to change the behaviour of the security forces. Beatings, abuse and degradation of Palestinians by Israeli security force personnel remain frequent, almost routine occurrences.'

Last week, something finally was done when two border policemen were each sentenced to eight months' imprisonment for aggravated assault on six Palestinians who had entered Israel illegally. The incident was by no means unusual, but what compelled the authorities to act in this instance was the fact that the assault had been caught on video and broadcast to the entire globe. No one who saw it will ever forget it.

Even while the trial was in progress, Israel Television interviewed two Palestinians in hospital who, it was alleged, had been savagely beaten by border police.

The police commander, Yisrael Sadan, said that the matter was being investigated, but that it was difficult to establish the identity of the culprits. This suggests that he is not fully aware of what his own men are doing.

There are brutes in every organisation and when one has armed men among unarmed civilians, some of them will always abuse their authority. But where brutality becomes routine, one can take it as a symptom of inadequate training, poor leadership and a collapse in discipline.

I had hoped that once the Oslo Accords were signed and Israel began to withdraw from the main centres of Arab population, *B'Tselem* would be able to wind down its activities. And, indeed, for a time there was a decline in the number of incidents, but not for long. *B'Tselem* has highlighted the injuries which 30 years of occupation have inflicted on the Palestinians, but it also suggests the damage inflicted upon the moral stature of Israel. The security forces are not the only institution to come out badly from its reports. Israel's judicial system is also called into question.

And the damage will continue for as long as Israel remains an occupying power and for as long as the Palestinians are not in charge of their own destinies. Whether they would be better off as a result is another matter. Arafatland has become a by-word for incompetence, cruelty and corruption without even acquiring the full panoply of statehood. I'm afraid to think what it will be like once it becomes – as it must – fully independent, but that is their problem, not ours.

The name *B'Tselem* derives from Genesis: *Vayivra ha'adam betsalmo b'tselem elohim* – and God created man in His own image. From which we may draw the inference that we are all equal.

We aren't, of course, and I'm afraid we never shall be, but we are all entitled to elementary justice, even under military rule. *B'Tselem* is devoted to assuring that no instance of serious injustice will pass unnoticed.

No publication I receive deserves closer study, but I still dream of the day it will become defunct.

22 August 1997

9
Religion

Judaism is essentially wholesome and benign, as long as it is distant from power.

Death of communism

THE DEATH OF Communism will have few mourners, even among Jews, though Jews have always been among its most loyal supporters, and for obvious reasons. It was Communism which toppled the hated tsars, Communism which removed Jewish disabilities and proscribed anti-Semitism, and Communism which, in its early days at least, opened the doors to Jewish advancement. But more than that, it stood for the right things and offered visions of a happier and more wholesome world.

Jews have often been accused of exclusiveness, but, in fact, where they have been offered free and full access to an open world they have joined *en masse*. Access, however, was never entirely free and they had to resort to all sorts of major and minor subterfuges, changing names and faith, and obscuring antecedents, to gain admission.

Not that Jews could dispense wholly with subterfuges under Communism, so that Bronstein became Trotsky, Wallach became Litvinov and Rosenfeld became Kamenev, but they were entering a faith which was partly of their own making. Here, as in the old faith, there was no debate on ultimates – it was all settled by history, though, of course, active effort could bring the millennium nearer.

And the Jewish Communist who combined his creed with a sense of Jewish history could even tell himself that he was making the visions of the Prophets manifest on earth, for there was hardly a humane sentiment among the slogans of Communism which had not received its first utterance in Scripture.

But it soon became clear that Jews, as Jews, were to have no part in the new order. The Communist Party formed a Jewish section, the Yevsektsia, which, though led by Jews, promptly busied itself in extirpating every vestige of organised Jewish life.

Then came the show trials and purges of the 1930s in which many of the leading victims, like Zinoviev and Kamenev, were Jews, but by then Jews were less concerned with events in Russia than in central Europe.

155

Fascism and Nazism seemed to be spreading in all directions and even Jews who were not attracted to the Communist creed saw Communism as the only effective bulwark against Hitler and Mussolini.

And finally came the greatest betrayal of all, the Nazi-Soviet Pact of 1939 which left Poland at the mercy of Hitler.

But all that was forgotten when Hitler invaded Russia in June 1941. At first he swept everything before him, but when the Russians finally held their ground before Moscow and Stalingrad all reservations about Communism vanished in the admiration for the achievements of the Soviet army. The other battles of the Second World War were side-shows compared to the fury and scale of the onslaughts which the Russians encountered and which they eventually threw back, and it was Russian soldiers who finally shattered the Wehrmacht.

The Russian victories were, of course, won in spite of Communism and not because of it, but it was difficult to dissociate Communism from Russia in the popular mind, and in the immediate post-war years the creed, with all its evils, spread in every direction.

When I first lived in Israel in 1951, the country was almost a People's Republic. The Communists had only four seats in the Knesset, but Mapam, which had 19, was Marxist. The economy was strictly controlled and largely in the hands of the Histadrut (Labour Federation) (and so indeed was Mapai). The kibbutz movement was the most dynamic element in the country, and the most dynamic kibbutzim were nearly all Marxist. And the great national *Yomtov* (holiday) was 1 May, with rallies and marches, red banners and red songs (the Communists always had the best tunes). It was not until the Slansky trial in Czechoslovakia in 1952 and the Doctor's Plot in Russia in 1953 that the grip of Communism on a large part of the Jewish intelligentsia was finally broken.

I remember meeting Professor Hyman Levy, a distinguished mathematician and an old and unrepentant Bolshevik a few years later. He told me Communism itself was all right but that the forms of Communism generally extant were merely perversions of it. It seemed to me that a creed so universally prone to perversion was inherently perverse.

No body of beliefs, not even Hitlerism, brought so much

156

misfortune to so many people over so many years as Communism, and when I heard that it was finally dead, I found myself uttering an old Jewish prayer: 'Blessed art thou, O Lord our God, King of the Universe, who has kept us alive, and preserved us, and has enabled us to reach this epoch.'

30 August 1991

Bruriah for our times

I WAS UNDER the impression that, according to Jewish law, Jewish women may be seen but not heard. Rabbi Ovadiah Yosef, the former Sephardi chief rabbi of Israel, has now ruled that they may be heard but not seen.

The matter arose over the case of Professor Nehama Leibowitz (sister of the famous – some would say notorious – Yeshayahu Leibowitz) who is something of a legend as a biblical scholar.

I used to attend her lectures regularly when I first lived in Jerusalem in the early fifties; I have listened to her on Israel Radio since and her commentaries on the Pentateuch, published by the Jewish Agency and ably translated by Aryeh Newman, are among my most cherished possessions.

It is easy to explain her legendary reputation. There is, first of all, the catholic range of her scholarship. She is familiar not only with all the major and most of the minor commentators, but where the need should arise, she does not hesitate to quote non-*kosher* thinkers like Moses Mendelssohn or Martin Buber, outright heretics like Berl Katznelson, non-Jewish scholars like Gottfried Herder, novelists like Howard Fast, and even poets like William Blake.

But more than that: she is never afraid to introduce her own scintillating ideas (some of which, I suspect, would not find much favour with the rabbis), and instead of regurgitating the old, one usually – no matter how familiar the text – comes away with something new.

She is also animated in manner and voice, shouts one moment, whispers the next, as if making a conspiratorial aside, walks up and down, throws her arms around, and there are times when one half expects her to take off. But whatever she does, one follows her every word.

She is, I suppose, the Bruriah of our age. Bruriah was the only female in the Talmud to be recognised as a scholar in her own right, but the rabbis, and especially her own husband, resented her presumption and her caustic wit and were anxious to put her in her place. I sometimes suspect that there could be a move afoot to do the same for Nehama Leibowitz.

Rabbi Shlomo Riskin, late of the Manhattan Lincoln Centre and now head of Efrat Yeshivah in Israel, is a man with a lively imagination who runs a seminar for diaspora rabbis. He had the brilliant idea of inviting Professor Leibowitz to join his faculty.

But hardly was she in place before he found himself in trouble, for Nehama Leibowitz, though deeply Orthodox (in so far as anyone so individualistic can be described in such terms) is, as her name may suggest, a w-m-n – a woman of 82, as it happens, but a woman none the less – while the rabbis she teaches are, of course, men, and Rabbi Eliezer Shach, former head of the Aguda Council of Sages, has ruled that she is unacceptable.

I am surprised at his attitude, for Rabbi Shach, the venerable head of Ponevesz Yeshivah, is one of the few members of the Council of Sages who is an actual sage, and one, moreover, who is respected far beyond the cramped confines of the Agudah. But there are times when even the greatest sage can be less than sagacious, and this, I am sorry to say, is one of them.

As Rabbi Riskin does not appear to have sought his opinion in the first place, he could have safely ignored it, or at least turned the aural equivalent of a Nelson eye by pretending he hadn't heard. He is, after all, himself a qualified rabbi of no small standing. There is nothing in Jewish law requiring one rabbi to defer to the judgement of another (especially where it isn't called for) and he was perfectly entitled to follow his own instincts in the matter.

Instead, he turned to Rabbi Ovadiah Yosef, who ruled that Professor Leibowitz may continue to lecture at the seminar, but – I swear I'm not making this up – *only from behind a screen!*

I am not, in fact, sure if that would solve the problem, for the professor has sometimes been known to burst into song, which is certainly against the law; so perhaps the screen will be of reinforced concrete, or in another room, so that she can be neither seen nor heard.

But whatever the arrangement, I am surprised that an independent figure like Rabbi Riskin should be prepared to submit so distinguished a scholar to so grotesque an indignity. I shall be even more surprised if Professor Leibowitz submits to it.

22 May 1987

Prince Charles and Islam

LIKE PRINCE CHARLES, I am a great admirer of Islam. But, unlike His Royal Highness, I have a problem. If Islam is so admirable in theory, why are Islamic states so dreadful in practice?

He was careful, in his expression of praise, to add that he was talking of 'Islamic civilisation at its best'. But where does one find it today? In the Sudan? Iraq? Syria? Afghanistan? Iran? Libya? Indonesia? The Yemen? Chechnya? Pakistan? Saudi Arabia?

There are over 50 Islamic states – more than 20 of which are members of the Arab League – comprising a population of almost a billion, and most are a byword for cruelty, incompetence and corruption.

It was not always so. The Ummayad Caliphs of Damascus, the Abbasids of Baghdad, the Fatimids of Cairo, were all beacons of light at a time when Europe was steeped in darkness; and there was a marvellous flowering of Islamic culture under Suleiman the Magnificent in the sixteenth century, and under the Indian moguls in the seventeenth, after which Islam sank into almost inexorable decline.

It has been enjoying something of a revival in our time but, as I have suggested, it has not made the world a happier place.

The fact is, few religions, no matter how sublime their precepts, work out all that well in practice. One may think fondly of

159

Christianity in decline, but it was often merciless while in power.

'Render unto Caesar that which is Caesar's and unto God that which is God's' was fine as far as it went. But it did not go very far once Constantine converted to Christianity and started acting in the name of God.

The first Crusade, which left a trail of Jewish blood across the face of Europe, and which culminated in the massacre of Jews and Muslims in Jerusalem – all in the name of the Prince of Peace – was a crime against humanity.

The Fourth Crusade, against the Albigensian heretics, was another. The expulsion of the Jews and Muslims from Spain was a third, and, until our own times, there was nothing to match the savagery with which Christian butchered Christian in the so-called 'wars of religion' in the seventeenth century.

Christianity became a moral force again only when it ceased to be a political one. When Stalin asked 'how many divisions does the Pope have,' he misunderstood the whole situation. The power of the Pope lay precisely in the fact that he had none.

Judaism, I'm afraid, is also one thing in theory and another in action. We tend to look back to the days of David and Solomon as the golden age in our history. It was certainly the most exciting age, but we acquired a moral influence out of all proportion to our number only after we ceased to be a political entity.

The governing precept of Jewish life as defined by Zechariah – 'Not by might, nor by power, but by my spirit sayeth the Lord of Hosts' – dates from the beginning of our dispersion.

Judaism is essentially wholesome and benign as long as it is distant from power. In Israel, where it exercises considerable power, it is neither the one nor the other. Those who claim to speak in its name are often indifferent to the rights of the Arab, and hostile to the secular Jew – or to Jews who do not embrace their brand of Judaism.

They also have a primitive idea of justice, a limited concept of ethics, no interest in other cultures, and if – heaven forbid – they should ever become an actual majority and attain real power, Israel would become as backward and barbaric as Christendom was, and Islamic states are.

But to return to Prince Charles. He is sickened, as any reasonable person might be, by many aspects of contemporary life – the mindless search for instant gratification, the indifference to

160

tradition, the decline of authority, the absence of discipline or restraint, the rampant materialism – and he evoked the spiritual claims of Islam in order to temper the excesses of secularism.

He was right in his diagnosis, but wrong in his remedy. Islam is indeed rich in qualities which we could all emulate, but it can also display an assertiveness, aggression and intolerance which are alien to the British character and, if the country should need guidelines to find its way back to a more wholesome way of life, they are to be found in its own Judaeo-Christian traditions.

One final thought. Adultery is a capital offence in many Islamic countries and one daren't think what fate might have befallen His Royal Highness had he lived in, say, Saudi Arabia.

27 December 1996

Praying together at the Kotel

WE ARE CONSTANTLY being assured that the Jewish world is in the grip of a religious revival, and that never in Jewish history have so many young men attended so many *yeshivot*.

But what is being taught in those *yeshivot*? We may presume that the love of God is one subject. Hatred of man would seem to be another.

How else may one explain the use of a *yeshivah* in the holy city of Jerusalem as a vantage point from which to pelt worshippers near the Western Wall?

The worshippers were not Orthodox. Worse, they were not all of the same sex. Furthermore, some of the women wore prayer shawls.

They were not, however, at the Wall itself, where, of course, men and women are strictly segregated, but among the milling crowds in the plaza outside, and their offence clearly lay not in the fact that they were standing together, but that they were *praying* together.

At first, they were merely subjected to verbal abuse. Then they were spat on, pummelled and pushed. Finally, when the foot soldiers had, so to speak, done their bit, the students joined in with their artillery from the *yeshivah* balcony. All, presumably, to the glory of God.

And it all happened on Shavuot, when the Torah was given on Sinai, and during the actual reading of the Torah.

A new race of zealots has been emerging among us who – given the reported array of projectiles – seem ready to defend Orthodoxy even to the last ounce of their excrement. One can take their missiles as a symbol of their sanctity.

The police, outnumbered, and taken by surprise – which they shouldn't have been – felt helpless to protect the victims, cut the service short, and hurried them to safety. They made no arrests and the *yeshivah* apparently made no attempt either to restrain its students or to discipline them.

The late Kingsley Amis, commenting on the multiplication of universities in Britain, said: 'More means worse.' The same is true of *yeshivot*. The very growth in their number and size has inevitably meant a decline in the quality of students and staff.

Among *charedim*, moreover, nearly all boys go to *yeshivah*, whether they have an aptitude for study or not. And not a few *yeshivot* are mere bucket-shops, haphazardly thrown together and haphazardly maintained, with students who are unwilling to learn and rabbis who are unable to teach.

Yeshivot in the area of the Western Wall, however, include some of the best-known in Israel. They tend to have the pick of students and, if even they behave like hooligans, then there is something seriously wrong with the *yeshivah* as an institution.

No two *yeshivot* are quite alike. They draw on different traditions and they do not have quite the same intake. But all inculcate a narrowness of outlook, all have a narrow curriculum – which is getting narrower as the years go by – and they all seem to believe that where a man accumulates sufficient learning, all the other qualities he may need will fall into place of their own accord. They don't, and one can become an *ilui* – a prodigy of learning – without becoming a *mensh*.

The most disturbing aspect of the whole affair, however, lies in the attitude of the municipal authorities. Mayor Ehud Olmert, a Likud man, described the incident as 'disgusting and unforgivable', but explained that he had no jurisdiction over the Kotel area. Well, yes, but, in the same way that, strictly speaking, he was not responsible for the decision to add a new entrance to the tunnel near the Temple Mount, in both areas his views carry potentially crucial influence. Still, at least he did offer something of an apology.

His deputy, Chaim Miller, of the Agudat Yisrael, did not – for men of religion are incapable of admitting that religious men can ever do wrong – and instead of berating the attackers turned upon their victims and accused them of 'provocation'.

David Hartman, one of the few rabbis in Israel to combine Orthodoxy with a concern for justice and tolerance, asked Olmert: 'Have you given over the Kotel to the *charedi* community?'

Well Olmert hasn't but Teddy Kollek did, years ago.

The real question he should have asked is whether Jerusalem itself is to be handed over to the *charedim*.

Even that would be rhetorical for while nobody is handing Jerusalem over to them, they are gradually taking it over. In this instance, at least the police tried to help the victims. Who knows if there might come a time when the police would be required to lead the attack?

27 June 1997

Do you know what your daughter's up to?

MANY JEWISH FAMILIES now send their sons to *yeshivah* and their daughters to seminary (or sem, as it is generally called) for a finishing education.

The *yeshivah* is a familiar institution. Sems are comparatively novel, if only because the idea of giving girls a Jewish education at all is itself comparatively novel, and they have become a growth industry in Israel. New ones are setting up shop as frequently as pizza parlours. Indeed, some of them, for all I know, may even be part of a franchise operation.

While females are trusted to learn, they are not as yet quite trusted to teach, at least in centres of higher education. Thus the sems tend to be headed by men, and are largely staffed by men. This is a pity, because I suspect that women teachers would adopt a more enlightened approach to their responsibilities.

The sems, like *yeshivot*, vary greatly in quality. The worst have second-rate teachers, third-rate students and fourth-rate facilities. The better ones have spacious accommodation, excellent facilities, highly qualified staff, and offer a three-year course in Jewish studies which, in many respects, is as good as anything available in the universities – with the following difference.

While universities try to encourage students to evaluate, assess and think for themselves, many sems demand conformity and devote a substantial part of their programme to what they call *hashkofoh*, which means 'outlook', but which might be better translated as brainwashing.

A friend of mine enrolled her daughter in one such sem. While there, she decided to attend a *hashkofoh* lecture and what she heard in the course of the next hour compelled her to withdraw her daughter on the spot.

The lecture was given in the aftermath of Yitzhak Rabin's assassination and the speaker, a rabbi, tried to explain how a young Jew, from a deeply religious home, and who was himself deeply religious, could have been guilty of such a crime.

His explanation was simple. Jews, and certainly religious Jews, don't kill, and if they do, it is due to their surrounding environment, and Yigal Amir's act was – wait for it – due to Muslim influence.

Muslims, he said, were the sons of Ishmael, who was the father of abominations, and were thus abominations in themselves. Their wives were whores, and they treated their womenfolk as chattels.

They had no true ideas of what was right or wrong. They may claim to pray to the one God but were in fact idol worshippers; when they prostrated themselves in prayer, they licked dirt, and for all their apparent religiosity, they were vicious, violent and treacherous.

His message in essence was that, where Jews do good, they

conform to Jewish teachings, and where they do evil, they have succumbed to alien ones.

What he appeared to mean, though he didn't spell it out, was that, as Amir's family stemmed from the Yemen, the Islamic strain in his background had proved to be more powerful than the Jewish one. In other words, the Jew who is truly Jewish can do no wrong, if only because, where he does do wrong, he cannot be truly Jewish. All of which was too much for my friend, and when the lecturer had finished, she rose to point out that everything he said was not only in stark defiance of elementary logic but it contradicted the teachings of Rambam, who was himself in many respects a product of Islamic culture and who had the highest respect for Islam.

The rabbi apparently didn't know what to say, perhaps because the presence of a knowledgeable woman was outside his experience, and, in the end, he said nothing. There were some 30 girls in the room, some of them from England, and all of them from English-speaking countries. In some ways, the most depressing part of the story is that only one – a London girl, bless her – had the independence of mind to question his assertions. She, too, was left unanswered.

The rest followed with rapt attention, nodding with approval. They clearly felt reassured by his message. Some had brought tape-recorders to capture every pearl of wisdom as it fell from the rabbi's lips.

I wonder how many parents take the trouble to find out what is actually being taught in such places, and what poison is being spread in the name of God?

I used to point to the growth in the number of such seminaries as proof of a religious revival. I am now beginning to wonder if they are not in fact a symptom of religious decline.

5 January 1996

Reforming the *Get*

WHEN THE LORD Chancellor, Lord Mackay, was drawing up his white paper on the reform of the English divorce laws, he was approached by the Board of Deputies with a proposal affecting Jewish law.

The Board does not usually dabble in such matters, but it was acting on behalf of our ecclesiastical authorities, who were too embarrassed to approach the Lord Chancellor themselves – as well they might be, for he was being asked to amend the English civil law, to redress a defect in the Jewish religious law.

The defect is well known. In Jewish law, only the husband can initiate a divorce, and although the wife can refuse to accept it, her refusal can be circumvented.

There is, however, no way of getting round a husband's refusal, and the Board therefore urged Lord Mackay to include a clause in his proposed reforms which would have enabled the courts to withhold a decree nisi where the parties refuse to accept a *get* (religious divorce). He rejected the proposal on the perfectly reasonable grounds that the civil laws of the realm should not be mixed up with the religious laws of a particular minority.

It is true that Ontario and New York state have included such proposals in their divorce laws, but this says little either for the Jewish lobbyists who pressed for them or for the politicians who accepted them.

The irony is that both Ontario and New York regard themselves as the most progressive and enlightened provinces of their respective countries; but far from being enlightened or progressive, they are, in this particular case, helping to perpetuate one of the most illiberal and unjust elements in Jewish law.

The readiness of our rabbis to resort to the civil authorities on such matters is a public confession of moral bankruptcy, for they have the authority to make the changes themselves, but lack the courage to do so.

The women's groups which have been seeking reforms have had to go about their work with the greatest circumspection. They cannot clamour loudly for change, because the rabbis cannot be seen to be bending to public pressure; and they have to measure their words carefully, because they are calling for something which dare not speak its name.

They cannot refer to reforms, because it would suggest that the laws need improving. They cannot speak of change, because Jewish laws are immutable. They must even hesitate about using such expressions as 'reinterpretation' because they, too, carry the connotation of change.

The simple fact is that Jewish laws can be changed, have been changed, and that Judaism would not have survived as a living faith had they not been changed. This does not mean, of course, that it must continually adapt to every passing vogue or quirk of fashion. Judaism is reactionary – and so it should be. It is perfectly right that it should approach every innovation with caution, especially in rapidly changing times.

Divorce, however, is not a new phenomenon, but where once it was rare, now it is commonplace. As currently applied, the Jewish divorce laws are a source of widespread injustice and distress, and a reproach to the entire body of Jewish law.

In 1954, Rabbi Saul Lieberman introduced a new clause to the *ketubah* (marriage contract) which allowed the Beth Din to dissolve a marriage in certain defined circumstances; and even though the Orthodox knew that Lieberman was one of the greatest Jewish scholars of his day, they dismissed his clause out of hand because he was a professor at the Jewish Theological Seminary. They even prohibited the study of his responsa, because they were published by the JTS and, as such, were 'non-kosher'.

Even worse was the case of the late Rabbi Eliezer Berkovits. He was not in the same class as Lieberman – very few people are – but he was a profound thinker, with a probing and original mind, and a man of impeccable Orthodoxy.

In 1967, he proposed that a husband should empower the Beth Din to dissolve his marriage retroactively in the event of a civil divorce. The proposal was accompanied by intricate arguments and a mass of learned responsa, but Berkovits's very readiness to put forward so radical a solution undermined his standing as a *halachist*.

Where does that leave Jewish women? In limbo, where they have always been. They like to think that if they show sufficient patience and restraint, justice and reason will ultimately prevail. So far, however, only the 'it-can't-be-done' brethren have prevailed – and I suspect they will continue to prevail for as long as the women show patience and restraint.

25 May 1995

Taking to the streets

IT'S NOT OFTEN that Jewish women take to the street to demonstrate against the action – or inaction – of rabbis, and the fact that they did so a week or two ago was a measure not so much of militancy as of desperation.

The demonstration was not only dignified, but altruistic, for, as we shall see, the women involved had no hope of benefiting personally from it, but no doubt it will be denounced in some quarters as a *chillul Hashem*, desecration of God's name, for it exposed Judaism to ridicule and shame.

But can the women be blamed for that? They have argued their case in private for long enough and, faced with injustice on the one hand and inertia on the other, they had no alternative but to take to the streets. I'm only sorry that they didn't do it sooner and the numbers weren't larger.

While this issue is allowed to fester, any homilies from Orthodox pulpits on humanity, equity, justice, the joys of Jewish tradition and the warmth of Jewish family life will sound like so much humbug.

And it is a purely Orthodox problem. The non-Orthodox have evolved their own procedures and have no problems with the *get* – the religious divorce – and, in effect, the devout Jewish woman is being punished for her loyalty to her faith.

One could argue that she has only herself to blame because, where women are concerned, it is difficult to have Orthodoxy and justice. That, however, is not the view of the Chief Rabbi and two

168

years ago he unveiled a pre-nuptial agreement (PNA) which, though it would do nothing to help the present victims of our divorce laws, just *might* have limited the number of new ones.

I have laid stress on the 'might' because it is by no means certain that it would have been enforceable in English law. I am also unhappy about the idea of resorting to the English courts to redress deficiencies in Jewish law. But the PNA was important as a symbol of intent. A beginning was being made.

There looked to be a glimmer of hope amid the despair but two years have now passed and nothing has been done to implement it.

Two years may be a short time in the eyes of rabbis and lawyers, but the injustice inherent in our divorce laws goes back more than 2,000 years, and they remain in force not because they are immutable, but because women accepted their fate – as some of them still do – with glum resignation. In any case, they were too few and isolated even to contemplate action.

Now that divorce is becoming almost as commonplace as marriage they are many and those of them who remain chained to their former husbands as a result of the *get*, are no longer prepared to stay silent.

One woman, who opposed the demonstration, said that the fault was not the Chief Rabbi's because he was trying to obtain a rabbinical consensus. But that is at the very heart of the problem.

The search for a consensus is a formula for paralysis – for rabbis will agree only on what can't or shouldn't be done. They never agree on what can or should be done, if only because some of them measure their standing as halachists by the measure of their obduracy.

One can have little respect for denominations or clergymen who change direction with every change of wind and who rush to consecrate every whim of fashion, but paralysis is even worse.

Everyone knows that the Jewish divorce laws as currently interpreted are morally untenable, and several outstanding Orthodox scholars have suggested ways in which they might be changed. But somebody has to take action, and the Chief Rabbi is well placed to do so.

He has the requisite standing, authority and brain power. All he needs is the will power. And, if he should take the initiative, he would, certainly on this particular issue, have the overwhelming mass of the community behind him. He does not have to wait for a *hechsher* from Stamford Hill.

In any case, now that women have taken their fate into their own hands there can be no going back. They began by demonstrating in the street, they may follow by demonstrating in the synagogues, perhaps even on Kol Nidrei night.

The idea may seem outrageous, but if we can disrupt the most sacred occasion in our calendar to raise money – as we have been doing for the past 50 years – I think women will be forgiven if they do the same to demand justice.

If Dr Sacks should succeed in making the necessary changes he will be regarded as the greatest Chief Rabbi we have had; if he should fail, he will inevitably be the last one.

3 November 1995

Drosnin Bible codes

DAYAN GAVRIEL KRAUSZ, head of the Manchester Beth Din, has banned the book on the Bible code by Michael Drosnin, not because it's drivel – which it is – but because Drosnin is a self-confessed heretic.

When I received the book a few months ago, I read it with a mixture of amusement, impatience and wonder. I was amused because there is a certain amount of fun in dabbling in futures and, as it was Derby week, I studied Drosnin's text meticulously in the vain hope of finding a winner at Epsom.

I became impatient once it dawned upon me that the book was but an elaborate variation of a very old game called Gematria. (As for the wonder, I shall come to that later.)

Hebrew letters represent both consonants and figures, and Gematria – which comes from the Greek for geometry – is a method of extracting the hidden meaning of a word or a phrase (presuming always there is one) by reference to its numerical value.

The Greeks played the game long before the Hebrews got round

170

to it. As a diversion, it is perfectly harmless, and as one is allowed to use variations in spelling, add a number here, remove a number there, and read the alphabet in reverse so that the first letter, if necessary, is given the same numerical value as the last, one can reach any conclusion one wants and indeed prove anything one likes.

For example, the word *eileh* in Exodus 35:1 is taken as proof that 39 different tasks were involved in the building of the Sanctuary. The numerical value of *eileh* itself, however, is actually 36 and one gets the necessary 39 only by a complex bit of borrowing from an adjacent word.

As a further variation, two different words can – if one is so minded – be given the same meaning where they happen to have the same numerical value.

Few rabbis now believe in Gematria, but even those who don't are prepared to use it when they have nothing better to talk about and it has become the ultimate resort of a preacher at the end of his homilies.

Drosnin's book, though not particularly concerned with numerical values, works on roughly the same principles as Gematria. For a start, he has reduced the entire text of the Bible to a gapless slab, adopting variations in spelling and, where necessary, reading the words back to front, as a result being able to show, at least to his own satisfaction, that every major event in world history – plus not a few minor ones – was presaged in Scripture more than 2,000 years ago.

But the main fault of the book lies not so much in its method as its attitude to prophecy. Prophets were not computer buffs and prophecy was not a word game. The aim of the prophets was not so much to presage events as to prevent them, much as Jonah, for example, was able to prevent the destruction of Nineveh. And, as we can see from the same example, the concept of prophecy is tied up with the concept of atonement, the one being a preliminary to the other.

Drosnin tells us, among other things, that the world will come to an end after a great cataclysm in 13 years or thereabouts.

Now I am not saying he is necessarily wrong – if only because I would looked damned silly if he turned out to be right – but such information is of more than passing importance and, if true, should be *en claire* and not in code.

When I finally finished reading the book – and it was anything but an easy read – it left me with a sense of marvel, not at the ingenuity of the author, but at the gullibility of readers, for the book was already then a best-seller in America (and has since become a best-seller in Britain).

Once it appears in paperback, as it no doubt will, it is likely to become more widely read than the Bible, or even Delia Smith's cookery books.

It seems to me that the Western world is on the brink of a new age of faith. People have become a little weary of this world and are searching around desperately for signs and portents of mysterious forces and transcendental powers. In such a situation, in the absence of any new creeds, they may even be ready to reconcile themselves to the old ones.

They are not, as yet, prepared to believe in God, if only because God has in recent years had rather a bad press, but they believe fervently in computers and, for many people, hidden meanings as exposed by a computer carry the strength of revelation.

In the beginning was the Internet . . .

8 August 1997

Rebbe and rocker

AN ANNOUNCEMENT EMANATING from Chabad House, London N16, declares:

'We eagerly await the fulfilment of the rebbe's clear statements made with the clarity of prophetic vision that the Moshiach is coming *immediately* [My italics]. It is apparent that, in our times, there is no one more fitting to assume the role of leading us to the redemption as the Moshiach than the rebbe. We therefore join in an expression of commitment and faith in the coming redemption.'

Mr Chaim Yitzhok Cohen, who is behind the announcement, was at the rebbe's funeral. Even so, he claims the rebbe is not dead but in hiding. (He is buried in a New York cemetery which, I

172

suppose, is as good a way as any of staying hidden.)

I should perhaps add that Mr Cohen is Irish, so that one must make some allowances for his claim. He insists that 'the majority of the Lubavitch worldwide support his view'.

The fact that the resurrectionist wing of the Lubavitch movement recently took a full-page ad in the *New York Times* to press its case suggests that, however prominent his voice, it is not a lone one.

The official Lubavitch movement has distanced itself from the campaign, without actually disowning it, possibly because it is anxious to keep all the options open.

In the absence of the rebbe, however – if, indeed, he is absent – it is by no means certain which is the official wing of Lubavitch and which isn't.

In the meantime, Mr Cohen and his colleagues have no hesitation in proclaiming Rabbi Menachem Mendel Schneerson as *Melech Hamoshiach*: The Messiah the King.

In the words of the old song, he knows that his redeemer liveth. In an age of uncertainties, it is good to find somebody who is certain about something.

But, as if to add to the confusion, back in Memphis, Tennessee, and, even beyond, a great many people are insisting that Elvis Presley, who died 20 years ago, is likewise still around.

Presley may, of course, have had a stand-in at his funeral or, rather, a lie-in, as Hollywood folk often did. Even if he didn't, special arrangements can always be made for special people.

The circumstances must be right, but if the rebbe can have a second coming I don't see why Presley can't. There is no copyright on resurrections and, even if there were, it must have lapsed by now.

I will no doubt be told that Presley wasn't Jewish, but I'm not at all sure about that. His very name is obviously a corruption of Priestly, which suggests that the family name was originally Cohen.

Moreover, his hit song, 'All Shook Up,' his long *peyot* (side curls), his very gyrations, carried obvious hints that he was a closet Chasid. He may even have been a Lubavitcher for I am told that his name – depending on how you spell it in Hebrew – adds up to 770, which is, of course, the address of the Lubavitch HQ in Brooklyn.

So, dare I say it, could Elvis Presley be the Moshiach? Probably not, if only because tradition insists that the Moshiach must stem from the House of David or, failing that, from the House of Joseph, whereas, if Presley was a Cohen, he must have stemmed from the House of Aaron, and there is no tradition linking the priesthood with the Redeemer.

But if he was a Cohen the first time round, there is no saying what he might have become during his concealment. People do change, especially after they're dead.

The problem as I see it, however, is not so much theological as psychological.

The Moshiach has always been referred to by the definite article in the belief that he is *sui generis*, one and unique; and the suggestion that there could be two around at the same time would strain credulity to its limits and undermine the belief in both.

I can see only two ways out of the difficulty. The Elvis Presley party could come together with the rebbe's followers and consult the oracle of our age, the Drosnin Bible code, to see what it might have to say in the matter and abide by its findings.

Failing which, they could have a rotation agreement on the lines adopted by Yitzhak Shamir after the 1982 election, with the rebbe as Moshiach for the third millennium and Presley for the fourth.

(As for what might happen in the fifth millennium, we shall deal with it when we come to it. One should never try to solve too many problems at once.)

May it all come speedily and in our day. Amen.

12 September 1997

Big brother's watching you

HULL USED TO be famous for fish. It was also famous to successive generations of Lithuanian Jews as the gateway to England.

Now it is known principally as the birthplace of Maureen Lipman, my favourite comedienne and one of the few women I have come across who can be witty without being smutty – although she can also be smutty if occasion demands, or even if it doesn't.

Hull is about to acquire a new claim to fame, at least in Jewish circles, as the source of a ruling by the London Beth Din which will go down in history as the '*Watchman* verdict'.

The *Watchman* is the official organ of the Hull Jewish Representative Council. The latest issue, which is likely to become a collector's item, and which could, one supposes, be the last one, carries the following announcement:

> From the Rabbi. To all concerned.
>
> Please be advised that the ruling from the London Beth Din to me (at the request of the *Shul* council, a while ago, to make the inquiry) – that a secular newsletter published by a secular organisation should not deal with religious matters – is now being fully implemented.
>
> It is therefore quite obvious that the *Watchman* has absolutely no right to publish any more the 'Times of Services' and the 'Yahrzeit lists'.
>
> These items are in the exclusive domain of the Hull Hebrew Congregation and they will be published in the monthly '*Shul* Bulletin'.
> [Signed] Rabbi Shalom Osdoba.

Forget the syntax. Consider the implications of the ruling.

A few years ago a genius at Bar-Ilan University in Israel developed a computer program which came up with an immediate answer to a myriad of *halachic* questions.

I, though no genius, was about to come up with a similar program, but decided against it because I already knew the answers, which could be compounded into one word: No.

The Hull ruling proves my point. No matter how banal the issue, how bizarre the question, or how misguided the questioner, the answer will always be the same. And the questioner would have to be misguided unless, of course, he is looking for a 'No' in the first place – which I suspect he was in this particular instance.

But it is still difficult to contemplate the issue without evincing a certain amount of admiration for the *dayanim* of the London Beth Din.

They could so easily have said to Rabbi Osdoba: this is your problem, you handle it.

Instead, they met in solemn conclave, brought out the ancient texts, and pored over them for 40 days and 40 nights. If not everyone will regard their verdict as proof of their wisdom, the very trouble they took is certainly proof of their zeal. And all this is on top of the trouble they have taken to warn rabbis away from the annual Limmud conference – and other such 'unholy' occasions. Yea, they sleep not, neither do they slumber.

I take my hat off to them.

I was always under the impression that there is no division in Jewish life between the secular and the sacred – though some things are more sacred than others.

The *Watchman* verdict shows that there most certainly is such a division, and that rabbis have the right to say which is which, and where the one finishes and the other begins.

It has also vested local rabbis with the copyright of the synagogue timetable and *yahrzeit* (anniversary of a death) lists, which, presumably, can be breached only at the price of ostracism in this world and damnation in the next.

What I suppose might happen now is that the *Watchman* will go underground and reappear in *samizdat* form. Or the forbidden messages will be circulated by word of mouth: 'Psst! *Minchah* next Sunday, four o'clock. Pass it on!' Or: 'I'll be saying *Kaddish* (memorial prayer) for my mother next Wednesday. Keep it dark.'

When I was in Hull on a brief visit some 30 years ago, it was an attractive and lively community with three synagogues, all of them Orthodox. It now has two synagogues, one Orthodox, the other Reform. At this rate, it will soon be reduced to one synagogue, and I leave you to guess what sort of synagogue that will be.

I sometimes wonder why so many people, some of them from traditional homes, are drawn to the Reform movement, with all its fads and 'with-itry', and all its half-baked doctrines. The simple answer would seem to be that it is not so much Reform which attracts them as Orthodoxy which repels them.

15 November 1996

What's happening to Manchester?

WHAT IS HAPPENING to Manchester? It used to be the home of English liberalism. But it is clearly not the home of Anglo-Jewish liberalism.

A couple of months ago it was the scene of a large rally to protest against the possible opening of a Masorti synagogue in the city.

Three weeks ago, some yobs in black, purporting to act in the name of heaven, tried to disrupt a meeting addressed by Rabbi Shlomo Riskin, on the grounds that he was a 'heretic'.

A few days later, four children were expelled from the Talmud Torah Chinuch N'Orim school on the grounds that their parents had attended the meeting ('for the sins of the fathers shall I bring down upon the heads of the children . . .').

In 1990, I published a collection of essays called *Murmurings of a Licensed Heretic* and was immediately denounced as a fraud by the doyen of Jewish journalists, the late Sam Goldsmith.

'*Ech mir* a heretic,' ('some heretic') he said, 'you haven't written a word to which any reasonable Orthodox Jew could take objection.'

Well I suppose one man's heretic is another man's fanatic, but Manchester has shown that the opposite is also true and that one man's fanatic can be another man's heretic.

There are many things one can say against Rabbi Riskin, and I think I have said them all, but just about the one thing he is *not* is a heretic. It is true that he invited Dr Nehama Leibowitz to address his *yeshivah* students in Efrat. Dr Leibowitz, though a very old, and a very learned woman, is still a woman, and Rabbi Riskin's action may therefore be construed as a sin of sorts, but it hardly makes him a heretic.

I can only presume he was mistaken by the men in black for Adin Steinsaltz, who was due to address a meeting in Manchester a few days later.

I can see how the mistake arose. Both are rabbis, both are from Israel, both are famous, both are short, and both have a fairly modern approach to Jewish issues. But whereas Riskin merely couches ancient platitudes in new words, Steinsaltz can be fairly outspoken.

A few years ago, he suggested, in the course of some broadcast talks, that some of our biblical heroes were less than heroic and that Samson, in particular, was a downright thug.

The spoken word among Jews does not have the same impact as the written word so that when his talks were subsequently published in book form, there were loud shrieks of dismay and he was denounced as a heretic and threatened with excommunication.

He had actually said nothing new. Scripture is not hagiography, and biblical figures are depicted as human beings with human frailties. This is one of the reasons why it has enthralled so many people over so many centuries.

And indeed, commentators like Nachmanides had some fairly harsh things to say even about the Patriarchs. Nachmanides, however, lived in the thirteenth century whereas Steinsaltz, a scholar of equal stature, is living in the twentieth.

Steinsaltz's forays into biblical biography were, however, a comparatively minor offence. He has also been charged with the wilful and indiscriminate diffusion of Jewish knowledge by vocalising the Aramaic text of the Talmud and translating it, first into Hebrew, and now into English.

The rabbis were unhappy about the translation of the Bible into Greek (the Septuagint) in the third century BCE and compared it to the creation of the Golden Calf (which, it will be remembered, was ground down into a powder).

The rabbis in our time would have liked to do the same with Steinsaltz. For, in vocalising and translating the Talmud, he has made it accessible to the intelligent layman, whereas they would have preferred it to remain a closed book accessible only to the *yeshivah* world, for their power, in a sense, rests on obfuscation.

If the events in Manchester represented a purely local phenomenon, they would have been good for a laugh, but would not otherwise have been worthy of comment.

They are, however, part of a larger effort to extend the *glatt kosher* philosophy, which has hitherto governed the supervision of meat, to the supervision of thought.

It is tempting to dismiss such attitudes as medieval but, as I have

178

suggested, medieval Jews were in some respects a good deal more open-minded than our contemporary brethren and it seems to me that Jewish Orthodoxy is entering – indeed, has entered – upon a new age of darkness.

17 March 1995

Navel-gazing

I ONCE ATTENDED a festive meal given by an Israeli friend and was digging pensively into my cous-cous when a half-clad female suddenly appeared from nowhere and began writhing, as if in agony.

I thought something she had eaten had violently disagreed with her and I hurriedly pushed my plate aside. It was only when people around me began clapping and cheering that I realised I was being entertained to a belly dance.

The young lady went though the motions an all-in wrestler might make when wrestling with himself. I was particularly mesmerised by the gyrations of her navel, which moved faster and faster as the music and clapping noises became louder, until she finally sank to the floor in a self-inflicted half-Nelson.

All that was a long time ago, but now belly dancers are to an Israeli celebration what After Eights are to an English one. (It used to be *petits fours*, but in England we do nothing by halves.)

Legend hath it that Eve was the first belly dancer, but legend hath it wrong, for Eve, of course, had no navel, and a belly dancer without a navel is like a clog dancer without clogs. And, in any case, for whom could she have danced?

It is, however, true that as an art form belly dancing is of great antiquity. Salome was a belly dancer, and John the Baptist was not the first man to lose his head over the spectacle. But it more or less lapsed in Israel until it was revived as part of the Maimuna festival celebrated by Jews of Moroccan origin on the last day of Pesach.

It is all very ethnic, like the Highland fling, the Irish jig and the Jewish jog (known otherwise as the *hora*). But – in the eyes of the Jerusalem rabbinate, at least – it is not very *kosher* and last year the rabbis threatened to withdraw their *kashrut* certificate from any catering establishment prepared to stomach a belly dance.

The rabbinate never made the threat public, but caterers got the message and belly dancers got the push, though they were never told why.

One of their number, Ilana Ruskin, made it her business to find out, however, and when she did, she sued the rabbinate for loss of earnings. The matter eventually came before the Supreme Court, which ruled that the rabbinate could say what people may eat at a *kosher* function, but not what they may see.

As I may have suggested, I do not regard belly dancing as particularly aesthetic, and given the choice between a belly dancer and, say, apple strudel to wind up a meal, I would opt for strudel every time. But I nevertheless regard Miss Ruskin as a heroine who has made the Jewish world that much safer for liberty.

Rabbis, like everyone else, have a habit of extending the authority they have into areas they haven't, and they will continue to do so for as long and as far as their intrusions are unchallenged.

I can understand their attitude in this particular case. A rabbi, sheltered from the outside world, who has to supervise the food in an establishment open to belly dancers, must feel a little like a musician who plays the piano in a house of ill repute.

Rabbis regard belly dancing as an 'immodest spectacle', but then they regard the sight of women's uncovered arms or heads as equally immodest.

There are also rabbis who object to men and women sitting together at the same table, or even assembling in the same room, and if they would get away with the ban on dancers, they would eventually go on to demand that all kosher functions be segregated.

As it is, any *kosher* hotelier in Israel who organises a New Year party imperils his *kashrut* licence, because the rabbis regard New Year celebrations as goyish.

The caterers, however, are even more culpable than the rabbis, for instead of uniting against unreasonable impositions, they have retreated cravenly before them; and instead of challenging the interdict against dancers the moment it was made, they left the fight to Miss Ruskin.

Kashrut observance in Israel was not nearly as widespread 20 or 30 years ago as it is now, and there may come a time – I fear it probably will – when the clientele of *kosher* hotels will insist not only on *kosher* food, but on *kosher* conduct.

Until that time comes, the rabbis should confine themselves to the kitchen, where they will at least be spared the sight of untoward navel displays.

15 June 1990

Status Quo

AN OPINION POLL published by the Geocartographic Institute of Tel Aviv suggests that nearly half the Jews in Israel believe that the growing animosity between the religious and secular could lead to civil war.

Surprise, surprise, but then opinion pollsters have always derived part of their livelihood from establishing what is perfectly obvious.

For the past 30 years, I've been saying that if there should ever be peace between Jew and Arab, there will be one almighty settling of accounts between Jew and Jew.

The trouble began in the good old days of good King David – David Ben-Gurion, that is (or that was).

B-G, though secular, was prepared to make concessions to the religious parties, not only because he needed them as coalition partners, but because they acted as a *yarmulke* (skull cap) to the bare head of Israel and accentuated the Jewish character of the Jewish state.

His policy, though right in general terms, was wrong in detail.

The biggest burden on the life of the Israeli is conscription but the sons and daughters of the ultras are largely, if not entirely, excluded from the provisions of successive national service acts.

He was wrong to allow everyone in a black hat to enjoy freedom from military service. And he was wrong to let the religious parties dictate when public transport could move, for it meant those with money to buy a car or hire a taxi could travel on Shabbat, and those who hadn't, couldn't. It extended religious rights to include religious coercion.

And, of course, it hasn't stopped there, for the Orthodox also assumed the right to say where even private vehicles could move on Shabbat. This didn't matter when they closed off their small side roads, but it does matter now that they are determined to close even major trunk routes.

This, for the time being, is only a Jerusalem problem. When Teddy Kollek was mayor of the city, he made it possible for Jew and Arab to live together in some sort of amity but, since Ehud Olmert took over, it has proved impossible for even Jew and Jew to do so.

In an ironic way, Olmert has become to the religious parties in Jerusalem, what the religious were to Ben-Gurion: he is there to suggest that the municipality is modern and even moderate in its attitudes.

In fact, it is thoroughly black and getting blacker and, for the secular, the finest prospect in Jerusalem is the highway which leads to Tel Aviv, and they are leaving the city in droves, while the highway is still open.

But lest they should have thought they were safe in Tel Aviv, some 20,000 men in black descended on the city last week to demand a greater degree of Sabbath observance.

I must admit that Tel Aviv is not my favourite city. Although it is great for a night out, I wouldn't care to live there on weekdays, let alone on Shabbat.

Its citizens, however, have evolved their own life style, and Jerusalem and Bnei Brak have no more right to impose their ways on Tel Aviv than Tel Aviv would have the right to impose its ways on Bnei Brak and Jerusalem.

But such considerations would not enter the Orthodox mind. They believe they alone have it right and that those who have it wrong – everybody else – must be put right.

The demonstration was a gratuitous exercise in insolence. The organisers must have known that they could not possibly do anything to change the habits of Tel Aviv, and could only provoke hostility to everything they stand for.

182

The Orthodox abused their power even when they formed some ten per cent of the electorate. Now that they form 23 per cent, their power has gone to their heads and they are even trying to undermine the authority of the Supreme Court, the ultimate defender of democracy and justice in Israel.

Yet, even if animosities should escalate, I do not envisage the possibility of outright war, if only because there will come a point when the secular parties will form a united front against the excesses of their religious brethren.

In 1974, about 8,000 *yeshiva* students received deferment from military service. Their number has since grown to 18,000,* and this in a small nation which has had to fight four major wars in its 38† years.

The ultras view Zionism as a damnable heresy, but if they think Israel is *treif* (not kosher), they regard its money as *kosher* and they have in recent years used their political influence to extort great fortunes from a semi-bankrupt exchequer. They have, in other words, obtained all the benefits of statehood without assuming any of its responsibilities – while presuming to tell others how they should live.

The emergence of a secular united front would, I think, show them how far they have been pushing their luck, and bring them to their senses.

20 June 1986/13 December 1996

Secular *Shtiebl*

I NOTICE THAT a number of British secular Jews would like to set up their own synagogue, a sort of infidels' Adath. Should they succeed, I shall offer my services as founder rabbi. And, even as I

*Now 29,000.
†Now 51 years.

write, the likely liturgy begins to form in my mind:

'Blessed art Thou, O Lord our God, King of the Universe, for not making me religious . . .'

Which would be followed by the Thirteen Principles of Faith-lessness: 'I believe with perfect faith that the Creator, blessed be His name, does not exist, never has existed and never will exist . . .'

Perhaps even a new version of the Lord's Prayer: 'Our Father, which aren't in Heaven (or anywhere else), unhallowed be Thy name, lead us not into temptation because we can find our way into it ourselves . . .'

The prayer is, of course, a Christian one but I believe that, if one is non-religious, one should be non-religious ecumenically.

In *der heim*, non-believers didn't believe with fervour. They used to have their own creed, their own anthem, and their own festivals and holy days. They would celebrate Yom Kippur with a banquet – though, given the quality of Jewish catering in those days, such a meal could have been a greater source of mortification than a fast.

In Britain, on the other hand, non-believers tend to be half-hearted. In the olden days they belonged to the United Synagogue, much as their Gentile counterparts belonged to the Church of England, which is to say they didn't treat their non-belief as an article of faith.

Since the United Synagogue began to take religion seriously, however, non-believers have become involved in a certain amount of soul-searching, which isn't easy if you believe you don't have a soul to search.

In Israel, one does not feel called upon to establish what sort of Jew one is – or is not – because one's Jewishness is defined by one's milieu. The same is to an extent true of New York, which is substantially a Jewish city, but in places like London or Oxford it's another matter.

I mention Oxford because the prime mover behind the secular scheme is Felix Posen, of the Oxford Centre for Post-Graduate Hebrew Studies. Now Oxford is the home not only of lost causes but of lost souls, though no one is irredeemably lost until he becomes a fellow of All Souls.

All Souls College is a rarefied meeting place of the great, the good and the wise. It showers its fellows with benefits without requiring duties in return. It has excellent dining facilities and a superb cellar, but while, as its name might suggest, it began life as a religious foundation, it is now a sublimely secular one.

That, I suppose, is only to be expected. What man in his senses would give a thought to the hereafter if he is offered everything he can want in the here and now? And to be a fellow of All Souls is to be a sort of anointed agnostic.

One such fellow is Sir Isaiah Berlin, a profoundly Jewish Jew, but not a profoundly religious one and, as if to show how profoundly non-religious he is, he has given Posen his blessing.

Another would probably be Dr David Daube, formerly regius professor of civil law. Dr Daube was extremely religious in his youth, but grew less so as he grew older, and is now, I gather, not religious at all.

Then there is Peter Pulzer, Gladstone professor of government and public administration, who is likewise a fellow of All Souls and also spurns all religious belief, I understand. And, finally, there was his predecessor in the Gladstone chair, Professor Samuel Finer.

I speak in the past tense, for Finer is, alas, no more. He died recently at the age of 77. Finer was almost classically Jewish in his utterances, manner, appearance and shape, but he never had a religious thought in his well-stocked mind nor a religious sentiment in his warm, Jewish heart.

Like Sir Isaiah, he would sometimes attend *shul*, but that, God knows, doesn't mean anything. If there is a heaven, then Finer is certainly there. If there isn't, he will have the pleasure of saying I told you so (or rather, he won't). Needless to say, he, too, was a fellow of All Souls.

Which gives me an idea. What better place than All Souls to join religiously in denying the existence of the mortal soul? In other words, why not take over All Souls as a secular *shtiebl*? I know it has some non-Jewish fellows, but I'm sure they would enter into the spirit – or lack of it – of the occasion, though the place might have to be renamed Non Souls.

Forget about my being a rabbi. I'll be their chaplain.

18 June 1993

10
The Morality
of
Orthodoxy

It is as if the very devotion to the mechanics of Judaism, has estranged the devout from its spirit.

Justice, justice shalt thou pursue

THE FIRST CHAPTER of Isaiah is read in synagogues on the Shabbat before the fast of Tisha B'Av. Last Shabbat the following extract was read by a young American rabbi, Jeremy Milgrom, in the unlikely setting of Umm el Fahm, a large Arab village in Israel:

> Hear the word of the Lord, ye rulers of Sodom; give ear unto the law of our God, ye people of Gomorrah.
> To what purpose is the multitude of your sacrifices unto me? saith the Lord: I am full of the burnt offerings of rams, and the fat of fed beasts; and I delight not in the blood of bullocks or of lambs, or of he goats . . .
> Bring me no more vain oblations; incense is an abomination unto me; the new moons and sabbaths, the calling of assemblies, I cannot away with it; it is iniquity, even the solemn meeting.
> Your new moons and your appointed feasts my soul hateth . . . And when you spread forth your hands, I will hide mine eyes from you; yea, when ye make many prayers I will not hear: your hands are full of blood.
> Wash you, make you clean; put away the evil of your doings from before mine eyes; cease to do evil.
> Learn to do well; seek judgement, relieve the oppressed . . .

These words have a tragic relevance to contemporary Israel. The Jewish state is undergoing what is often described as 'a religious revival'. New synagogues are opening everywhere, and nearly all are crammed to capacity; and the same is true of *yeshivot*. *Kashrut* has never been more widely or meticulously observed. The covered head, once the badge of a shrinking minority, is now *de rigueur* with a growing majority, and many heads are now twice, or even thrice covered. The tassels and side locks which used to characterise the inhabitants of this or that minute quarter, are becoming ubiquitous. Comes Succot and tabernacles sprout on every balcony and in every back-yard, and a growing number of people – not all

189

of them mad – are clamouring for the rebuilding of the Temple and the restoration of sacrifices.

There is even an establishment known as Ateret Kohanim which for some years now has been training priests to perform sacrificial rites. The Holy Land is, on the face of it, becoming the land of the holy, yet it is as if the very devotion to the mechanics of Judaism has estranged the devout from its spirit. Injustice and oppression have grown with the very growth in religious zeal, and we now have the nemesis of an Orthodox rabbi who, if his name is anything to go by, is also a *cohen-tsadik*, a 'holy priest', who is trying to hasten the day when he may offer up sacrifices of rams, bullocks, lambs and he-goats.

In the meantime, however, he is preparing to sacrifice the Arabs of Israel and the West Bank, and yet the entire religious establishment has stayed silent in the face of his blasphemies. One of the chief rabbis has criticised his ideas in vague, ambiguous terms, without criticising him. The other said nothing. The Council of Sages has uttered not a word. Some rabbis, like Chaim Druckman of the Morashah party, have stayed silent for the good reason that their own ideas are not all that far from his, and others because ideas in general are a little outside their province. They are concerned with *mitzvot* and not justice.

When Mosley sought to draw attention to his cause in the thirties, he concentrated his efforts on the area in which he could excite the most violent opposition, the Jewish East End. The *kosher* Mosley of Israel is planning to do the same in the Arab village of Umm El Fahm. Last Shabbat Rabbi Jeremy Milgrom sought to forestall him by taking part in a march through that same village. He was joined by four rabbinical colleagues, three of them Conservative and one Reform, and by a number of Orthodox families, but – although the chairman of the local council made all the arrangements necessary for the observance of Shabbat – there were no Orthodox rabbis on the scene. Part of the trouble is that the Prophets, Isaiah, Amos, Micah and the rest are closed books in some *yeshivot*, and forbidden books in others.

It could be argued that the new adherents of Orthodoxy should be allowed time to find themselves and get beyond the outer trappings of Judaism to its inner meaning.

Yet who is to guide them if their religious leaders have lost all capacity to lead? If one regards the religious faith with misgivings, one regards the rabbinate with despair, and it is left to young men like Jeremy Milgrom, who are not even officially recognised as rabbis in Israel, to remind the world that the ways of the Torah 'are ways of pleasantness, and that all its paths are peace.'

10 August 1984

Darkness and light – Israeli rabbis

THE GREATEST THREAT to the character and integrity of the Jewish State comes not from Arabs, but from Jews.

This was the gist of an important speech made by President Chaim Herzog on the first anniversary of the murder of Emil Grunzweig, and I cannot imagine that any reasonable person would disagree with him.

He referred to the attempt to blow up the Al Aksa Mosque and to numerous other attacks on Muslim and Christian religious institutions, which, he said, were 'often committed ostensibly in the name of Heaven,' and he called on religious leaders to denounce such acts of terrorism. To which one must ask: what religious leaders?

The last Israeli chief rabbi to enjoy any standing with the secular as well as the religious community was the president's own father, Rabbi Isaac Herzog, and he's been dead for 25 years. His successor, Rabbi Isser Unterman, was a decent but ineffectual man, and *his* successor, Chief Rabbi Tweedledum (né Goren), devoted most of his energies to doing battle with his Sephardi counterpart, Chief Rabbi Tweedledee (alias Ovadiah Yosef).

Nothing, however, so ill became them in office as their leaving of it, and when they were required to retire, they clung to their posts as drowning men cling to a raft and they almost had to be wrenched free.

Between them, they made the religious establishment a laughing

191

stock. Their successors are an unknown quantity, but given their silence on the major moral issues affecting Israel, they would seem to prefer to stay unknown.

As for the heads of the great yeshivot, the so-called *gedolei hatorah*, their attitude may be summed up as indifference tempered by cupidity. They will accept government subventions – indeed, through their spokesmen in the Knesset, they will clamour for them – but they are only vaguely aware of what is happening in the country.

They have always been able to use their influence to stop the buses on Shabbat; they have now stopped the planes; given half the chance they would stop all life. But I have never heard them utter a plea for tolerance, decency, justice or any of the qualities which make human society civil and human.

Scholasticism, however, has always gone with unworldliness and the failings of such men arise partly out of the nature of their calling.

It is when one turns to some of the younger rabbis that one really begins to worry. There is Rabbi Waldman, the head of Kiryat Arba Yeshiva, a slight, amiable figure with a pair of kindly, smiling eyes gleaming out of a wilderness of hair. He can argue with all seriousness that it is the destiny of Jews to rule and of Arabs to be ruled and that to oppose the occupation of the West Bank is therefore to oppose the will of God.

One can warm to such a man, even if one shudders at his philosophy. The same cannot be said of Rabbi Chaim Druckman, founder and head of Or Etzion Yeshivah; he simply makes one shudder.

Rabbi Druckman is the most dynamic and probably the most influential rabbi in Israel, not because of his spiritual attainments, but because of his political connections. He was at one time in the National Religious Party, but has since moved so far to the Right as to have moved right out, and he is now in a party of his own.

When there was an attempt on the life of three Arab West Bank mayors a few years ago, instead of condemning the attack, he virtually condoned it. He once said (and perhaps more than once) that he was not averse to the state of war between Jews and Arabs, because if there were peace, there would be intermarriage, which makes one wonder what God he could be worshipping.

And whenever some trigger-happy thug is taken into custody on suspicion of killing or maiming an Arab, one can be fairly certain that he will immediately intervene with the police to explain that the culprit meant no harm, that he was 'a good Jewish boy with a good Jewish heart' who was only doing it in self-defence. As far as he is concerned, there is no closed season for Arab-baiting. He is, one is not surprised to learn, the spiritual head of Bnei Akiva.

Against the Druckmans one can set Rabbi Lichtenstein of Alon Shvut Yeshivah, who has expressed the strongest reservations about the direction which religious Zionism has been taking; but, unhappily, Rabbi Lichtenstein is an isolated individual while Druckman is, in many respects, a representative figure.

In the war of attrition now being waged in Israel between the powers of light and powers of darkness, the rabbis are largely on the side of darkness. We are in this respect, at least, more fortunate in the diaspora.

10 February 1984

Enemies of mankind

IT HASN'T BEEN a good time for God.

In Beirut, 40 Americans are still being held hostage by Muslim extremists, and about eight of the hostages 'with Jewish-sounding names' have been singled out for special attention by the Hizbollah, the Party of God.

On Sunday, 322 innocent travellers, including many children, were blown out of the sky. The cause has not yet been finally established, but all the available evidence suggests that it was the work of religious extremists, adherents of another party, of another God.

Our own men of God have, happily, never taken to hijacking or placing bombs on civilian airliners, and have limited their efforts to cars and buses. What is more to the point, they have been apprehended and are now on trial (the prosecution closed its case last week and judgement may be delivered any day now), but one sometimes hears remarks so insensitive and outrageous that they amount almost to a form of violence in their own right.

Thus, for example, Israeli interior minister, Itzhak Peretz, a leading member of the Torah Guardians Party (which could be roughly translated as the Party of God), sought to comfort the bereaved with the thought that the recent bus–train collision in which 22 people, most of them children, died was not, in fact, an accident, but the work of God, and was intended as a punishment for the desecration of the Sabbath. Earlier this year, a colleague of his, Mr Shimon Shlomo, suggested in a newspaper interview that Israeli troops were dying in Lebanon because of the promiscuity of women soldiers.

How, if God can punish the innocent for the sins of the guilty, can man – who is, after all, made in God's image – be blamed for doing the same?

Any body of individuals which purports to be doing the work of God sooner or later enters into a conspiracy against man, and this is – paradoxically enough – true even of the godless, who, instead of invoking the name of this or that deity, invoke some remote ideal such as the nation or the people, or equality, or peace, or brotherhood, for it is often the case that men in love with concepts hate their fellow beings.

The men of God, as I have suggested, have a lot to answer for, but no crime committed in the name of heaven, not even the Fourth Crusade, or the Inquisition, can approach the scale of the crimes committed in Europe in the name of the Herrenvolk, or in Russia and Kampuchea in the name of Socialism.

The latter crimes are not a thing of the past, for they are still being committed (if not with the same ferocity) in our time, and if they rarely impinge on our awareness, it is because they are part of a continuing process.

And, to give a more banal example, here in this country we have people who are prepared to desecrate the dead and poison children's sweets in furtherance of what they call 'animal rights'. The bomb in Frankfurt airport, which killed three children, was, apparently, planted by a group claiming to be friends of the environment.

The friends of the environment, the defenders of animal rights, the promoters of equality and freedom, the guardians of the

Torah, the parties of God, the friends of mankind, all have this one thing in common: they are the enemies of man.

George Bernard Shaw once said that he would rather be in the company of a lion than in the company of men, because if the lion didn't want to eat him, it would leave him alone, whereas men might tear him apart for any of a dozen reasons, all of them for his own good.

If there is one lesson to be drawn from the tragic events of the past few weeks – or, indeed, the past few millennia – it is that society has no greater enemy than the zealots, whether sacred or secular, people who feel their cause enables them to rise above the law.

In Israel, they tend to be of the sacred variety, and they seem to think that their beliefs entitle them to control the habits of non-believers, to halt traffic on the Sabbath, to close swimming pools (or prevent them from being built) and to shut down theatres. In other words, to impose their views upon others and make the Kingdom of Heaven manifest on earth.

Some madmen sought to expedite the process by conspiring to blow up the mosques on the Temple Mount, but they, at least, were known to be madmen and were caught before they could do any damage. Who will vouch for the sanity of the Guardians of the Torah, one of whom happens to be the minister of the interior?

God, I feel, should be left to fight His own battles, for if He is the deity we think He is, He can manage without our help. And if He isn't, our help will be unavailing.

28 June 1985

Graveyard desecration

THERE IS NO more hated figure in Jewish life or, indeed, any society, then the *moser*, the informer, and I can think of none who is regarded with greater contempt. What, then, is to be said of someone who actually informs on the *dead*?

195

It happened about a year ago in Rishon le Zion – which is in some respects the birthplace of our new Jewish state – when some Holy Ones took it upon themselves to whisper to the rabbinate that a Mrs Theresa Engelovitz, a Romanian immigrant, who was buried in the local Jewish cemetery, had not been properly converted to Judaism.

If the rabbis had shown an ounce of compassion or sense, they would have sent the *moserim* (informers) home with one of the many imprecations against such people which fill our liturgy. Instead, they took the matter further and, with the consent of the chief rabbis, they ordered the remains be exhumed and buried beyond the cemetery fence.

Now, I do not know whether Mrs Engelovitz was, or was not, properly converted, especially as the definition of what constitutes a proper conversion seems to vary from place to place, but let us presume the worst, namely, that she was not properly converted. Is there no Jewishness to be acquired from the fact that one had lived, suffered and died as a Jew, or is a moment in the *mikveh* more important than decades of immersion in Jewish life?

Yet the rabbis continued to insist on their ruling, and the bereaved family had to appeal to the Supreme Court – the last resort of compassion in Israel – to prevent, or at least delay, the exhumation.

The intervention of the civil authorities in what they regarded as a sacred issue upset local zealots. Last December they removed the headstone over Mrs Engelovitz's grave. Last week they went further; they removed her skeleton and dumped it in a plastic bag in the Ramle Muslim cemetery.

And this in a country where archaeologists are harassed and threatened, and where hardly a year passes without mass demonstrations against archaeological digs because of fears that human remains could be disturbed which, though they had been in the earth for a thousand years or more, *might* possibly have been Jewish.

Why are the ancient dead given the benefit of such doubts, and not the more recently dead? And why is so little thought given to the feelings of the living?

Mrs Engelovitz is not, was not, a solitary figure; she had, and has, a family. Or are their sentiments of no account because they may not be quite Jewish?

The Morality of Orthodoxy

We read reports of the desecration of Jewish cemeteries, here and abroad, every week, but has there been an act of desecration so black and revolting as the one now perpetrated in Rishon le Zion?

I am rather sorry for Rishon, which is rightly proud of its place in Zionist history, but which may, hereafter, be remembered not as the first in Zion, but as the last in infamy.

Ten good men would have been enough to save Sodom. Was there not *one* rabbi among the several thousand in Israel who would have been readily prepared to lay Mrs Engelovitz to rest in consecrated ground? If I should be proved wrong, I should be happy to be proved wrong, but I doubt it.

Where there should be concern with life, there is a preoccupation with death; where there should be charity, there is legalism; and where there should be pleasantness, there is bloody-mindedness.

And in this I refer not only to the formal religious establishment, but to their Right-wing brethren of the *gedolei hatorah*, who somehow think they are absolved from moral responsibility because they are not directly on the government's payroll.

Even as I write, however, reason has prevailed. The Israeli Supreme Court, acting on a petition from Mrs Engelovitz's daughter, ruled this week that the bones be reburied in Rishon's Jewish cemetery.

It was left, you will note, to the Supreme Court to issue a ruling. Israel's two chief rabbis were themselves sufficiently embarrassed by the events in Rishon to condemn the desecration, but they did not say that the bones should be returned to their former resting place.

Perhaps the remains should have been put on display in Hechal Shlomo, the seat of the chief rabbinate, in Jerusalem, to symbolise the ossified state of the Israeli rabbinate as a whole.

9 March 1984

197

A long, dark shadow

ISRAEL HAS NOW entered upon her fortieth year, as crucial a phase in the life of a state as in the life of a man.

Up to the age of 40 a man tends to ascribe his failures and failings to the inexperience and indiscretions of youth and can draw comfort from the hope that the best is yet ahead, that he still has qualities to develop and powers to enhance and more fields to conquer and peaks to climb.

At 40 such hopes begin to fade and he has to reconcile himself to the thought that he has probably got as far as he is likely to get and that where he was up and coming he is possibly down and going.

Forty years in terms of Jewish history may be a blink in time, but it is a significant period in the life of a state. Israel is no longer an emerging or developing country, but an emerged and developed one and, in technological terms, a very advanced one.

Her technology, too, is at the source of her military might. She is a small country with a small population, but what she lacks in numbers she makes up for in skills.

She is still the only democracy between the Atlantic and the Indus and the one Middle Eastern country which, though devoid of oil and largely devoid of other natural resources, enjoys a European standard of living. Left in peace she could become another Japan (except that not everything about Japan and the Japanese is worthy of emulation).

Her achievements in the arts – in music, drama, ballet, painting and above all, literature – are a source of wonder, and it is only when one turns to politics and religion that the horizons darken, possibly because the one has become intermingled with the other to the detriment of both.

Israel, in terms of observance at least, is obviously a much more religious country than it was a generation ago and there are now more students in its *yeshivot* than in its universities.

One can sometimes hear murmurings of regret that the energies of *yeshivah* students are not put to more practical use, but Israel

198

herself could not possibly employ the intellectual talents she produces, and if the *yeshivot* did not absorb so many of them, they would be seeking employment abroad.

Yet the great religiosity has not given rise to a more benign social climate. Israel has not become a more considerate, more just or more tolerant society, for what we have is not so much greater religiosity as greater Orthodoxy, and an Orthodoxy, moreover, which was formed by the exigencies of exile rather than of nationhood.

We have prayed 2,000 years for the restoration of Zion without preparing for the possibility that our prayers might be answered, and though the Jewish state has now been in existence for well over a generation, the rabbis have yet to adapt themselves to their new responsibilities.

They still have the mentality of exile, except that where they were once timid, they are now arrogant; where they once beseeched, they now demand; where they looked to the Gentile *Shabbos goy* to cope with the intricacies of observance, they now have Jewish ones; and the disdain with which they regarded the Gentile is now applied to the Jew, while the Arab hardly impinges upon their reckoning.

They have no commitment to democracy – indeed they scorn it – but they have learned to manipulate the defects of the political system and the deficiencies of politicians for their own ends.

A few years ago people spoke with dark foreboding of 'the ethnic divide' and the growing friction between Sephardim and Ashkenazim. Some friction did exist, but it was not endemic or widespread and it was exploited by second-rate politicians, who saw in their ethnic origins a compensation for their lack of talent, and puffed up by journalists hungry for headlines.

Intermarriage between the different ethnic groups in Israel is commonplace and the children of such marriages tend to assume a European identity. As a result, what there is of Sephardi tradition and culture is being rapidly eroded and the easy-going tolerance which used to characterise Sephardi religious life has given way to the rigidities and intolerance of the Ashkenazim.

In other words, there is not, and never was, an ethnic divide, but there is a religious divide which is growing wider and which, I believe, casts an ominous shadow over the future of Israel.

8 May 1987

A light unto the nations?

CHIEF RABBI SIR Immanuel Jakobovits recently had some controversial things to say about Zionism and he was attacked not so much for what he said, but for where he said it – in *The Times*.

Whether we like it or not – and I suspect that most of us do like it – what happens in the Jewish State is of interest to more than Jews, which is why the chief rabbi's opinions are so often sought by the media.

It so happens that I disagreed with some of his conclusions, but his arguments were well put, and if the resulting controversy showed that Jews do not always think alike, it suggested that they at least do think, and I, for one, prefer honest divisions to spurious unanimity.

Sir Immanuel's main point is that Zionism took too little account of the fact that Jewish national aspirations were at source religious and that the attempt to create a secular state was therefore doomed to failure.

But Zionism, as he must know, evolved in the teeth of religious opposition. One could find a Moshe Mohilever here or a Rav Kook there who were prepared to go along with it, and even bless it, but the mass of religious leaders condemned Zionism with bell, book and candle, not because it was secular, but because it was presumptuous. The Jewish state, they believed, could be restored only by divine intervention.

There was a paralysis of will in the great ghettos of eastern Europe. Zionists had to be secular to get off the ground at all – and by God they did.

They drained swamps, laid roads, set up kibbutzim and other settlements, established schools and institutions of higher learning, built cities, fought and won a prolonged war against impossible odds, and created a state out of chaos. They took their fate into their own hands and succeeded with 50 years of strenuous effort where 2,000 years of prayer had failed.

But that was not the limit of their achievements. A country with fewer than a million Jews, bled white by war and on the brink of bankruptcy, immediately applied itself to the ingathering of exiles and absorbed more than 600,000 immigrants, most of them penniless and few of them skilled, in three years, without economic upheaval or civil strife. I doubt if any nation in history, large or small, surmounted so many difficulties in so few years.

And yet Sir Immanuel talks of failure. If that was failure, what is success?

Mistakes were made, of course, and the country had its critics, but in the main it was a source of wonder and for a while Israel – unashamedly secular though she may have been – was 'a light unto the nations', a model of what a small, democratic country could achieve.

She was crowded with delegations from other new nations who hoped to learn from her experience and emulate her ways. She had (to adapt the words of Pitt) saved herself by her exertions and hoped to save others by her example.

Israel is now, in formal terms, an infinitely more religious society than it was 30 years ago. There are more synagogues, *yeshivot* and religious day schools and a far greater degree of religious observance.

But would Sir Immanuel lay his hand on this heart and say that it is therefore a more just, tolerant and equitable society?

I would invite him to quote one action or utterance of a leading Israeli rabbi or leader of a religious party to suggest a concern with humanity or justice, for I could quote any number to show a perversion of everything that Judaism has traditionally stood for.

Yet Sir Immanuel is right. Zionism *has* failed, though not because it was secularist, but because it has abandoned secularism and been hijacked by messianism.

In the last resort, however, the chief rabbi and I are arguing about words. I believe that a man is religious if he acts religiously, and not because he festoons himself with the appurtenances of religion and spouts religious teachings. In that sense, Israel was a good deal more religious in its secular phase than it is now.

Abraham Isaac Kook, the first Ashkenazi chief rabbi, who always defended secular Zionists against their religious detractors, argued that godless men can sometimes do the work of God. The corollary of this is that godly men can sometimes do the work of the devil.

26 June 1987

Black American flag

WHEN A LARGE number of rabbis agree about anything, you can be almost absolutely certain that they are absolutely wrong.

I may have said this before, but my view has been confirmed by the 3,000-strong International Rabbinical Coalition for Israel, which has declared with one voice that:

'Uprooting Jewish settlements in the Golan, Judea, Samaria and Gaza, as part of the false Israeli peace, is a national crime, and it is forbidden for a Jew to lend a hand to such a deed.'

The so-called International Rabinical Coalition is a New York-based organisation consisting overwhelmingly of American rabbis. American rabbis have, generally speaking, been foaming at the mouth ever since the peace initiative was launched, but they, unfortunately, are not alone.

On that particular issue, they enjoy the support of most Orthodox rabbis everywhere, which, if anything, is further proof that they are wrong.

There is a cherished refrain which we repeat before the open ark every Shabbat:

' . . . forsake ye not my Torah. It is a tree of life to them that grasp it . . . Its ways are ways of pleasantness, and all its paths are peace.'

Which may be true of the Torah, but sadly not of the self-proclaimed 'Torah-camp' as represented by the International Rabbinical Coalition for Israel.

Peace, of course, has its hazards, as we have already seen, and there will be more to follow, but the rabbis in this rabbinical assembly have never for a moment weighed up the consequences of a continued occupation, not only for the Palestinians, but for Israel itself. But then, they appear indifferent to the one, and ignorant of the other.

In Britain I know of only two Orthodox rabbis who have openly and consistently supported the peace process, Chief Rabbi Sacks and ex-Chief Rabbi Jakobovits. I know of two or three in Israel who have done the same. I know of none in America, or at least none of any eminence.

Shulamit Aloni, who was physically assaulted by a Zionist zealot during a recent visit to America, has said that 'a group of anarchic Fascists – the same kind that prevailed in Germany – are taking control of American Jewry.'

That, I think, is something of an exaggeration. It is, however, true that American Jewry is sick and that American Orthodox Jewry is very sick. If present trends of the sort embodied by the Rabbinical Coalition continue, there may come a time when a self-respecting Jew will hesitate before setting foot in an American Orthodox synagogue, or shaking hands with an American Orthodox rabbi.

Years ago, I attended a gathering in Israel addressed by Rabbi Shaul Yisraeli, the legendary founder of Kfar Haroeh Yeshivah, who died last month at the age of 85. He was everything a rabbi should be – learned, compassionate, prescient, wise – and radiated amiability and grace.

All that, however, was before 1967, when Israel, unfortunately, became 'Greater Israel', and where he had once preached on the sanctity of life, he then began preaching on the sanctity of land.

He became the spiritual leader of the Gush Emunim and, last year, he joined with two other rabbis to issue an edict requiring soldiers to disobey orders if they were called upon to evacuate any settlement in the occupied territories. Sedition in the name of the Lord!

We often comfort ourselves with the thought that, with all our problems, we are going through a golden age. Never in our history have we had so many students attending so many seats of Jewish learning, and it has become almost *de rigueur* for Jewish youngsters to spend a period of years in a *yeshivah* or a seminary after they have finished school.

Yet what is the value of Jewish teaching where the teachers themselves – and rabbis, of course, are essentially teachers – are corrupt, and propagate a hollow and debased form of Judaism?

The words of Micah come to mind in this context: 'What doth the Lord require of thee, but to do justly, to love mercy and to walk humbly with thy God?'

But, in place of humility, these rabbis of the American Orthodox

203

persuasion preach arrogance; in place of mercy, they preach cruelty; and in place of justice, they preach injustice.

7 July 1995

Meimad

RABBI YEHUDA AMITAL, whom Shimon Peres has appointed minister without portfolio, is a throwback to an earlier age when rabbis were thought of not only as learned, but reasonable, kindly and benevolent.

The far-sighted, tolerant Judaism he preaches was the sort which used to be preached by the National Religious Party, but which it has since betrayed in its efforts to convince the electorate that it was no less bigoted than the *charedim*, and no less patriotic than the Likud, nor even, in some cases, less rabid than Techiyah.

In 1988, Rabbi Amital launched a new party, Meimad, in a bid to recover the middle ground abandoned by the NRP. Though flanked by candidates of the highest order, he failed to win a single seat, while Rechavam Ze'evi's Moledet Party, with a creed so vile one daren't call it by its true name, secured three.

I suspect, however, that the rational elements in the religious camp felt that it was no time to vote for a religious party no matter how moderate its policies and opted for Labour or even Meretz instead.

Peres has now, so to speak, gone over the heads of the electorate and brought Amital into his Cabinet as a bridge-builder. It is in many respects an inspired choice, but I fear that Amital will have his work cut out, because, even before he took office, Yisrael Harel, head of the West Bank settlers, let it be known that they would not co-operate with him.

Among rabbis in general, if a man wants to establish a reputation as a halachist, he has to be stricter than his colleagues, and, if he hopes to acquire a reputation as a true patriot, he has to be more rabid.

Amital may be – and to an extent already has been – marginalised by his very reasonableness. He is certainly unlikely to make much headway among the most prominent of West Bank opponents of the government: the Waldmans and the Druckmans and the Nachum Rabinovitches.

We can see the process at work even in Britain. The tribute paid by Chief Rabbi Jonathan Sacks at the Yitzhak Rabin memorial meeting in the Albert Hall on 12 November was the most moving and passionate of his career. It may be useful to recall some of his words:

'For months before Yitzhak Rabin died, the warning lights were flashing. The positions taken were growing more extreme. We began to hear the rhetoric of hate. And, what was worst of all, some of those voices were religious voices, and what they said, and what it led to, make me hang my head in shame.'

I doubt if there was an Orthodox rabbi anywhere in the world who expressed himself with such sincerity and contrition. But the final echo of his words had hardly died away before at least one leading voice of the *charedim* of North London let it be known that he wasn't speaking for them.

Such words were hardly necessary for, as the thousands who had packed the Albert Hall, or were milling around outside, could see for themselves, the *charedim* had virtually ignored the meeting.

There was a mass rally in Israel last week, attended by some 50,000 people protesting against archaeological excavations at a Hasmonean site, which they see as a desecration of Judaism.

Such strictly Orthodox demonstrators appear able to summon more passion for the remains of Jews who have been dead for over 2,000 years, than for a Jew – forget the fact that he was prime Minister of Israel – struck down before their eyes by a religious fanatic.

But then, the *charedim* have always been largely indifferent to the fate of the Jewish state, and have been interested only in any largesse they could extract. And it must be added that a few of them were involved in the agitation which culminated in Rabin's death.

The real problem arises from the attitude of the so-called 'modern Orthodox' rabbinate. It is no secret that the chief rabbi, his predecessor, and two or three colleagues, who represent the humane traditions of Judaism, are a minority among British Orthodox rabbis.

Rabbi Sacks was even reproved by some of his colleagues for the tenor of his Albert Hall speech, and he is becoming increasingly marginalised in the Orthodox world. A few rabbis, Shlomo Riskin on the West Bank for example, have, to some extent, recanted.

But some seem to follow the view of Nachum Rabinovitch, a guru of the settler movement, who in a *JC* column the week afterwards could not bring himself to utter a clear word of reproach or contrition, in Chief Rabbi Sacks's vein, in connection with the Rabin assassination – and who still dreams of a Greater Israel.

8 December 1995

Rabin's murder

WHEN CHAIM ARLOSOROFF, the political secretary of the Jewish Agency, was gunned down on Tel Aviv beach in 1933, Chief Rabbi Abraham Kook was convinced the assassin could not have been Jewish because Jew did not kill Jew.

How little he knew his own people and how forgetful he was of Jewish history, for there is no enormity to which men will not stoop when they think they hear the voice of God, and Jews are every bit as prone to the illusion as others, perhaps even more so.

It is uncertain who actually killed Arlosoroff but the campaign of vilification and hatred launched by the Revisionists – the forerunners of the Likud party – against the Labour movement and the Zionist leadership, prepared the way for the murder.

The same was true of the slaying of Yitzhak Rabin.

Israeli elections have never been particularly clean but the 1981 election was the filthiest I have witnessed. Likud mobs roamed the streets trying to break up Labour meetings with incessant chants of 'Begin, Begin, Begin!'

Begin himself denounced Shimon Peres, then the Labour leader, as a traitor – and that was long before the peace process was ever heard of. But the Likud was almost chivalrous compared to the allies it acquired once the peace process was launched. These so-called men of God, the ayatollahs, altered the very context of the Jewish liturgy to rain down anathemas upon Rabin and his government and preached sedition to the armed forces – all, of course, in the name of God.

The *Jerusalem Report* describes how a group of cabalists stationed themselves before Rabin's house this year on the eve of Yom Kippur, put on tefilin, lit black candles, blew the *shofar* and cursed the prime minister with the *pulsa denura* – 'lashes of fire'.

'And on him . . .' they intoned, 'Yitzhak, son of Rosa, known as Rabin, we have permission . . . to demand from the angels of destruction that they take a sword to this wicked man . . . to kill him . . . for handing over the Land of Israel to our enemies, the sons of Ishmael.'

Yigal Amir, a student at Bar-Ilan – a university founded by the National Religious Party – answered their prayers with three bullet shots. One could perhaps describe him as a practitioner in applied cabalism.

I would ask the thousands of rabbis in Israel, America and elsewhere, who joined the campaign of hatred and vilification against the late Yitzhak Rabin to search the dark recesses of their souls and ask themselves if they were not, however obliquely, accessories before the fact.

Various commentators have described the assassination as a crisis for the Jewish state and the Jewish people, but essentially it is a crisis for the Jewish faith.

As Lord Jakobovits, one of the very few sane voices in the Orthodox fold, has observed: 'This represents a challenge to the religious community, since this was born out of religious fanaticism . . . The Jewish community will have to do some very profound stocktaking. We may have to revise our educational system to ensure such a thing can never happen again.'

'We *may* have to revise?' We *must* revise, and pay more attention to the actual text of Scripture, rather than the commentaries, and the commentaries on the commentaries, some of which are perverse distortions of the text. As a result of such distortions we have never been able to forgive Ishmael for the wrongs committed against him by Abraham.

And we have never even allowed ourselves to contemplate the possibility that we may have been less than just to the sons of Ishmael.

Many people who like to think of themselves as moderates, and who in principle support the peace process, complain that Rabin was giving away 'too much too soon'.

Too soon? After 28 years of occupation and two of negotiation? Too much? Israel is retaining over 70 per cent of the West Bank, and the enclaves returned to the Arabs are criss-crossed with roads under Jewish control.

Rabin was no bleeding-heart liberal, but a tough, resolute and stubborn man. He was the Right-wing head of what was essentially a Right-wing party. But, in the last resort, he was a decent man who had no wish to keep two million Arabs under his heel.

He was a great prime minister, greater perhaps even than Ben-Gurion. Ben-Gurion had to contend only with Arabs. Rabin was also compelled to battle against Jews and, like the soldier he was, he fell in battle.

10 November 1995

11
The Festivals

There is no harm in being reminded, even within the sacred precincts of a synagogue, that the earth is an exceedingly beautiful place and that we are in origin a pastoral race.

Blowing my own trumpet

FOR, LO, THE summer is past, the rain is over and gone (or should be), the leaves are thick on the earth, the time of the singing and the preaching has come, and the voice of the *shofar* (ram's horn) is heard in the land.

The shofar interludes form, in some respects, the high point of the Rosh Hashana service because, apart from anything else, they are about the only parts of the service which most people understand, and, of course, there is always drama attached to the performance.

The synagogue is packed; the congregation is hushed. The *baal tekiah* (horn blower) pulls his *tallit* (prayer shawl) over his head and puts the horn to his lips. He inflates his chest. The *baal makreh* calls the tune, *tekiah!* and 2,000 people hold their breath for the blast off.

But instead of the shrill sound which should follow, one often gets a dull *phut!* or a prolonged hiss, like air escaping from a burst tyre. The *baal tekiah* shakes the water from his instrument, tries again and again, and turns from red to scarlet to blue.

It is generally accepted, even among fundamentalists, that one does not shoot the *baal tekiah*, for he is trying his best, yet it is no easy thing to admit failure in front of 2,000 people, and he keeps on trying, and he continues to try, but the harder he tries, the worse it gets.

I speak from the heart, because I recently underwent such an experience, not in front of 2,000 people, or even 20,000 people, but – so to speak – *two million* people.

But first, a bit of history. My late father, of blessed memory, was the Menuhin of the *shofar* and gave a virtuoso performance every time he played. His pitch was perfect and one could, so to speak, pass one's finger over the sound without encountering a notch.

I had hoped to follow in his footsteps and was given my chance before a small, uninvited audience in a breakaway Glasgow *minyan*. My performance was faultless and my skill must have been trumpeted abroad, for when I moved to London, I was invited to give a recital, in an old-age home.

211

Again I played well, but I may have applied myself to the final *tekiah gedolah* with excessive vigour and at excessive length, for even before the final echo died away, one of the residents keeled over, never to rise again. He was about 119 at the time, and deaf into the bargain, so that the fault could not have been entirely mine; but the incident did nothing for my reputation.

We are all aware that at the end of time 'the trumpet shall sound, and the dead shall arise,' but I appeared to have reversed the process and I was never invited back.

Thames Television have a late night programme, *Close Down*, which is presumably designed for insomniacs, people on night shift, and others who are so glued to their set that they haven't the willpower to switch off while there is anything on the screen at all, and who total some two million in number. From what I can see, the programme is peopled mainly by dons, divines and other worthy gentlemen, who offer their thoughts on this world and the next; and a few weeks ago I was invited to give my thoughts on the Jewish New Year.

Now, who can talk about Rosh Hashanah without blowing his *shofar*? I couldn't, for one, and saw myself – and, indeed, heard myself – redressing all the frustrations and disappointments I had suffered over 20 years in one mighty blow.

I brought out my whole collection of instruments – tenor, baritone and bass. They went well at home, they went very well in the limousine on the way to the studio (though a car which tried to overtake me while I was in full blast came off the road). They went superbly at rehearsal. But came the take and – *phut!* I tried again – *phut, phut!* Once more, and – *phsssss!*

There are about 30 people involved in making the programme, all of them drawing astronomical salaries, and I feared that if this went on, Thames TV might be passing its dividend, and I could pass out. As I may have hinted before, I verge on the hirsute, and a barber was brought in to hack an opening between my moustache and my beard. I cleared my throat, filled my lungs and made one last, mighty effort, and the result was beautiful, like a sustained chord from a Haydn concerto. But, alas, just as I was holding the chord, my *kipah* flew off with the effort.

A lengthy conference followed. Did I want to continue? I did, indeed, for I had invested too much wind to give up; whereupon a carpenter was summoned with his mate who, between them, secured the *kipah* to my skull with a rawlplug and I tried yet again. This time the *kipah* stayed in place, but, try as I might, I could not repeat my earlier performance.

If you also suffer from insomnia, you will be able to see the result next week, but my ambition to be a *baal tekiah* has been finally and irrevocably exorcised. I shall auction off my collection of *shofars* (*shofarim*?) and will send the proceeds to the Hospital for Respiratory Diseases. Instead I intend to take up the bagpipe, so that even if I can no longer aspire to pipe out Yom Kippur, I might still be able to pipe in the haggis.

10 September 1982

High Holy-days

THE DAYS OF AWE, or the High Holy-days, as they are quaintly called in this country, have sometimes presented me with something of a quandary. Where to go?

In *der heim*, which is to say Latvia, the matter was settled for me. My father, of blessed memory, being a rabbi, officiated in the main *shul*, and to the main *shul* I went. And in the main *shul* I stayed.

Other boys, with less exalted connections, could nip out to play tig, or munch apples, or pull faces at the girls, or even float paper boats on a nearby pond. I, ever mindful of my status as *ben harav* (rabbi's son) and of my seat of honour by the East Wall, remained in place with prayer book in hand (if not always with prayer in mind), and about the only time I got out for a breather, even on Yom Kippur, was during *Yizkor* (Yom Kippur memorial prayer). I sometimes feel that the account I stored up in heaven during those years of enforced piety should have entitled me to a few escapades in later life.

When we moved to Britain, my father was no longer rabbi, or at least not *the* rabbi, so that I was a freer agent, but we had hardly

213

settled in when the war broke out and I, in common with most of my contemporaries, was evacuated to a remote corner of Scotland. It was a marvellous feeling of liberation, for we were suddenly sans parents, and it looked for a time as if we might be sans God until the elders of Glasgow Jewry sent down the headmaster of our *cheder* as His representative.

He took over two shops, which I thought would both function as synagogues (on the principle of having one *not* to go to), but the one was to serve our spiritual needs, and the other our temporal ones, so that when the *Yomtovim* came, I again had no choice in the matter of venue.

It was only after the war that I had alternatives to contemplate, and the struggle was, so to speak, between the upper world and the lower one. The former was represented by the local cathedral synagogue, which had an ornate interior, an ornate service and, most important of all, some very ornate females.

The front rows of the ladies' gallery were occupied by a solid wall of solid matrons in Persian-lamb coats (what has happened to Persian lambs, by the way? Have they been phased out? Have they married out? If there should be a furrier among my readers, perhaps he could enlighten us), but behind them, at the back, were the *jeunes filles* in bright costumes and fancy hats.

The thoughts they inspired were not those one normally associates with the Days of Awe, but, as I told myself, they were, after all, God's creatures, and to behold them was in itself an act of worship.

The drawback to the cathedral synagogue was that it had a full complement of minister (one didn't talk of rabbis in those days), reader, second reader (one didn't talk of *chazanim* either) and choir, with each trying to outdo the other in their different ways, so that the service could last all day, and Rosh Hashanah felt like Yom Kippur.

Moreover, there was no overflow service. Instead, they placed chairs in front of the *bimah* (raised platform from which prayers are conducted), behind the *bimah*, in the gangways, along the aisles; I'm a little surprised they didn't suspend them from the chandeliers. And they were only for adults. Youngsters were there on sufferance, and one was hardly settled in one's seat before one received a tap on the shoulder and had to move on to another. It was an extended game of musical chairs, which is why eventually I found myself drawn to the local *shtiebl*.

It cannot be claimed that that particular *shtiebl* was the last resort of holiness in the city, for it included congregants who were too poor or too mean to pay for a seat in the main *shul*, and one of them, at least, came by bicycle. (He would park it discreetly round the corner, but spoilt it all by forgetting to remove his bicycle clips.)

The service, however, was brisk and informal. There was no minister and no ministrations, no cantor, canticles or, indeed, cant. A small area was set aside for women, but they were not of a type to form a distraction: if anything, they disposed one to prayer.

I have since prospered sufficiently to have an assured place in a cathedral synagogue, but I still feel pulled in different directions, not only by my own inclinations, but by the different members of my family. In the end, we divide our patronage among three or four different places of worship, but that should, at least, improve the chance of one of us getting through to the right number.

28 September 1984

Yom Kippur

I RATHER ENJOY Yom Kippur, the sense of occasion, the rituals, the crowds, the prayers, the tunes, even the sermons.

This is possibly a sin in itself, for it is meant to be a time for self-mortification, but as we have turned festivals like Passover into occasions for self-mortification, it is perhaps only right that we should have converted an occasion like Yom Kippur into a festival.

We are, of course, required to abstain from the pleasures of the table – to mention only the more mentionable pleasures – for a night and a day, but we make up for it both before and after the event. (The Jewish grocery trade would be ruined without our fasts.) In any case, abstinence can be pleasurable, or can at least induce a sense of well-being, for a little of what you don't fancy does you good. I think it was Lord Jakobovits who said that we pray not to propitiate our Maker, but to improve ourselves. The same is true of self-denial. It offers a passing sense of virtue to the self-indulgent, but what does it do for the pious?

If you cast your eyes round the synagogue on Yom Kippur, you will find that the raffish characters with the roving eyes who look as if they might have something to atone for are completely relaxed, while the good and the true, who rarely raise their heads from the yellowing pages of their prayerbooks, shake with agitation.

I once spent Yom Kippur at the Western Wall in Jerusalem and was surrounded by wizened figures with sunken eyes and sunken cheeks who looked as if they subsisted on a diet of Psalms and snuff. When the service reached the confessional – 'We have transgressed . . . we have violated . . . we have robbed . . . we have lied . . . we have ensnared . . . we have wrought iniquity . . . we have gone astray and have led astray . . .' – they pulled their prayer shawls over their heads, shut their eyes and beat their breasts in an agony of contrition.

I am aware that the Jewish confessional is a collective one and that we seek forgiveness not only for our own failings, but for those of others; but even so, would men thump themselves with such fervour without an acute awareness of their own personal shortcomings?

What could they have been up to? What laws had they broken, what enormities had they committed? Or were they merely, in old age, seeking forgiveness for the sins of youth?

There is, to adapt the words of Ecclesiastes, a time for everything – a time to be born and a time to die, a time to plant and a time to reap, a time to transgress and a time to seek forgiveness for transgressions. And old age is the time, not only because one is nearer the day of reckoning, but because it is rather easier to mend one's ways. (Or, as Rochefoucauld put it: we think we abandon sins in old age, whereas it's the sins which abandon us.)

But the worshippers at the Kotel weren't all old, even if they nearly all looked it, and it seems to me that one's sense of guilt is a measure not of one's iniquity, but of one's innocence.

Put otherwise, the more innocent the man, the more likely he is to feel guilty, which doesn't mean that he is necessarily blameless. The innocent have higher standards, and the higher one's standards, the easier it is to go wrong and the worse one feels for going wrong.

One's standards can, of course, be too high, which is almost a sin in itself, for it is a form of hubris. Judaism, fortunately, doesn't require us to be saints, and even suggests that the pleasures of life are there to be enjoyed. It merely insists that we don't overdo it, and that we keep our shortcomings within tolerable limits.

On the other hand, standards can also be (and often are) too low, and in a society where almost anything goes, there is almost nothing to feel guilty about. Or, as I once put it in another context: the world is divided into miserable sinners, cheerful sinners and people who don't even know that they have gone wrong.

Which brings me finally to the words of Solomon: 'The wicked flee when no man pursueth, but the righteous are bold as a lion.'

One hesitates to question the wisdom of the wisest of kings, but in this particular instance, I believe he had it wrong.

If anything, it is the other way about. The wicked lack the measure of their guilt and tend to be complacent, while the innocent lack the measure of their innocence and tend to be contrite. Which is why the most blameless elements in a community apply themselves to the demands of Yom Kippur with the greatest dedication. And why those who are most in need on Yom Kippur will not be in synagogue at all.

13 September 1991

Second mortgage needed

WHEN ONE READS in Exodus that the Israelites left Egypt 'with great wealth', one's first thought is that they needed it to pay for Pesach.

Judaism may or may not be a rich man's religion, but Pesach is assuredly a rich man's festival.

Out of the simple verse, 'There shall be no leavened bread be seen with thee, neither shall there be leaven seen within all thy quarters,' there has developed a vast supervision and labelling industry which imposes a tariff on everything we eat and drink and which has now grown to the point where we have supervised *mehadrin min hamehadrin kosher-le-Pesach* (ultra-*kosher* for Passover) water.

Our atmosphere is thick with *chametz* (leaven) particles, and even now I can see bearded figures in earnest conclave wondering whether they should not perhaps insist that the air we breathe over Pesach should be supervised and be dispensed among the faithful in cylinders. But one hesitates to joke about such things, lest – as in the case of water – the joke is overtaken by reality.

But all this is a minor matter. No one is under any obligation to eat three gourmet meals a day throughout the length of Pesach (though some have a good try) and one can celebrate the festival without supervised water, or supervised Swiss chocolate, or supervised crystallised fruit, or supervised smoked salmon, or supervised gherkins or even supervised wine.

In Latvia, when I was a child, only the head of the household had four cups of wine at the *seder* (ritual service on the first two nights of Passover). Everyone else had to be content with four cups of mead (which is made out of fermented honey and which may have been specifically designed to drive one to sobriety – not that the wine normally consumed at the *seder* is much better).

The luxuries with which we overload our *seder* tables and undermine our health derive from Jewish habit and not from Jewish law, while the basic necessities are reasonably priced, and *matzah* – now the staple fare of the overweight – is in fact cheaper over Pesach than at any other time of the year.

There seems to be a growing belief that the more burdens we assume, the more Brownie points we accumulate in the hereafter, like some celestial pension fund. But we don't. To add is to detract, and expensiveness, certainly, is no measure of holiness.

Our rabbis, in the main, are doing well and move mainly among the well-to-do; and while they are trained to give a thought to the destitute – especially at this time of the year – they give no thought at all to the merely solvent, to those who try to get by on their meagre earnings without resorting to charity. They are not even aware that they exist, because such people can rarely afford to live in Jewish districts.

It is no longer hard to be a Jew, but it is damnably expensive, and the traditional invocation, 'Let all who are needy come and celebrate the Passover,' should now read, 'Let all who are needy take out a second mortgage.'

One can find any number of rabbinical tirades against ostentation in food and dress, but none against religious ostentation, as exemplified by two or three kitchens or four sets of utensils. If anything, it is encouraged and sanctified, so that the extravagance of the wealthy becomes the norm of the less-than-wealthy.

But there is not only extravagance in expenditure; there is extravagance in precaution. Some rabbis, for example, insist that one should immerse one's dentures in hot water for 24 hours before Pesach.

But why stop there? Tiny particles of *chametz* can also lodge in the ears, nose, larynx, pharynx, epiglottis and oesophagus; so, to be on the safe side, one should perhaps also immerse one's head in hot water for 24 hours. Come to think of it, it wouldn't be a bad thing if some people did.

Pesach should be a sublimely happy event, and I should imagine that it originally was, for, after all, it celebrates the beginning of our nationhood.

But we have burdened ourselves with so many mindless impositions that the season of our liberation has become the season of our mortification.

14 April 1989

Making Pesachdik

ROUND ABOUT THIS time of the year I am always tempted to leave home, and my dear wife, for her part, wishes that I would, for she is in the throes of an annual catharsis known as making Pesachdik. This is sometimes translated as spring-cleaning, except that spring-cleaners merely clean their homes, whereas Pesachdik-makers attack them, and everything in them, and newcomers to the scene must feel that in the weeks before Pesach the Israelites replay some of the travails experienced by their forefathers in Egypt.

Making Pesachdik derives from an innocent verse in Exodus: 'Seven days shall there be no leaven found in your houses,' which one might think meant merely that one should not have bread in one's household over Pesach, and that, indeed, may have been the original intention; but since then precaution has been piled on precaution, and it is now generally accepted that even if an infinitesimal speck of *chametz* is suffered to remain, one's house is not fit for Pesach. Hence the annual catharsis.

Some women with large homes who take a particularly strict view of their duties have hardly rested from one Pesach when they begin work on the next; others regard the fourteen weeks between Chanucah and Pesach as specially designated for their effort; most give themselves about a month. All begin at a fairly calm pace, like the opening bars of Ravel's 'Bolero', but they gather velocity as the days go by until in the final week they are like whirling dervishes, hair battened down, sleeves rolled up, a pillar of cloud by day, a pillar of ire by night, and virtually out of control.

Nothing is safe from their fury. Furniture and furnishings are turned upside down and inside out; bedding is ravaged; carpets are subjected to assault and battery; books are pulled from their bookshelves, and files from their filing cabinets; cupboards are bared, drawers ransacked, shelves dishevelled, and anyone who gets in the way may suffer grievous bodily harm. Normal services, such as regular meals, are suspended, and anyone who cannot shake off ingrained habits, such as eating, must make his own arrangements (Bloom's comes into its own at this time), or make furtive forays into the fridge.

I must admit that as a child I enjoyed the whole thing hugely, but then all children enjoy chaos, at least for a while. My immediate task was to search pockets and turn-ups (which should tell you something about my age) for *chametz*, but I also helped with shifting furniture and rolling up carpets, and was often rewarded for my efforts which a rich harvest of coins, marbles, tin soldiers, Dinky toys, and other long-forgotten treasures. In fact, the usual refrain in our family when something seemed to be irretrievably lost was: 'It's all right, it'll turn up before Pesach' – and it almost invariably did.

The whole operation sometimes feels like one long retreat. One loses use of the lounge; one stops eating in the dining-room and is confined to the kitchen, where one is able to make something of a last stand, until, as the festival draws nigh, one is banished even from the kitchen and one has to eat in the garage. At least that is our custom and I cannot imagine what the garageless do during the last fateful hours.

(Come to think of it, when we spent a year in Israel we made do with the kitchen balcony, but as we were clearing up the last of our *chametz*, a cloud burst of *chametz* descended from the balcony above. Taking this to be the local custom, we quickly swept the lot on to the balcony below. I daren't think what the people on the ground floor did. Perhaps they weren't Jewish.)

And when the last of the *chametz* has been ceremoniously burned (which is easier said than done, for the sort of bread we eat is either made of asbestos, or could serve as a substitute for it), one returns to a house transformed, with floors gleaming and windows glowing, and objects more clearly defined, like a hazy television picture which has been re-adjusted, and the air is rich with the aromas of Mansion Polish and silver polish, Brasso and Windolene, Ajax and teak oil, until, as the day proceeds, they give way to the more familiar smells of cooking.

And what smells! Fish, flesh and fowl, on the range and in the oven, boiling, broiling, roasting, basting, exuding their souls as a foretaste of things to come. Pesach is no occasion for weight-watchers. Tonight we dine, tomorrow, we repine. This week we are here; next week we shall be in Grayshott.

Is it all worth it? Most men will readily agree that it is. Tradition has it that the Israelites were liberated from Egypt because of the chastity of their womenfolk, which seems to me to put rather too high a premium on chastity, and I suspect it was their industry which really counted, and which is repeated to this day in the preparations for Pesach.

I suppose it does help, when performing a necessary chore, to feel that one is engaged in a timeless ritual, but it is demanding, an annual endurance test, and by the time most women reach Passover they are ready to pass out, and not a few do. And therein lies the best – and, to my mind, the only – acceptable argument for a second *seder*: most women are too exhausted to enjoy the first.

26 March 1982

221

Passover

NOTHING SO MARKS the passing years as Pesach, and we look back on the festival as a series of milestones. We scan the faces round the table and wonder if time has been as unkind to us as it has to them. Alas, it has. One has hardly finished asking the Four Questions before one finds oneself answering them.

It is also a time of reckoning, the ideal occasion to catch up on family gossip, who is doing what, and with whom, where are they doing it, and when are they likely to stop? There is a silent roll-call. At no time are absent friends more absent, and never are gaps more glaring, and in quiet moments the dead almost seem to crowd in among the living. That's one of the reasons why everything is built round the young; they muffle the intimations of mortality.

Each *seder* has the same pattern as dictated not only by formal tradition, but by the incidence of mishaps which have almost become traditions in their own right: the children's Hagadah which falls apart the minute a child lays his hand on it, the radishes wolfed by some starving delinquent before the *seder* has even begun, the wrong *beracha* (blessing) (or, for that matter, the right one) made over the wrong herbs, and mislaid *afikomen (piece of matzah eaten at the end of the seder meal)* (and the same puns made by the same people at the same point – such as '*af-a-komen* is better than none') and, throughout, the clatter of toppling wine-cups, so that by the end of the evening the spotless, damask table-cloth is a collage of wine stains and *matzah* crumble. (I have a suspicion that the awkward top-heavy wine-cups normally used on Pesach were designed by wine-merchants.)

And yet, if every *seder* is the same, each one is different, made unique by the recollections attached to it. The rest of the year passes in a blur, but each *seder* remains fixed in the memory like a tableau, as if the family posed for the occasion.

I know Jews who do not keep Rosh Hashanah or Yom Kippur, but I know of none who pass over Passover, and if there are 400,000 Jews in Britain, we may feel fairly certain that the country will experience a slight tremor tonight as 400,000 sets of teeth

222

attack 400,000 panels of *matzah* (or rather more, for Jews now frequently have Gentile guests at their *seder* tables), for the observances of Passover linger even where all others have lapsed.

Of course, any festival whose central features include a sumptuous meal is assured of a firm hold on Jewish loyalties, especially where the meal itself assumes the status of a holy communion (we do have a genius for sanctifying our carnal pleasures, possibly on the principle that if you can't stop 'em, bless 'em), but there is more to the *seder* than stuffed carp and *matzah* dumplings. There is, first of all, the folk memory evoked not only by the Hagada, but by family lore, of earlier travails (of which the years in Egypt were perhaps the least painful), and the satisfaction of knowing that, for all we've been through, we are still around and are probably here to stay, so that the meal before us is not just another beano, but an act of thanksgiving for the fact of survival. Pesach celebrates not only our redemption, but our resilience.

Time heals. For all the mementoes to hardship and afflictions (and the sort of *matzo* eaten by our more devout brothers not only evokes them, it recreates them), the occasion is light-hearted and given the quantity of wine we are enjoined to consume, even light-headed (those who drink grape-juice are observing the letter of the law, but not the spirit), and there is, I think, something almost symbolic in the fact that all the bitter herbs assembled to recall past vexations strike us as merely piquant, and the bitterest of them, *chrane*, has become almost institutionalised as the classical Jewish relish. (Gentile guests should be warned of its effects: one man's *hors d'oeuvre* can render another man *hors de combat*.)

And finally, there are the evocations of childhood. In days when children were expected to be seen but not heard (I doubt if there were ever such days among Jews), the *seder* was the prime occasion for the young to hold the stage. Nowadays, of course, they hold it all the year round, but the *seder* is fashioned to their tastes. It is then that they have their first (and one hopes last) experience of inebriation and the joys of staying up late (strange how even the smallest among them remain lively and boisterous long after the adults have begun to wilt). It is their night, and it is this which makes it so different from other nights.

In Proust's *À la recherche du temps perdu*, the narrator dips a biscuit in his coffee (slovenly habit) and, as he puts it to his mouth, the whole of his past comes flooding in upon him. Do we not experience a similar sensation when we dip our bitter herbs in salt water or swallow a morsel of *charoset* (mixture of nut, fruit, spices and wine)? To celebrate the *seder* is to hear the echoes of our younger selves.

13 April 1979

Shavuot

SHAVUOT IS, WITHOUT doubt, my favourite festival.

It is short, undemanding, with attractive customs and happy associations. I suppose, too, the fact that it usually coincides with the beginning of summer adds to its many pleasures.

Judaism not only impacts on the soul, it can be – and should be – tasted on the tongue. And no other festive fare, not Channucah latkes, hamentaschem on Purim, honey or honey-cake on Rosh Hashanah, galuptzi (or holiskshes) on Succot, or matzah balls on Pesach can compare to cheesecake, blintzes and borscht on Shavuot. Different sages have suggested different reasons for their origins, but have overlooked the most obvious one. This is, of course, the fact that milk curdles quickly in summer.

There have been moments in my life when I have had the deepest reservations about Judaism, but I have always come round to the view that a faith which actually requires the faithful to eat cheesecake and blintzes must have something to commend it.

It is, of course, one of the three pilgrimage festivals, the other two being Pesach and Succot. All three are associated with different phases of the agricultural year, Pesach being the feast of spring, Shavuot the festival of the first fruits, and Succot the harvest festival.

Pesach seems to have been observed in fairly cursory form until it was revived in its full splendour – and, one imagines, at great expense – in the time of Josiah, while Succot lapsed altogether until it was revived by Nehemiah.

224

There is no evidence that Shavuot suffered any such fate and, according to Josephus, it was particularly popular in Roman times:

'. . . on the approach of Pentecost, which is a festival of ours from the days of our forefathers, a great many ten thousands of men got together . . . Galileans and Idumeans, and many men from Jericho, and many others who had passed over the Jordan, and inhabited these parts.'

What made the occasion particularly memorable was that, in the course of the celebrations, the multitudes who had gathered in Jerusalem joined in an uprising against Sabinus, the Roman tax collector, a unique way of mixing business with prayer. Many Jews died in the uprising, but Sabinus was forced to flee.

Once the Temple was destroyed, all three pilgrimage festivals lost much of their point. Pesach still celebrated the Exodus from Egypt, while Succot commemorated the wandering in the wilderness. Shavuot, however, had no such links, and in ancient times, must have been celebrated purely as an agricultural event.

The Book of Ruth, which is read on Shavuot, describes harvest time in Judea in the days 'when the Judges judged'. It is a rustic idyll, probably written in exile, pithy, moving and full of sighs for distant scenes and a bygone age. But it is also earthy and bucolic, and, once the crops were in, the wine flowed freely and even Ruth's future husband Boaz, who otherwise seemed to be a rather lugubrious old man, ate, drank and was merry.

While our rabbis commended farming as an occupation, I suspect they were rather nervous of agricultural festivals and rustic merry-making – or, indeed, merry-making of any sort. It was the sort of thing that surrounding tribes went in for, and suggested too close a link with the seasons, the soil and nature. Agricultural festivals, in other words, encouraged an awareness of this world rather than the world on high and smacked vaguely of paganism.

The Book of Jubilees, written during the second century BCE, claimed that Shavuot commemorated the renewal of the covenant between God and man after the Flood, but the rabbis could not accept that because they never regarded the book as quite kosher, and they eventually gave Shavuot a new emphasis by designating it as *zeman matan Toratenu* – the season of the giving of our Torah.

It was never referred to as such in Scripture, and never celebrated as such in biblical times, nor is there anything in the text to show that the Torah was actually given on Shavuot but, as it was certainly given in Sivan, they had it approximately right.

Yet even the efforts to give the festival an extra dimension of holiness have not impaired its beauty, and its rustic associations remain intact.

Our synagogues used to be dingy. They are now rather flashy (how gaudy are thy tents O Jacob) and my favourite place of worship used to be the Carmel College synagogue, not because it was particularly beautiful itself, but because it looked out on to lawns, trees and flowers. My favourite now is the private chapel of a close friend which looks out on to a splendid garden and, beyond it, to Hampstead Heath.

Prayer and plants don't mix in Jewish lore, except on two occasions. One, is of course, Succot, when we bring our *arba minim* (four species [of plants]) to synagogue, and the other is Shavuot, when the synagogues are bedecked with plants and flowers.

Plants do bring one down to earth, but there is no harm in being reminded, even within the sacred precincts of a synagogue, that the earth is an exceedingly beautiful place and that we are in origin a pastoral race.

13 May 1994

Miracle *succah*

WHEN IT COMES to any do-it-yourself job, I am undone. I can rarely knock a nail in to the wall without demolishing my thumbs and, indeed, a good part of the wall, yet over the past 20 years I have somehow contrived to erect a *succah* (booth or tabernacle), using odd bits of lumber and trellis-work strewn about the garden.

My family called it a miracle-*succah*, for it was a miracle that it stood at all, and it sometimes remained standing for the entire length of the festival, though it not infrequently fell about my head at the first breath of wind, and my children grew up thinking that we build a *succah* to commemorate the fall of the Temple.

This year I decided to put my travails to an end once and for all and planned a permanent *succah* through the simple expedient of cutting a hole in my garage roof (in common with most of my neighbours we keep everything in the garage except the car), but in the event it proved less simple than expected and it would have been easier, and probably less painful, to have had a hole in my head.

The hole needed a window, the window needed a parapet, the parapet needed building permission, which meant architect's drawings and an architect, and the whole operation, of course, needed a builder – all for one wretched hole.

And so I got myself a builder. He was a good builder as builders go, but even good builders sometimes go bust, and bust he went, leaving us without a garage and without a *succah* (to say nothing of the substantial sum I had paid him in advance); but somehow I managed to get the job finished and we again have a miracle-*succah* – the miracle in this instance being that I survived without going bankrupt.

In a way, however, I feel I've been cheating. My friend and mentor, Rabbi Chaim Wilschanski, came round to survey the structure and assured me that it was perfectly kosher, but isn't a permanent *succah* a contradiction in terms? I'm aware that Chief Rabbi Nathan Adler had a permanent *succah* abutting on the Great Synagogue and used it as his study all the year round, and that some synagogue halls have moving roofs so that they can double as a *succah*, but I feel that such structures are against the spirit of the law, even where they conform to the letter.

The same is true of what might be called super-*succot*. The Israel Government Tourist Office used to run a competition for the grandest *succah* in Jerusalem, which to my mind is a little like having a competition for the most leavened *matzah*. It was inevitably won by the Sheraton Hotel with a pleasure-dome worthy of Kubla Khan ('In Xanadu did Kubla Khan a stately *succah* decree . . .'.)

Vast in size, with thick carpets, silken drapes and crystal chandeliers, it was not unlike Mrs Schuldenfrei's idea of an Anglo-Jewish suburban home, except that one half expected a line of semi-clad dancing girls to escape from the folds. If the Israelites had had booths like that in the wilderness, they would never have left it.

The fare, I may add, matched the furnishings: it was infinitely better than manna, or even quails, though infinitely more expensive. I remember sitting there and thinking: *c'est magnifique, mais ce ne'est pas la* succah.

I am told that in America, where the competitive spirit is as rife in religion as it is in other areas of life, they are trying to out-*succah* one another by bringing in architects and interior designers, so that one has ranch-style *succot*, and colonial style, and rather elaborate wigwams, not only in the suburbs, but on top of skyscrapers in Manhattan; and, for all I know, they may wear outfits to match the styles.

And even here one can find *succot* whose decorations would make the hanging gardens of Babylon look austere; but decorations, at least, are sanctioned by tradition, and a cheerless interior would go ill with what is, after all, meant to be a joyous event (though, strangely enough, the most joyous part of Succot – the water libation celebration – is almost defunct).

A *succah*, even if richly emblazoned, should ideally be frail, shaky, open to the winds, and look and feel as if it's been put together with pieces of string – and one should, I think, be involved in its making. If a thing is worth doing, it's worth doing badly, or, to put it another way, there is immense satisfaction to be had from performing a task for which one is inherently ill-equipped (in my case, almost everything practical).

I doubt if Sir Christopher Wren ever regarded St Paul's with the sort of pride that I used to contemplate my *succah*. I would gaze out of my window every morning and, if it was still standing, I would mutter the prayer: 'Blessed be he who sustaineth the infirm.'

My garage with the hole-in-the-roof may save me an annual headache, but it has deprived me of an annual challenge.

12 October 1984

Purim

I'VE GRUMBLED OFTEN enough about the Jewish festivals, about Rosh Hashanah (too holy), Succot (too draughty), Pesach (too costly), but you might think that I would approach Purim, at least, with joyous anticipation. I don't. In fact, I regard it with something like dread, for I have many children (bless 'em) and with the blessing of many children comes the curse of many Purim costumes.

I have scoured the holy texts to find the origins of the costume custom, but there is no reference to it in Scripture and none in the Talmud and it seems fairly certain that it was something we picked up from the pre-Lenten carnivals of our Gentile neighbours. There is also, I suppose, some sanction for it in the rabbinic injunction to drink to the point of intoxication, for intoxication is but a quick means of acquiring a temporary change in personality, while dressing up is a sober means of doing the same thing.

I have by chance been reading a fascinating book by Alison Lurie, *The Language of Clothes*, in which she shows how far one's garments are a public declaration of one's private self. As an example, she quotes the Chasidim of New York, whose gear, she says, 'indicates six different degrees of religious commitment, from the near-secular *Yid*, who wears only the standard dark double-breasted suit, buttoning from right to left, to the *Rebbe* who also has a full beard, sidelocks, *kapote*, sable hat, *bekescher* (a *Chasidic* coat of silky material), and *shick* [sic] and *zocken* (slippers and white knee socks).'

I am not sure if I agree with her. If one gets up in the morning and throws on the nearest clothes to hand, they could be a true expression of oneself, but where one actually takes pains to dress up, one defines the sort of person one would like to be taken for.

One masquerades. Still, it's to a man's credit that he likes to be taken for a saint. The sort of gear sported by most young men nowadays suggest that they would prefer to be taken for Starsky and Hutch, or even for the last of the Mohicans.

Purim, carnivals, fancy-dress parties are licensed occasions to play out our fantasies.

When I was a lad, we had no difficulty with Purim costumes, for I grew up during the war and just after, and we all had yards of blackout material to play with (to say nothing of gas masks), but we were restricted in the sort of personae we could adopt. You were either Mordechai, Ahasuerus or Haman, or you were nothing, and most of us, almost to a man (or boy), opted for Haman.

This may suggest that most small boys are villains at heart, except that one couldn't help noticing that during the reading of the Megillah, the Purim scroll, Mordechai and Ahasuerus were passed over in silence, while Haman caused all the commotion and got all the cheers; and many of my contemporaries grew up to believe that he was, in fact, the hero of the piece.

It was also easier to impersonate Haman. Mordechai needed a beard, Ahasuerus a crown, but all that Haman required was a black mustachio. (Why is it, incidentally, that the moustache, or, at least, the mustachio, is regarded as a symbol of villainy, while the beard has always been accepted as a badge of sanctity?)

In Israel, children dress up as soldiers and sailors and national heroes. The untimely death of Moshe Dayan has robbed them of an easy option (and must have ruined the eye-patch trade). Golda was a godsend to the girls (and the boys) while she was around, but neither Menachem Begin's appearance nor his style offers much scope to the costumier.

In this country, children tend to dress up as batmen or spidermen or vampires or things from outer space if they are left to their own devices, but more often they are dressed by their parents, and one finds a parade of queens and princes and princesses (Princess Di has made things easy for them now), and doctors and surgeons (replete with masks), film stars, pop singers, newscasters, barristers, judges, Little Bo Peeps, Little Jack Horners, but never, or hardly ever, a rabbi, which tells one something about public attitudes to the cloth.

Among adults, I suppose, Purim and Purim dress offer a passing opportunity to escape from anonymity for a day and to play at being a more brazen, more conspicuous self, except that it is rather difficult to be conspicuous these days.

I was travelling in the tube last week when a man entered with baggy yellow trousers tucked into red boots, an embroidered kaftan under a tabard, huge gold earrings, a shaven head, green eye-shadow and a brown moustache running like a thick trickle of gravy along his upper lip and down the sides of his mouth. No one gave him a second look, though the thing which particularly caught my attention was that after he had settled himself in his seat, he pulled the *Daily Telegraph* from under his arm and began to read it. I suspect he was something in the City.

It's difficult to make something of Purim in a world in which it is Purim all the year round.

5 March 1982

A holiday from Jewish holidays

WE NEED FESTIVALS, if only as a diversion to the workaday week. When the French revolutionaries abolished the old religious festivals, they had to introduce new secular ones. The Communists did the same.

The new secular festivals, however, could never attain the appeal of the old, precisely because they were new and secular, and most of them fell out of use.

A festival, to be truly festive, needs ghosts – a link to the past, childhood echoes, hallowed customs, ancient usage, shared sentiments, an awareness of worlds beyond our own. But they should be reasonably spaced and reasonably brief, otherwise their frequency and number can reduce their festive character and make them *vochedik* (workaday).

You can guess what I'm about to say next if only because I have said it before (though in different words). It's rather like Mark Twain's famous complaint that everyone grumbles about the weather but no one does anything about it.

The same is true of the spate of festivals through which we have just passed and from which we are still reeling.

We all know that one can have too much of a good thing; but

231

one can also have too much even of a holy thing. Maimonides said that one should leave the table before one has had enough. The same, I think, can be said of synagogues.

It is possible to have a surfeit of sanctity and, after spending the better part of a month bent over a prayer book, one needs something akin to a decompression chamber before one is ready to face normal life.

I approached the festivals this year with particular apprehension because the small *shtiebl* I normally attend is no more. I found myself in the unfamiliar ambience of a large synagogue and, I must say, I was pleasantly surprised.

The services were well conducted; the *chazan* was in good voice; the sermons were brief and to the point; and the decorum on most days verged on the exemplary.

I especially enjoyed Succot – though the security people must have had a hard time of it, for nearly everyone came armed with what looked like Kalashnikovs in cardboard cases.

But, as worshippers unsheathed their *lulavim* (palm branches), the synagogue began to resemble a moving forest, which is ideally what a synagogue should resemble.

There must have been about 400 of them and, when it came to *Hoshanot* (procession with the four species), the congestion was so acute that they tried – ineffectually – to introduce traffic wardens.

Succot, in days of old, was also a libation festival and I was glad to see the customs revived. Libations within the synagogue and without were liberal (though not half so liberal as they were in our dear old *shtiebl*).

Yet, much as I enjoyed the festivals, I would have enjoyed them more had they been fewer. Their incidence this year was particularly unfortunate for it meant that, for three weeks out of four, we had three days in a row in synagogue.

The last of the three was, of course, Shabbat and, where Shabbat follows immediately on the heels of two-days' *Yomtov*, it loses it's sublime sabbatarian quality.

The day of rest presumes a day of toil. Only the toiler can approach it with pleasurable anticipation, so that even the frantic, last-minute rush on Friday afternoon adds to the joy of the event.

Where one works only three days a week, one does not deserve the Sabbath.

The trouble with our rabbis, bless 'em, is that they can never leave well alone, whereas they are disposed to leave the ill undisturbed. Did they really have to add an extra day to our holidays? Or, having added them, are they really unable to remove them? One has only to pose the question to know the answer.

I may indeed have made the point before; but one should not give up too easily. I have been grumbling about this issue every five or six months for about 30 years. If I should continue for a further 300, I may yet get somewhere – and what's 300 years between Jews?

In the meantime, let me turn to a happy event. The month of Marcheshvan is upon us. In biblical times, it was known as Bul, which I much prefer. It has a cheerful sound to it which goes with its character, and what makes it cheerful is that it is mercifully free of festivals, major or minor, and even fast days.

In fact, there is nothing in sight until the end of Kislev – a clear run of a least seven working weeks in which we can enjoy Shabbat to the full. Marcheshvan – or rather Bul – is the month in which Jewish life comes to life.

31 October 1997

12
Gourmet

Judaism not only impacts on the soul, it can be,
and should be, tasted on the tongue.

Winter's golden *cholent* and golden mists

ALMOST EVERYONE I know has over the past week or two been making for warmer climates – Barbados, Eilat, Miami, even Melbourne – but I don't mind the cold, at least in winter. I even revel in it, especially at weekends, for though I am fond of Shabbat at any time of the year, I sometimes think it was specifically designed for winter.

The same is true of the marvellous tales about Jacob and Esau, Joseph and his brothers, and Moses and Pharaoh – *die winterdike sedras* (the wintertime readings of the law), as we used to call them in Yiddish – which come with the winter months.

I suppose I have been over them now about a hundred times, but, as long as one avoids the less likely commentaries and the more improbable legends, they offer new pleasures every time one reads them.

There is, of course, nothing wintry about the stories themselves and the word 'winter' occurs but once in the entire Pentateuch. If one often reads of 'the heat of the day', there is never a reference to the cold of the night.

Joseph didn't wear his coat of many colours to keep warm, and the settings – whether in Aram, Canaan or Egypt – are invariably sunny; but the narrative is best enjoyed in the depths of winter.

A good story calls for long nights, swirling snows and howling winds; but the stories apart, I feel that the character of Shabbat as we know it was formed not by our experience in Palestine, or Babylonia, or even Spain, but by our sojournment under northern skies.

I remember reading about Joseph and his dreams on a balmy night in Mobile, Alabama: the story didn't sound the same and Shabbat didn't feel the same. I sometimes wonder how they manage to keep Shabbat – if, indeed, they do – in South Africa or Australia, or the American south and west, where everything is topsy-turvy and where what they call winter is a good deal warmer than our summer.

It's the Friday night which establishes the festive mood of

Shabbat, rather than the day itself. It is heralded by the declining sun and glowing skies.

The service, if one overlooks the blemish of *bameh madlikin* ('Women die in childbirth for three omissions: because of negligence during their period of separation, in failing to consecrate the first cake of dough, and in failing to light the Sabbath lamp'), is the loveliest in our liturgy.

The six psalms which open it are particularly beautiful, and so is the *Yigdal* (hymn in praise of God) with which it closes. And then home through the chilly night to the glowing candles, the gleaming silver, the assembled family.

In the summer, proceedings are a bit hurried and attenuated, for there is no Friday night to speak of, while the day itself can seem a little too extended. If Friday nights can never be too long, Saturdays can rarely be too short.

The winter, moreover, is the *cholent* season. There are people who eat it all the year round (and on weekdays, too, which strikes me as a sort of sacrilege), but *cholent* on a hot day is like ice-cream on a cold one – it can be eaten but not relished. It is best eaten at lunch, by which time it acquires its optimum flavour.

(I speak, of course, of the classical, or Lithuanian, *cholent*, not the Hungarian variety, which is really a dehydrated bean soup and has the consistency and flavour of ready-mixed concrete.)

A good *cholent*, with a *kugel* on top like the crust on a volcano, presumes winter. Break the crust and the steam comes hissing through, to reveal the *cholent* itself, rich, golden and burbling, like molten lava. It is a form of central heating.

The windows become misted, its flavour pervades the house and hovers over the household like a temporal *shechina* (spirit of God), and those who cannot enjoy it actively enjoy it (or suffer it) passively.

Doctors tell me it's a slow poison, but what enjoyable food isn't – and in any case, who's in a hurry?

It is certainly richly soporific. Golden mists begin to form before one's eyes as one eats, near things seem hazy and distant, voices become discordant, and one gradually sinks into sleep.

And when one wakes, it is dark, *Shabbat* is over, the phones are ringing, the children are in jeans, ready for their night out, and one is, a trifle reluctantly, back in this world.

25 December 1987

Kosher braindrain

THE GOOD NEWS is that Fruity Pops, Fruity Rolls, Ju Ju Coins, Large Winkies (and presumably Wee Willie Winkies), Lollies, Small Tulips (and presumably large ones), Niblie Cones, Small Ju Jus, Sour Balls, Battle of the Planet Bars, Buttons 'n' Bouches, Chewy Fruit Rolls, Marzipan Challah, Sesame Crisps, Mint Chocolate Lentils, Strawberry Ministicks, Chocolate Umbrellas, Cric Crac Parev, Giant Ragusa (and presumably diminutive ones), Creepy Crawlies, Bumper Bunnies, Dr Who Bars, Dormice, Chewits, Assorted Chunks, Sour Rain Drops and even Coloured Kisses are all *kosher*.

The bad news is that Alpha Bricks, Boneheads, Bubble Gum Cigarettes, Chewing Nuts, Chunky Chicks, Flootie-Tooties, Double Deckers, Curly Wurlies, Biarritz Assortments, Skippy, Daredevil Cigarettes, Elizabeth Shaw Mint Creams and, more seriously, Bassett's Liquorice Allsorts are not.

I am indebted for all this information – and much else – to the *Kashrut Guide* compiled by the London Beth Din, which, if not in the Rushdie class as a best-seller, has gone into its third edition and is likely to cause less offence and more amusement.

The Jewish dietary laws are dealt with by Scripture in a few paragraphs. The *Kashrut Guide* extends to 148 pages, but then Scripture doesn't have an index, which the *Kashrut Guide* does.

Scripture makes no references to Flootie-Tooties and Creepy Crawlies, which the *Kashrut Guide* does; and Scripture has nothing to say about disinfectants, water softeners, metal polishes and stain removers.

The *Kashrut Guide*, on the other hand, has something to say about everything you could imagine, and a few things you couldn't, such as *kosher* drain cleaners.

Did I say *kosher* drain cleaners? I did. At which point it occurs to me that as we are in the middle of the Purim-April Fool's spoof season, you may think I am making this up.

But my imagination, if fertile, is not that fertile and I would refer you to page 120 of the *Kashrut Guide* (hereafter to be known as

239

the *Guide for the Perplexed*), where you will find two different brands of drain cleaner listed: Amway Drain Mate and Michael D'Avid.

Neither is actually produced under rabbinical supervision, but the Beth Din is satisfied that both may be used, and though it doesn't name them in order of preference, the latter sounds marginally more *kosher*.

You've heard of the brain drain? Well, here we have the drain brain. The next time your drains get blocked, don't call for Dyno-Rod, call for the *dayanim*, who will leave no stone unturned to make sure that everything in, around and under your home is *glatt kosher*. It is not enough merely to scrutinise Creepy Crawlies and Curly Wurlies, one has to get down to the nitty-gritty.

But in case you should think that such zeal is confined to London, let me refer you to a 'Koshergram' (which should not be confused with a Kissogram) issued by the Layman's Association of the Vaad Harabbonim of Greater Detroit.

The 'Koshergram' deals with such joys as 'Famous Amos Cookies', 'Meatless Salami' (it hadn't occurred to me there was any other sort) and 'Vegetable Scallops'; but its main concern is so-called '*kosher*' wine. Before going further, however, I had better explain a term which is apt to erupt in the 'Koshergram' with some frequency – and that is *mevushal*.

Wine, even '*kosher*' wine, can be rendered non-*kosher* if touched by a non-Jew, or even by a non-observant Jew, but if it is *mevushal* – i.e., boiled – it becomes inviolate (the principle, I hasten to add, does not extend to pork, scampi, shrimps or oysters, but as lobsters have a cloven hoof, they might be half-*kosher*. If anyone could train lobsters to chew the cud he would be a rich man).

Now let me quote the 'Koshergram' on 'imported and Baron Jaquab De Herzog brand wines and Champagnes'.

'Those that are *mevushal* state so in Hebrew on the label. However, many are not *mevushal*, even in the 750-ml size. If the label does not say *mevushal*, that bottle is NOT *mevushal*, even if other identical bottles do say *mevushal*.'

I hope you've got that, otherwise there is more than a chance that you may end up drinking non-*kosher* wine. To be on the safe side, you may prefer to make do with Michael D'Avid drain cleaner, which may be consumed *mevushal* or not.

17 March 1989

Duck soup

IN THE OLD days, if someone took you out for a *kosher* meal, you could look forward to all the familiar pleasures – chopped herring and *lokshen* (vermicelli) soup, salt beef and *latkes* (small potato pancakes), with maybe a gherkin, *lokshen* pudding and Russian tea.

Well, you can't any more, at least not in America. When I was last there, I was taken out to three or four different *kosher* restaurants and never even caught wind of a herring, nor any of the other joys of Jewish cuisine.

It was all Peking duck, and Nanking hen, and bird's nest soup (don't they know what birds do in their nests?), and seaweed, and chow mein with *chrane* (or rather, without), and won ton soup, and half a ton of gravy and oodles of noodles. (Noodles, you may think, are merely *lokshen* in disguise, but a *loksh* under any other name has not got the same flavour.)

And instead of closing the meal with a glass of Russian tea (including a generous slice of lemon), they serve you something with a fancy name like Lapsang Orangutang, which has the appearance and flavour of hot water filtered through a nylon sock.

From which you might conclude that I have a bias against the Chinese and Chinese food. I have not, but I do have a bias against the unfamiliar, and I note with alarm that the sinisation of Jewish cuisine has now spread to Britain, so that one is no longer sure of traditional Jewish fare even at a traditional Jewish wedding.

Perhaps it was always so. The Chinese have been around for even longer than the Jews, and in infinitely greater number, and their influence may have spread further than we think.

When the Israelites wandered in the wilderness, they lived on a diet of manna, which was 'like coriander seed, but white; and the taste of it was like wafers made with honey'.

Monks at St Catherine's monastery in Sinai aver that it was derived from the secretion of insects on tamarisk trees. In other words, it is all rather unsavoury, but the Chinese go in for that sort of thing and it suggests an affinity with bird's nest soup.

Legend also has it that *cholent*, the king of Jewish dishes and the best-known antidote to chronic longevity, was originally known as Chow Lent, a meatless dish designed for consumption by Chinese Marranos in the seven weeks before Easter.

Which brings me to a rather sad story. There were three good men in the *kosher* catering trade, one of them a Mr Ung, who owned the Moshe Dragon, a Chinese restaurant of some repute in Washington DC.

Now Mr Ung, as his name might suggest, is not Jewish and he therefore engaged a *shomer* (kashrut supervisor) appointed by the Union of Orthodox Jewish congregations of America.

When I was last in his establishment, every table was taken and his clientele was loud in praise of his food (it was even louder in eating it). Ung seemed to be riding a crest of prosperity, but then came the fall.

His troubles began – as troubles usually begin in kosher establishments – with the *shomer*, who claimed he had found a non-*kosher* duck in the fridge. Had the charge been substantiated Mr Ung would have been finished – hence, possibly, the expression 'out for a duck' – but it was not.

Mr Ung claimed that there was no duck in the fridge; that it was not his, but his cousin's; that it had flown in through the window and had settled in the fridge; that it was put there by the Chinese mafia; that it was not a duck, but a hen; and that, in any case, it was kosher.

The local rabbinate considered the charge for 40 days and 40 nights, found the case against Mr Ung unproven and appointed a new *shomer*.

But he did not last long either, for though he found no dubious ducks in the fridge, he had alighted upon dubious practices in the kitchen. Ung's staff, he complained, were dedicating food and drink to a statue of the Buddha.

Mr Ung, I gather, insisted it was not the Buddha, but the Lubavitcher Rebbe. When it was pointed out that the statue was both bare-headed and bare-chinned (and, indeed, bare all over), he replied that he meant the Chinese Lubavitcher Rebbe, known otherwise as the Admor of Kai Feng.

As the argument continued, Mr Ung collapsed and was rushed to the Holy Cross hospital, which more or less settled the matter. If only he had been admitted to the Mount Sinai hospital, he might have still been in business.

14 September 1990

Horseradish by any other name

WHEN ONE IS young, one learns that not a few of the things in life one yearns for are not *kosher*. As one gets older, one discovers that even if they are *kosher*, they are not healthy, and the most obvious examples of this are dairy foods.

When I was a lad, cream, butter and eggs were regarded not merely as food, but as elixirs, so that if someone was rundown, one topped him up with all three.

The household remedy for most childhood ailments was a *goggle-mogel* composed of the yellow of an egg beaten into a cream with sugar, and then mixed with boiled milk. Even if it did not always cure the ailment, it was a compensation for it.

Today, all three would be condemned as poison, and the very festival of Shavuot, with its sanctification of dairy foods, is regarded as a health hazard. Friends pull one aside with the warning: 'Put not thy trust in *blintzes* (a kind of stuffed pancake).'

The dreaded word is, of course, cholesterol. I used to think it was an engine oil and wondered what it could have been doing in the blood. Now I know.

Every time I see my doctor, she drains off half a pint of blood to check my cholesterol count (that's her story, though I half suspect she's a closet vampire). My cholesterol count, you may (or may not) be glad to hear, is all right, only I'm beginning to suffer from anaemia – and acute cheese-cake deficiency.

It used to be said that a little of what you fancy does you good, which was taken by Jews to mean that a lot of what you fancy does you better. That, however, was long before we allowed rabbis and doctors to run our lives.

If they had their way, we would all be subsisting on a diet of distilled water and *shemurah matzah*. It doesn't mean that every-one who followed their prescription to the letter would live to be 120, but they would feel as if they did.

Doctors are trained to be killjoys, but British doctors are not half as bad as their American colleagues. In Britain, at least, a food is presumed to be benign until it is shown to be harmful; in America it is taken to be harmful unless shown to be benign.

I was therefore not entirely surprised to come across an article in the *Journal of the American Medical Association* by a Dr Chaya Rubin and Dr Albert Wu (sic), which condemned even *chrane* as poisonous.

(I was a little mystified by the involvement of Dr Wu in the piece and can only conclude that there are now so many kosher Chinese restaurants about that they serve chop suey with *chrane*.)

Chrane, or *armoracia lapathifolia*, is generally known in the English-speaking world by the unflattering name of horseradish, which suggests that only horses would eat it, and as a matter of fact only horses would touch the sort of bland preparations generally available in English shops.

Real, five-star, high-octane, *heimishe* (home-made) *chrane*, of the type I normally prepare (there are some things which cannot be trusted to one's women-folk), is another matter, for even a tiny dollop sends steam hissing out of one's ears and down one's nostrils, while a large one can induce a sense of levitation.

Dr Chaya Rubin says she was moved to write the article when her aged father keeled over after swallowing a mouthful of *chrane* at a *seder*. She didn't say how much *shemurah matzah* he had had before he ate the *chrane*, or how much *charoset*, and in any case, the good man soon recovered, which suggests that he may have merely passed out in a fit of ecstasy.

Horseradish is of Iberian origin (hence, no doubt, the saying: 'The *chrane* in Spain stays mainly in the plain'), but oddly enough, it never took root among Sephardim and it was Polish and Lithuanian Jews who discovered its unique properties and who still cherish them.

Though marvellously piquant, *chrane* is not a food as such, nor even a condiment, but rather a local anaesthetic which temporarily deadens the taste buds so as to render almost any food – such as *gefilte* fish (boiled fish cakes) – palatable. No Jewish table should be without it, and few Jewish tables are, and any attack upon it is an attack on Jewish tradition and Jewish life.

But not only that. The pious, as we read in our Shavuot liturgy, will be rewarded for their self-denial in this world with a feast of leviathan in the next – and whoever feasted on leviathan without *chrane*?

20 May 1988

A Jewish obsession

DR JOHNSON DESCRIBED remarriage as 'the triumph of hope over experience'. One could say the same of the *kosher* catering trade.

Hardly a week goes by without one *kosher* restaurant closing down and another opening up. What is even more remarkable is that the people who close and open are sometimes one and the same, even if they don't always operate under the same name.

I know of one purveyor who has surfaced under a variety of different names, on different sites, under the supervision of different *kashrut* authorities. I don't know what his food is like but, my God, I admire his persistence.

You can't keep a good man down, at least not if he has a good lawyer. The real challenge, of course, is to find a good cook.

All this may explain why we have so many *kashrut* authorities. For what is about to pass into the hands of the receiver, may the Lord make us truly thankful!

Yet, if some establishments are ephemeral, their number is growing. And so is their variety. Golders Green Road is becoming like a cosmopolitan Dizengoff Street and, where a *kosher* meal once meant salt beef and *latkes*, one now has pizzas and mezzes and shishliks and kebabs, and stir-fries and *shmir*-fries.

Where *lokshen* pudding used to put the seal on a meal – and one's digestive tract – one is now offered flaming crêpes Suzette (which is not a dish I would recommend to anyone with a beard).

Some point to the growth of *kosher* restaurants, cafés, snack-joints, take-aways and throw-aways as proof that we are in the grip of a religious revival, which, in a sense we are, the religion being food.

Jews have always approached their food with a certain amount of religious fervour because it forms such an important part of their faith. There are three statutory meals to the Sabbath and, in winter, when it begins to get dark about four, one has barely finished the second meal before one gets down to the third.

Nearly every festival, major or minor, has its culinary associations: honey and honey-cake on Rosh Hashanah; *matzah* and *matzah*-balls on Pesach; cheesecake and *blintzes* on Shavuot; *latkes* and doughnuts on Chanucah; *hamantaschen* on Purim. The way to a man's soul is through his stomach.

Moreover, the very fact that so many foods are forbidden to Jews has led them to over-indulge in permitted ones. But what may have begun as a purely Jewish obsession has since become a national one.

Food now dominates the air waves, the newspapers, the publishing industry. There are more cookery books sold in Britain than all other books – including the Bible – put together. In fact, cookery books have replaced the Bible in most British homes. The restaurant has become a sort of church. And gluttony, once denounced as a deadly sin, has become almost a form of devotion.

Switch on the television and, more often than not, you will be confronted with a food programme. Chefs are the chief attraction, some young, some old, some drinking, some drunk. Chefs, indeed, sporting their white hats like mitres, have become the high priests of the new cult, with steam rising from their stoves like incense from an altar.

I used to enjoy TV nature programmes but they are, in the main, also concerned with food, with lions doing the eating, zebras providing the fare, and jackals standing by for the leftovers.

The papers – at least the serious ones – are in some ways worse, especially at weekends. The news pages are generally dominated by food scares and the feature pages by food columnists, wine columnists and restaurant critics.

I should perhaps be the last one to complain, for I am not particularly abstemious myself. I was also for a time restaurant critic on a national newspaper, until I began to attract more writs than readers. (One of the writs was from a *kosher* restaurant which, perhaps inevitably, has since closed down, though another, which I happened to praise, continued to quote my commendations even after it set up under a new name.)

All I can say by way of mitigation is that, if I hadn't been fired, I would have given up of my own accord. Eating may be all right as a pleasure but it has its limitations as a topic and its dangers as an obsession. 'One should eat to live,' said Molière, 'not live to eat.'

There is a little-known Yiddish expression which deserves wider currency: *reib und schweig* – meaning, grind and be silent, or eat up and shut up.

7 February 1997

Harangue on herrings

I HOPE MY readers will forgive me, but I'm about to indulge in a harangue, and in what I take to be the original sense of the term. In other words, I'm going to talk about herrings.

In *der heim* (oh, not again, I hear you say) when they selected a *Chatan Torah* (bridegroom of the Law) and *Chatan Bereshit* (bridegroom of Genesis) for *Simchat Torah* (Rejoicing of the Law), they would pair a rich man with a pauper and have the former supply the whisky and the latter the herring. Well, no pauper could supply the herrings today; if anything, it would be cheaper to supply the whisky.

In our family, we normally break our Yom Kippur fast on herrings and I found that this year we had to pay something like *£1 a herring*! If that isn't a ramp, what is? Every spring this paper is full of (justified) complaints about the cost of Passover foods, but we seem to be content to pay through the nose for our basic necessities for the rest of the year – and what necessity is more basic than herrings?

A distinguished member of the Anglo-Jewish community – the late Redcliffe Salaman – gained an international reputation through his study of the social impact of the potato, but as far as I know, no one has as yet attempted to examine the social impact of the herring. Perhaps I'll do it, for if Irish social history can be explained in terms of the potato, and Scottish social history in terms of oatmeal, Jewish social history may be explained in terms of the herring.

I once attended a symposium which tried to discover why the

247

Jews of the Pale of Settlement, while sunk in poverty, enjoyed greater longevity than any other section of the population. One scholar pointed to the Jewish laws of hygiene, another suggested greater health care, a third ascribed the cause to greater abstinence (by which, I take it, he meant sobriety), a fourth believed that the main cause may simply have been divine protection. But no one alighted on the most obvious reason of all – namely, that every Jewish family, no matter how poor, could always afford a diet of herrings.

One can live on herrings – indeed, I have lived on them. In *der heim* (here he goes again!) one celebrated the Sabbath and festivals religiously with white fish and fowl, but on weekdays, the fare was more varied.

On Sunday, one had pickled herring, on Monday, soused herring; on Tuesday, smoked herring; on Wednesday, baked herring; on Thursday, herring fried in oatmeal (delicious!); and on Friday, one had herrings in sour cream (and as few Jewish households could afford a calendar, one could tell the days of the week by the herrings one ate).

Herrings, of course, were always eaten with onions, and the herrings and onions were consumed either with potatoes or with *khleba*, good, solid, black Russian bread – and not the cotton-wool and plastic that passes for bread in this country – which made it a perfectly balanced diet. One would have to be rich to afford a diet like that in London.

When I moved to Scotland, I was able to adapt myself readily to my new environment because the Scots are second only to the Jews in their adoration of herrings. It may also explain why they have been so successful in every conceivable walk of life, and it was in Scotland that I discovered the herring in its supreme form – the kipper.

I was once involved with a Scotsman in a debate on who made the greatest contribution to civilisation, the Jews or the Scots. I naturally invoked the Ten Commandments and anticipated that the Scotsman would come up with whisky (for which I had a reply), but instead he trumped me with kippers.

They really are – especially when grilled with tomatoes – the most delectable food I know. Like other forms of herring, they used to be a poor man's dish, but like the others, they have gone so far up-market as almost to have priced themselves out of it.

They are, of course, golden in colour, but one might think from the cost of a pair that they were actually dipped in gold.

According to Jewish tradition – we in fact say a prayer to that effect at the end of Succot – when the righteous attain the hereafter, they will feast on the leviathan. Most commentators agree that the leviathan is some sort of fish, but few agree on what sort of fish it is. I, for my part, have no doubt whatever that it is a good Scotch kipper – the hereafter would hardly be worth attaining if it were anything else.

That, however, does not solve the short-term problem of the here and now, or, indeed, the long-term problem for those of us (and I suspect we may be in the majority) who are less than righteous. How can Jews be expected to survive as Jews with even common-or-garden herrings at £3 a pound? Did I hear someone say, 'Let them eat salmon'?

19 October 1984

13
Animal
Magic

*Cats are the most beautiful things in creation
(especially when small) . . . and the one constant
element in a constantly changing world.*

Pet theories

WHO SAID THAT rabbis live in ivory towers and rarely concern themselves with the practicalities of Jewish life?

Well I did for one, and must now withdraw, for I have come upon a rabbi, and a very eminent one, who has his ear to the ground, his nose to the grindstone, his eyes on the ball and his finger on the pulse. He is Ovadiah Yosef – long may he live – the former Sephardi chief rabbi of Israel, who last week ruled that one can use a monkey or a dog, and by extension other household pets, as a Shabbos *goy*.

The ruling suggests a commendable readiness to lighten the burdens of Sabbath observance and, for a start, it could revolutionise the trade in household pets. In future when a Jew buys a dog, a cat or a monkey he will want to know not only if it is house-trained but whether it is Sabbath trained. (Somebody may even open a *cheder* to this purpose.)

It could also have an effect on various public services in Israel.

It has always been difficult to recruit Orthodox Jews into the Israeli police force because of Shabbat and Yomtov, but chimpanzees and gorillas could be trained to stand in for them on such occasions. They could not perform all the necessary duties and it would not, I think, be a good idea to arm them, but chimpanzees could probably control traffic, and gorillas cope with demonstrations.

When it comes to hospitals I doubt if either could be trained as doctors or medical auxiliaries, but they would make perfectly adequate porters. They would be particularly useful to the hotel and catering trade. I doubt if monkeys could act as chefs – though to judge by the cuisine in some Israeli hotels, some may already have done so – but they could make beds, clean rooms, receive payments, and act as waiters, porters and lift attendants.

Most hotels do have Shabbat lifts, but they stop at every floor and are extremely slow. I remember when I used the Shabbat lift in the Jerusalem Plaza that, by the time I got to my room on the top floor, Shabbat was out.

I can see some difficulties with the Histadrut, which would

253

probably want to unionise monkeys, and even dogs and cats, in regular employment, but such problems are not insurmountable.

One could certainly have football teams composed of primates, who would probably play a damn sight better than some of the Israeli teams already in existence, though I doubt if they would be up to cricket.

On a domestic level, Rabbi Yosef's ruling may have come a bit late because, in northern climates at least, every Jewish household needed a Shabbos *goy* to light a fire on Shabbos morning, but with the advent of central heating, Shabbos *goyim* have gradually become redundant.

There is, of course, still the problem of television. Many rabbis argue that television should be banned from Jewish homes, and should certainly not be used on Shabbat. Few Jewish families, however, are that strict, and I know of one where they have trained their poodle to switch on their set during Shabbat. The trouble is he is only disposed to switch on programmes he wants to watch. He is all right when it comes to *Neighbours* and *Coronation Street*, for example, and he loves the pet-food ads, but when it comes to the news, he generally switches off. (I knew of another family with a parrot which cried 'Shabbos, Shabbos,' every time one touched a light switch, but as it made the same cry all the week round, it wasn't much use.)

We ourselves are not what one might call a doggy household, but we are a catty one (we also used to be a fishy one, until the cat ate the fish) and we used to have a tom-cat, who, after a night on the tiles, would ring the door bell to gain admission (we eventually had him doctored). I could, I suppose, have trained him to switch the lights on and off, but it was, on balance, easier to buy a time switch.

The ideal animal for religious duties is one which is rarely thought of in such a context. I refer to the goose.

We are all familiar with the legendary Goosey Gander who wandered upstairs and downstairs and in his lady's chamber. There he met a man who wouldn't say his prayers, and took him by the left leg and threw him down the stairs.

Such an animal would possibly be better as a *shomer* than as a Shabbos *goy*, but it would have one immeasurable advantage over cats, dogs and even monkeys. If it failed to perform its duties one could always eat it.

22 November 1991

Elephant rites

SURELY YOU'VE HEARD the one about the father who wanted something different, but completely different, for his son's barmitzvah.

His first thought was to have the barmitzvah on ice in the Wembley Arena, but the ice rink had already been booked for a Satmar wedding.

His next idea was to have the barmitzvah on water, but the barmitzvah boy, among his many accomplishments, had not yet learned to swim, so he had to think again. And finally, after taking professional advice, he decided to take all his guests out on safari.

And so he chartered a jumbo jet and flew them out to Nairobi, from where they flew in a succession of smaller planes to Dar es Salaam. There a long line of elephants, with porters and guides and police outriders and postilions and a brass band, awaited them for the trip through the jungle.

There was a bit of difficulty with Zeida and Booba, who found it all a bit strange and who, in any case, did not have a head for heights. But after they had been coaxed on to their elephant, the column set off, with the barmitzvah boy, the rabbi and the principal guests ahead, and the father bringing up the rear.

What with the band and the elephants and the native bearers and the police escort and the many guests in their fancy best, it was an impressive sight, but they hadn't moved far when the whole line suddenly pulled to a halt.

Father waited five minutes, ten minutes, then shouted impatiently: 'What the hell's keeping us?'

And the word went up the line: 'What the hell's keeping us? . . . What the hell? . . . What . . .'

And back came the message: 'Another barmitzvah . . . Another bar . . . Another . . .'

Well, Mr Leslie Jacobs, a shoe repairer from east London, took no such chances and instead of *schlepping* his guests out for a safari to darkest Africa, he brought the safari to darkest Ilford, and there, mixing with his family and friends, were an elephant and two dancing bears, one male and one female. (The local rabbi stayed away because he disapproved of mixed dancing.) Also present were a ringmaster, two stilt-walkers, a strongman, a clown and a knife-thrower.

I have been to barmitzvahs where they threw not only knives, but forks, spoons, fish balls, bridge rolls, rum babas and mushroom vol-au-vents, but this was a more orderly affair. The ringmaster and the strongman saw to that.

One gathers that Mr Jacobs and his family live in a modest terrace house with a modest garden, and one wonders how they managed to accommodate their 180 guests as well as the elephant, the bears, the stilt-walkers, etc: but according to legend, the courtyard of the holy temple in Jerusalem expanded to accommodate all comers and as this was, after all, a religious occasion, the same may have happened in Ilford.

Mr Jacobs, it is said, is not one to do things by halves and some guests may have been disappointed by the fact that the elephant was but a baby elephant and not fully grown, that there were no performing seals or lions, or lion tamers, or jugglers, or trapeze artists, or bareback riders. But we live in straitened times, England is not America, and to have brought in a whole circus would, I believe, have verged on the ostentatious.

It is always difficult to balance the demands of hospitality with those of restraint, and Mr Jacobs just about got it right. In any case, there is another barmitzvah in the offing and, no doubt, other family celebrations, and a considerate host has to have something in reserve.

Press and cameramen were invited to witness the spectacle and record it for posterity and the headline in the local papers was, 'Bear facts of a jumbo celebration.'

'How many barmitzvahs do you see like this?' said Mr Jacobs, proudly. Not many – as yet – but the idea could spread, for what Ilford does today, Edgware could be doing tomorrow, and in the years ahead no barmitzvah boy will feel that he has really attained manhood until he has an elephant at his *simcha* (joyous occasion).

In the meantime, we have shown that, like other ethnic minorities, we, too, can bring a splash of colour to the drab streets of London, and even if the new custom should remain localised, barmitzvahs may yet do for Ilford what the Caribbean carnival has done for Notting Hill.

27 September 1985

Dog days

I HAVE SO far withheld comment on the batmitzvah, or rather, the non-batmitzvah of Shana Racquel, the 13-year-old Pittsburgh English springer spaniel, but it is not a matter on which one should speak from the top of one's head or, indeed, from the bottom, and I have been cogitating on it for the past few weeks and although I was not myself invited to the affair and therefore have reason to feel aggrieved, I have tried to be as objective as possible.

I think Shana Racquel's owner, Suzanne Brandau, has shown a lack of judgement in the matter. Every dog has his day, while she proposed to give Shana Racquel a series of celebrations extending over *two* days, culminating in a black-tie dinner for 125 guests. Moreover, Shana Racquel is not a dog, but a bitch and while it may not have been unreasonable to have two days of celebrations for a dog's barmitzvah, to do the same for a bitch does seem to verge on the excessive.

What is perhaps more to the point, a batmitzvah is usually celebrated at 12, whereas the bitch, as I have said, is already 13, and finally, as dogs mature much more rapidly than humans, the proper age for a muttmitzvah is four. At 13 Shana Racquel is of an age to be celebrating her silver wedding, which is perhaps what Mrs Brandau had in mind. (What, incidentally, does one give a dog for a barmitzvah present? A tree certificate, I suppose, or better still, a tree.)

Poor Mrs Brandau has been in the dog-house ever since her plans became public but I suspect she may have been wishing to make a point and that by staging a two-day affair for her bitch she hoped to make a batmitzvah to end all batmitzvahs and, with them, all barmitzvahs, for most observers would agree that they have been getting more than a little out of hand lately.

When I was 13 my mother got together with my aunts, baked a few cakes, cut up a few bridge-rolls, sliced a few herrings, my father opened a bottle of whisky. I delivered a *pilpul* (subtle argumentation) (not a word of which made sense to me or, I

257

should imagine, anyone else), and that was my barmitzvah. We didn't even hire the *shul* hall for the occasion for in those days *shuls* had no halls (and our particular *shul* didn't even have heating).

Nowadays the festivities are rather more elaborate, which isn't so bad where the boy has made the effort to prepare the *sidrah* and perhaps a learned discourse, but in general the scale of the celebrations tends to be in opposite ratio to the attainments of the celebrant, and a lad only has to stumble through his *berachot* (blessing) to be assured of a round of festivities so sumptuous and prolonged as to make poor Shana Racquel seem deprived.

This is true even of Israel where I notice one now has to employ not only a butcher and baker, but also a candlestick maker, for a new custom is evolving whereby every immediate relative of the barmitzvah (and a few less immediate ones) is required to come to the fore and light a candle. At the end of it all there are so many people holding so many candles that they resemble a procession of penitents at a Lady's Day Mass.

The true home of excess is, of course, America. Jews like over-doing things a bit, and so do Americans, so that there is nothing quite like the excesses of American Jewry and when one has a bar/bat/dog-mitzvah these days one has to employ not only the usual corps of caterers, florists, musicians, photographers and security guards, but a director to stage-manage the whole affair and give it a particular theme.

The theme can vary. Indeed, they must vary, the idea being that every celebration should be unique but they have one thing in common in that they are completely removed from anything to do with *mitzvot* or Judaism, or even maturity.

One may have a *Guys and Dolls* theme where the family of the celebrant dress as gangsters and molls (appropriately so, in some cases) and guests are invited to do the same, or an Old Tyme theme, where they dress as recent immigrants from *der heim*, or a Western theme, with stetsons and high-heeled boots or a Red Indian theme, with feathers flying, or even a Tarzan theme ('Me barmitzvah boy, you batmitzvah girl').

I have not yet heard of a barmitzvah with a nudist theme, but it will no doubt come (and when it does it should give more than usual meaning – or less, as the case may be – to the familiar claim: 'Today I am a man'), and I am looking to San Francisco for news of the first gay barmitzvah ('Today I am a man, or am I?')

In the circumstances the two days of celebrations which Shana Racquel had planned for Suzanne Brandau (or is it the other way about?) seem to verge on the restrained.

But why a black-tie affair, why not dog collars?

24 February 1984

Kosher Pig

YOU WILL NO doubt have read of the kosher pig. Israel was agog with the news and for a time people spoke of nothing else, partly no doubt, because it made a change from inflation.

I, for my part, have hitherto refrained from comment because I wanted further and better particulars, for even if it is wrong to look a gift horse in the teeth, one can, I think, be forgiven for probing in the tonsils something which purports to be a *kosher* pig. In other words, I wanted to see the animal face to face to establish whether it had not only cloven hooves (which all pigs have), but fins and scales (which most pigs haven't), and to date, I confess, I have failed in this endeavour.

My first reaction was to suspect that our friends in the Hebrew University had been up to some new mischief. It was, you will remember, scientists at the Hebrew University who crossed a goat with an ibex to produce something called a *yaez*. What was to stop them from crossing a sow with some sort of kosher computer to produce a *kosher* pig? I, however, gather that this particular pig evolved without the benefit of scientists and that it, or rather its forebears, did their own dirty work.

The idea of a *kosher* pig may, on the face of it, seem a contradiction in terms, but, as I have already pointed out, it has cloven hooves, which suggests that it is already half kosher. Moreover, the Hebrew for pig (*chazir*) can also mean return, and there are

259

eminent sages who have argued that it is so called because one day 'the Holy One will return it to Israel', which is to say that it will become as acceptable on Jewish tables as boiled chicken or *gefilte* fish.

The Talmud, which has something to say on everything, refers to a fish called the *sheebuta*, which sounds like a cross between a sheep and a boot, but which, apart from the grunt, was said to have many of the properties of a pig and which, according to Rashi, tasted exactly like pork. (If you should think I'm making this up, which I suspect you may, you will find it mentioned at the bottom of page 109b of the tractate Chulin.)

My own fishmonger has never heard of it. Harrods, too, confessed that the name didn't ring a bell, though they were prepared to look into it for me; and it is not on the menu of Wheeler's, Manzi's or the Trattoria Di Pescatori, but the Talmud speaks not whereof it knows not, and if one can have sea-lions and dog-fish and cat-fish and wolf-fish, why not pig-fish?

If *sheebuta* tastes exactly like pork, smoked *sheebuta* could make a passing substitute for bacon, and would probably be cheaper than smoked salmon. Think of it, *sheebuta* and eggs! It would revolutionise the Jewish breakfast, though first, of course, you've got to catch your *sheebuta*.

But this is taking us away from our subject, for no one has suggested that the *sheebuta*, for all its porcine properties, is in itself a porker. The *kosher* pig should offer a taste of the real thing, and I can envisage a time when no barmitzvah celebration will be complete without a boar's head (with apple in mouth) at the top table.

The rabbis, in the meantime, have approached the matter with circumspection, and who can blame them? It's all they need. They have trouble enough establishing that the beef, mutton and poultry we eat is *kosher* (or not, as the case may be), and to add pork to their burden would test the wisdom and integrity of even a Federation Beth Din.

One rabbi, however, was apparently so bold as to suggest that a pig could be *kosher* provided it displayed all the characteristics of a *kosher* animal and provided its mother was of unimpeachably *kosher* origin – say a cow – which, I think, is asking a lot of a pig, but then Judaism has always demanded more from newcomers to the fold than from those who are, so to speak, born into it.

If the *kosher* pig should, indeed, prove to be *kosher* – and it will not only need a cow as a mother, but a fox as a father, to pass the scrutiny to which it will be subjected – it will blunt the edge of many a popular Yiddish expression. *A chazer bleibt a chazer* (a pig remains a pig), for example, is clearly meaningless when some pigs don't, and the even more familiar *treif vi chazer* and other such colourful expression will become obsolete.

There are, I should imagine, a whole host of people who will relish the thought of going the whole hog – of *leben a chazersher tog* (living a pig's day) – without imperilling their mortal souls, but most Jews I know prefer sea food to meat of any variety, and they would be much more excited by the prospect of kosher lobster.

No doubt it will come. Lobsters' hooves are even more markedly cloven than those of the pig. Let someone discover a variety which chews the cud and his fortune is made.

30 November 1984

The sad story of Arthur

PIGS IN ISRAEL lead a dog's life, for at best they are only tolerated, and even then within limits.

One cannot, or at least one should not, import them, breed them, sell them or eat them, but there are still a few of them snorting around, either in Christian areas, or in zoos or more surprisingly, as pets – and thereby hangs a tail (albeit a short and curly one).

While urban children in Israel have to make do with gerbils, guinea pigs, hamsters, or white mice, kibbutz children do rather better and have private menageries, and at Kibbutz Har Amasa in the Negev, the menagerie included – but, as you will hear, no longer includes – a stout porker called Arthur.

The thing to be said for pigs as pets is that they don't have to be exercised, and are not too fussy about their food, and Arthur,

261

genial, uncomplaining and cuddly, became the darling of the *chaverim* (male kibbutz members), young and old, and, almost the kibbutz mascot and something of a tourist attraction. But, as so often happens, he soon tired of kibbutz life – he may have found it too egalitarian for his tastes, or perhaps, as the only pig around, he was lonely – but whatever the cause, he fled to a nearby forest.

Now while forests elsewhere are dark, mysterious places full of hazards, Israeli forests are full of plaques and ring with the happy voices of tree-planters cheerfully planting trees.

Arthur's experience, however, was less than cheerful. He encountered a party from Kibbutz Livna, who looked at him, looked at each other, looked about them, and before you could say oink, he was no more.

Meanwhile back at Har Amasa there was consternation and grief. The young were inconsolable and would not eat their muesli and would not attend school. The old abandoned bridge and moped for their portly friend. All work stopped while *chaverim* and *chaverot* (female kibbutz members) searched every sand-dune and wadi in the Negev for some sign of their beloved pet.

Prayers were offered up for his safety, rewards were promised for his return, but no trace was found, until towards dusk one day a cloud rose up in the east and the entire Negev began to smell like a Blackpool boarding house after a Sunday morning fry up; for while they were gnashing their teeth in Har Amasa, they were noshing on Arthur in Kibbutz Livna.

Word of the feast soon spread to Har Amasa. They descended on Livna in a solid mass and there in the dining-room was Arthur with his head on a platter, an apple in his mouth, while the tables were laden with pork chops and pork pies, and gammon, and spare ribs, and black puddings, and chopped liver, and crackling, and sweetbreads, and kidneys, and trotters and hams, like a medieval banquet, with young and old digging in, from each according to his ability, to each according to his needs.

Caught thus red-handed, or rather greasy mouthed, Livna insisted that Arthur had fallen off the back of a lorry, that they had won him at a tombola at the Beersheba JIA ball, that they had received him from Oxfam, that he had arrived in a hamper from Fortnum & Masons, that he had strayed into their microwave, that in any case he wasn't a pig but a rare variety of hairless sheep, and that if Har Amasa didn't want their wretched beasts to be eaten they should jolly well keep a better eye on them. And having thus made their denial, they went on to swallow the evidence.

An altercation followed. Angry words were uttered, angry letters exchanged. The matter was taken to the highest councils of the kibbutz movement and finally Livna came clean, admitted that they had done the dirty on Arthur and promised Har Amasa another pig in lieu of Arthur, or cash in lieu of another pig.

They have not replaced Arthur in Har Amasa, but they have planted a forest in his name.

When news of the affair leaked out (as everything in Israel does) there was much shaking of heads and wagging of fingers and clicking of tongues, for Livna is no ordinary kibbutz but a member of the Gush Emunim, Greater Israel brotherhood, known otherwise as the Bloc of the Faithful, and they had eaten Arthur without even porging his rump, but they have purged their sins – hence the expression *chazir b'tchuvah*.

It also goes to show that where one insists on the whole hog in one area of life, one tends to apply it to others.

8 April 1988

Antisemitic cat

I HESITATE TO speak ill of any man, woman or beast and do not suffer from paranoia, but the cat next door is an anti-Semite.

He is a large and attractive animal called Hadrian, black all over, except for a fluffy white dicky and white spats, and everyone else in the street finds him the friendliest of creatures. He goes out to greet them with face beaming and tail up high, rubs against them and purrs till he crackles like a Geiger counter.

Yet he turns tail when I approach, glowers at me from a distance, or swears at me silently under his breath, and when I try to go near him, he will recoil, arch his back and hiss like a serpent.

Everyone else speaks of him as an angel of a cat, but to me he has become a heap of brooding malevolence. I even think he's laid a curse on my car, for it won't start in the mornings when he's around. (It sometimes won't start in the afternoons even when he isn't around, but that's another matter.) I have half a mind to report him to the Race Relations Board.

I am told that animals can reflect the bias of their owners, but that applies only to dogs. Cats have always had a mind of their own, and, in any case, I am on the friendliest terms with Hadrian's owner, who is embarrassed by his behaviour and frequently apologises for it.

Now, if Hadrian had been a dog, it would have been a different matter, for dogs are notoriously anti-Semitic and always have been, which is perhaps why they do not feature favourably in Jewish literature.

There is a curious passage in the Talmud (Pesachim 13b), in which we are cautioned not to live in a town without dogs, and where the head of the community is a doctor. I suspect it was garbled and what it meant to say was that we shouldn't live in a town without doctors and where the head of the community is a dog, for holy writ treats dogs in much the same terms as pigs and there is some doubt whether one may even keep a dog in a Jewish household.

Put otherwise, cats are kosher – not, of course, in the sense that one can eat them – and dogs are not. (When I first met my wife, they had a dog and a cat and a parrot in the house – to say nothing of innumerable children – and I thought she was the product of a very mixed marriage.)

Cats are praised in the Talmud (as well they might be) for their cleanliness and hygiene and their general demeanour, and one sage went so far as to say that, if we had not learnt modesty from the Torah, we would have learnt it from the cat.

When we last lived in Jerusalem we shared our abode with a huge ginger tom who was something of a Jekyll and Hyde. By day he was placid, playful, friendly, even affectionate, but by night, when the moon was full (and even when it wasn't), he turned into a monster.

His fangs grew longer, his eyes reddened, his hair stood on end and he would emerge to terrorise the neighbourhood; and he would return at cock-crow, mangled and matted with blood, but meek and contrite.

He was, of course, Israeli and therefore a trifle difficult, but other cats we have had have been less troublesome and I don't think I've ever lived in a totally catless household. I have even written the biography of one of our cats, Belshazzar, of blessed memory (for, alas – as if sensing that he was in any case about to be made immortal – he gave up the last of his lives just as I completed the final draft of the book.)

I once knew a cat with a curious stomping walk, as if he had a wooden leg, but even he was oddly graceful in his movements. Cats are the most beautiful things in creation (especially when small) and the one constant element in a constantly changing world.

Cats remain as one has always known them – undemanding, intelligent, dignified, even majestic, whether in motion or in repose, and if they are sometimes a trifle distant and aloof, I have never known one to be positively hostile – until, that is, I came upon Hadrian.

I cannot think what I might have done to earn his disfavour, but I have alighted on the following possibility. In his youth he underwent an operation, which effectively deprived him of his manhood. I don't know if the vet responsible for the atrocity was Jewish, but I understand he was bearded, and I can only imagine that the poor beast associates me with the unkindest cut of all.

30 May 1986

Mad cows

MAD COWS HAVE finally hit the *kosher* meat market, which has never in any case been quite sane, though they have highlighted its insanity in a peculiar way.

As a result of the cow scare, beef prices have virtually collapsed, which might lead one to expect that the price of *kosher* meat must likewise fall – except that it never does. Here is one area which is an exception to the rule that everything which goes up must come down. But in this instance they have not only failed to fall, they are actually set to *rise*, and thereby hangs a tail – or rather there doesn't.

As is generally known, kosher butchers in this country, as distinct from their counterparts in Israel, America and France, are allowed to sell only the fore-quarters of an animal, but they recoup something of their costs by selling the rear-quarters – which, incidentally, contain the choicest cuts – to the general market. It means, of course, that they have to slaughter twice as many animals as they need, and as *shechitah* (ritual slaughter) is expensive, it adds considerably to their costs.

That was the situation when cows were still sane, but now that they have gone round the bend, there is almost no general market for beef, and the front has to bear the cost of the rear, hence the higher prices.

But wait – if there is almost no general market for beef, shouldn't the fore-quarters also be cheaper? Well they are, but the costs of *shechitah* supervison – what one might call the *kosher-* quotient – remain resolutely the same.

I don't know if you've followed me this far, because I'm not sure if I've followed myself, but I do have a dark suspicion that somebody is making a killing out of this, and it isn't the customer. It is a classical instance of heads I win, tails you lose, which is where I came in.

Could we not get round the rumpless beast difficulty by breeding two-legged animals with fore-quarters only, and fixing them up with wheels and maybe an outboard motor to help them get about?

If that should prove impractical, can we not follow the example of other communities, and porge the rear-quarters and make them *kosher*?

I fear that the second suggestion is even less likely to be taken up than the first, for just as meat prices can only go up but never down, it also appears that we can only add to prohibitions, but never diminish them. All of which may explain why kosher meat – at more than double the price of the other variety – has become the food of the rich.

There is no great mystery to porging. Two parts of an animal must be extracted before it is fit for kosher consumption. One is the fat attached to the stomach and intestines, which can be removed without difficulty, and the other is the sciatic nerve in the thigh, which involves a more intricate operation, but one does not have to be an FRCS to master it.

As we have three – or is it four? – different *kashrut* authorities in Britain, one might think that at least one of them would take the measure of the times sufficiently to break ranks and establish a porging unit, but none will, because each is afraid of the other. Supervisory bodies spend much of their nervous energies supervising each other. The whole issue, however, is becoming academic, for the way things look we shall soon have no *shechitah* in Britain at all.

A few years ago, the chief rabbi, after consultations with his colleagues, agreed to the introduction of a new restraining pen in place of the casting pen hitherto used for *shechitah* in Britain. For a time there was near consensus, which suggested a rare degree of reasonableness in the Orthodox community, but first one dissenting voice, then another, were heard to complain that the arrangement was not quite *kosher*, and they have since grown to a chorus.

Now if there is one area in which there is no room for a holier-than-thou tournament, it is *shechitah*, for where the public attitude to ritual slaughter has always been less than friendly, it is now positively hostile, and if the chief rabbi's proposals are opposed even within the Jewish community, then there can only be one outcome – a total ban.

There would be a certain amount of poetic justice to such an outcome, for the conduct of the *kashrut* industry, with the United Synagogue, the Federation, the Kedassia and the Sephardim all battening on one small declining community has made the whole concept of *kashrut treif*, and if they were all to be forced out of business we might be better off.

29 June 1990

14
Sport . . . and Transport

*There may come a time when Israel will be at
peace with its neighbours, but it will never be at
peace with itself until the principles and practice
of cricket are more widely understood.*

Olympic Games

I WAS AMAZED at the coverage given by Israel's television to the Olympic games, for apart from an hour's summary, at peak viewing times, there were live transmissions right through the night. It left one with the feeling that Israel was among the principal contenders at the games, and that its athletes and players would stagger home bent under the weight of their medals.

As it is, of course, they did not even come within sight of a bronze, and it is perhaps typical that the one event in which they had entertained any hopes at all, was in the millionaire's sport of yachting.

Yet I am not in the least disturbed by Israel's hapless performance. A country faced with so many real challenges can be forgiven for not devoting its energies to the pseudo-challenges of sport, and given what happened at the Munich games in 1972, one wonders whether Israel should have taken part in the Olympics at all.

I draw comfort from the fact that the Olympic games are held every four years, for it means that only one summer in four is darkened by the event. I hate everything about it, the hoo-ha which precedes it, the ballyhoo which accompanies it, the recriminations which follow it. It may only last a fortnight, but it seems to reverberate in the media for months, and it gives rise to insufferable displays of chauvinism. Remember the fuss when a British contender won a bronze (or was it silver?) in the aptly named small bore event? I'm told that people actually stayed up half the night to watch it live. For me the high spot of the games was the sight of this chap Bud Zola tripping up the American runner in the 3,000 metres (or was it the high jump?), though I kept asking myself what he was doing in a women's event? (To which I must add that when I watched some of the Russian women athletes at the Moscow games, I had the feeling that the Olympics had turned unisex.)

I enjoy watching tennis, football, or even cricket (wasn't this a black summer, by the way? I know of someone who, after sitting through the final débâcle at the Oval, decided to go on *aliyah*), but the Olympic games have ceased to be fun, and with their flaming rituals and ritual flames, and their flag waving and their anthems and their sermons, they have assumed something of the portentousness of a religious event. One does not have to be brought up within the Jewish faith to find something repellent about the worship of physique and physical excellence. (One can, of course, go to the other extreme, as we have sometimes done, and regard all form of athletic endeavour with distaste. There is in this, as in all things, a golden mean.)

The most laughable thing about the entire Olympic circus is the talk of the Olympic 'spirit' as a cause of international harmony and friendship. The Olympic games might have been expressly designed for the promotion of international animosity. The Montreal games, it will be remembered, were boycotted by the African states, the Moscow games by the Americans, and the Los Angeles games by the Muscovites and their satellites. Even the friendship one might expect to find among the actual participants is rarely in evidence and was completely absent at the Munich games when competing athletes had no qualms about running over the dead bodies of their murdered Israeli colleagues.

The Olympic 'ideal' is, and perhaps always was, a sham. The Communist states, which begin to train their athletes from the cradle, and who therefore come away with more than their share of medals and medallists, use the occasion to suggest the superiority of their way of life, while the Americans, who in the absence of Communist contenders, almost ran away with the Los Angeles games, showed a braggartry which would have been unbecoming even in a banana republic and which, in a super-power, was grotesque. The games consistently bring out the worst in the participating nations and, not infrequently, in the individual contenders.

That they should have been followed avidly in Israel is understandable. They provided a welcome diversion from events at home.

Israel regards itself as an honorary state of the American union, and Americans as honorary Israelis, and Israelis follow American events almost as closely as their own. Thus they stayed up all night to follow the results of the last American elections, and they will no doubt do the same during the next ones. It was therefore predictable that they would stay up o'nights to watch the Olympics, especially as Los Angeles features in the Israeli imagination as a sort of Tel Aviv on high, and if there was little joy to be had from the performance of Israel's own athletes, there was *naches* (proud pleasure) in abundance from the hon Israelis.

24 August 1984

Basketball in Israel

WHAT CRICKET IS to the Englishman, fitba' to the Scot and baseball to the American, basketball is to the Israeli.

The game has none of the spaciousness one finds in cricket, no green acres, no outfield, or even infield. There is no scope for the wild dash up the wings that one has in rugby or football, or the home runs that one sometimes sees in baseball.

It is a compact and constricted game and, given the fact that most of the players are anything but compact, they need only step out of their own penalty area to be in that of their opponents, which may be why it has become the national sport, for Israel (even 'Greater' Israel) is a small country and a basketball pitch occupies about the area of a drawing-room carpet.

I have watched the game a number of times, with bewilderment rather than pleasure, for it seems to consist of a succession of fouls interspersed with penalties. (The Hebrew for 'foul' is *averah*, which is usually translated as 'sin', and a basketball game is a dramatic confirmation of the talmudic belief that 'sin begets sin'.)

Everyone is running hither and thither, presumably to show that they are not inert, but the movements of the players seem unrelated to the whereabouts of the ball. Occasionally, though, there is a pause while some seven-foot giant leans over the basket and casually drops a ball into it, an action which calls for about as much skill as popping a can of baked beans into a shopping trolley.

But that's how the Israelis like it and when there's a major game

273

in the offing, all life – and, indeed, all death – comes to a halt. Roads turn into pedestrian precincts, shops and restaurants empty out, even *batei midrash* (houses of prayer and study) are deserted, while the nation sits at home, eyes glued to the television screen.

And there is no damned nonsense about playing for the sake of the game – they play to *win*:

> There's a breathless hush in the Close tonight –
> Ten to make and the match to win –
> A timbered floor and a blinding light,
> An hour to play and the last man in.
> And it's not for a place in the world to come,
> Or the selfish hope of a season's fame.
> But his captain's hand on his shoulder smote:
> 'Play up, and win, or I'll cut your throat.'

The trouble is that, while Israelis are good at about everything you could name (plus a few things you couldn't), they are not all that great at sport. They are more eager spectators than participants, and even where they participate, few of them grow to the height necessary for a game of basketball, which is to say, about the height of a mature palm-tree. As a result, clubs anxious to get to the top, and to stay there, have taken to importing their players from America, fully grown and ready made.

There is, of course, an international trade in sportsmen of all sorts. Players are imported and exported like cattle, and Liverpool, for example, at one time fielded an Israeli striker (who promptly struck the ball into his own goal – but that's probably because he was used to reading from right to left).

Such things, however, are – in common with almost everything else – more complicated in Israel for in order to play for a local team, one has to be Israeli, and (given the Law of Return) about the quickest way of becoming Israeli is to become Jewish.

There was an American divine, who became known as 'The Basketball Rabbi' – or the 'Basketballer', to distinguish him from, say, the Bobover or the Lubavitcher – who specialised in instant conversion and out of whose efforts there evolved a new species of Israelite (to add to the three already in being) known as 'the Basketball Jews'.

The Israeli rabbinate has, however, closed that loop-hole (or should one say, hoop-hole?), possibly out of a suspicion that the Basketballer has been pursuing his holy work with an eye to material gain, and hungry though it is for new immigrants, it has refused to accept any new converts from him. As a result, Petach Tikva Maccabi, which is a second-division team, but which recently imported two American players in a bid for promotion, has had to negotiate a different route.

It appears that if one way to instant citizenship is to become a Jew, another is to become the spouse of a Jew or Jewess, and so the two players were taken from Israel (where mixed marriages are not allowed) to Cyprus (where they are) and given Jewish brides. The grooms were in their twenties, the brides in their forties, so that in a sense they acquired not only Jewish wives but Jewish mothers.

I am not sure if it's cricket, but it is the latest trend, and, in the words of the old song, 'it's all in the game'.

2 December 1983

Cricket

IF TWO OCCASIONS were ever made for each other, they are cricket and Shabbat. Has there ever been – can there ever be – a sport so entirely in keeping with the spirit of the Day of Rest? It is not only restful to watch, it is restful to play, and, with the possible exception of listening to sermons, I know of no experience which is more soporific.

The only time (touch wood) I have ever been involved in a road accident was when I inadvertently tuned in to *Test Match Special* and found myself driving in my sleep. (The chap I ran into must have been walking in his sleep, for he was found under my car with a transistor to his ear.)

Fishing, which is but an active way of staying inert, is perhaps even more restful, but it can be cruel, whereas cricket is never less then benign, and what with its white vestments, elaborate rituals,

275

ancient codes, arcane language and mysterious incantations, it is almost a sacred activity in its own right.

The very sights and sounds evoked by cricket, the green fields, the leafy trees, the sunny skies, the click of bat on ball, suggest a benevolent deity smiling on a happy land, and men at ease with their Maker. And is it not written somewhere that 'the beginning of Wisden is fear of the Lord'? – which may also explain why to many a Jew, the Lord's Day means a day at Lord's.

Cricket is, with the exception of teatime, Marmite and wellington boots, England's greatest contribution to civilisation, and if the Empire has receded, the game has not. It is still played in the Antipodes, the Indian sub-continent, the West Indies and South Africa (better, in fact, than in England itself). It never took on, however, in Canada, but then Canada is half French, and the French have never had the serenity necessary to appreciate the game; and, of course, Canada is too cold.

And it never took on in the Holy Land, but then the Holy Land was under British rule for only 30 years, which is hardly more than the duration of an extended innings and, as any groundsman will aver, it can take more than 300 years to prepare a good wicket.

It may, I think, be readily admitted that the hundreds of thousands of immigrants who have poured into Israel since 1948 have, on the whole, not been cricketing types, but they have included a few ex-colonials, like Indians and South Africans, and sundry Anglo-Saxons, whose influence has been out of all proportion to their number and who have imported, along with other elements of their culture, an ingrained love of cricket.

This does not mean that all life stops when a game is played, or that one can hear ball-by-ball commentaries on Kol Yisrael. In fact, cricket is almost completely ignored by the local media, enjoys neither patronage nor even passing goodwill from the sports authorities, and, if anything, suffers from tacit discrimination.

On a recent Saturday, a number of Indian immigrants were enjoying a quiet game of cricket in an Ashdod park, when about 1,000 spectators suddenly invaded the pitch. When I first read of the incident, I thought they may have been Australians protesting against a decison of the umpire, but they did not look Australian, for apparently they were bearded and in black and they were not brandishing cans of Foster's lager.

They were also shouting 'Shabbes!' 'Shabbes!', which is not an expression to be found in any cricketing almanac, either English or Australian, and it appears they were, in fact, religious zealots protesting against the *desecration of the Sabbath*, which shows how far our religious academies are removed from the realities of life.

Now, if the game had been rugby, as currently played in this country – or basketball as played anywhere – one might have been able to understand their feelings, but there is nothing to cricket which can be construed as a breach of the Sabbath, and the invasion of the pitch, and the threats to the players were a double desecration, both of the day and of the game. And what is worse instead of shielding the victims, the police urged them to draw stumps and move to another part of the town, where they could play unobserved, as if they were engaged in something obscene.

There may come a time when Israel will be at peace with its neighbours, but it will never be at peace with itself until the principles and practice of cricket are more widely understood, and until every *yeshivah* student is given a thorough grounding in the game, for it is not only the ideal recreation for those excessively engaged in study, but it can, given the normal pace of a game, actually be combined with study, especially when fielding. And, of course, it also teaches patience, tolerance and the idea of fair play.

It would, I suppose, be difficult for a *yeshivah* to field a team in white (except on Yom Kippur), but there is no reason why players should not be kitted out in black. Nor can I imagine such a team abiding by the verdict of a solitary umpire (or two) and one might have to supply a Beth Din. But, apart from that, the spread of the game would give a new meaning to the spirit of the Sabbath, and lead to greater amity throughout the land.

28 May 1982

Back to their routes

FORGET *KOSHER* WINE, *kosher* milk, *kosher* lettuce, or even *kosher* drain-cleaners. We now have *kosher* buses – at least they do in Bnei Brak, courtesy of the Dan bus co-operative which, in turn, is subsidised by the Israeli taxpayer. As bus companies nowadays like to give their vehicles snappy titles, the Bnei Brak bus will no doubt come to be known as the Kosher Rusher, or maybe even the Sheitl Shuttle.

It was, I suppose, inevitable. Hitherto, there were men and women sitting together in the same part of the bus, and sometimes even – *chas vecholilleh* (perish the thought) – in the same seats.

And it was not only a matter of sitting together. One daren't describe the scenes which ensued when the buses had to brake suddenly – as they do so often in Israel. All that has now stopped, for the Bnei Brak Beth Din, after deliberating on the matter for 40 days and 40 nights, has, in its infinite wisdom, ruled that, henceforth even unto for ever, local buses will be segregated, with male passengers sitting in the front half, and female passengers in the back. Women are also required to buy season tickets, so that there will be no physical contact between them and the driver.

Ideally, they should have separate buses for the different sexes, with men drivers and women drivers; except that, in Bnei Brak, women of an age to drive a bus are usually pregnant and they might experience some difficulty in getting behind the wheel, or even reaching the brakes.

What I think will eventually happen is that – in the time-honoured tradition of the Orient – men will go by bus and women on foot. The new *kosher* buses are thus probably an interim measure and, in fact, represent something of a concession to modernity. Even so, certain questions arise. Why should the women have to sit at the back? Rabbis never tire of telling us that Jewish women are treated like queens and placed on a pedestal. If this is so, should they not be at the front?

This is not merely a matter of courtesy. Bnei Brak ladies, as I have already suggested, are usually laden internally. They are also often

278

laden externally and clamber on to buses *sheitls* askew, dripping with sweat, encumbered with infants, shopping and pushchairs. Why, then, should they have to push their way to the back?

It would also be interesting to know if there is a no-man's land – or, for that matter, a no-woman's land – to separate the two halves. Or, to put it in another way, do they have a desexualised zone, akin to the demilitarised zones to be found in various other parts of the world?

What do children do? Are they free to travel in either half of the bus, or are they also segregated? And what happens if the women's half is full and the men's half is half-empty – or vice versa? Will passengers be expected to stand and leave the empty seats vacant?

The maximum penalty for smoking on a British bus is £1,000. What is the penalty for mixing on a Bnei Brak bus?

Do the buses carry external signs of identification, like a *kashrut* certificate, on their windscreens? Do men and women embark and alight at different stops?

And, finally, what happens when the buses go beyond the sacred purlieus of Bnei Brak and penetrate the unholy reaches of Tel Aviv? Are passengers free to jump to their feet and mix promiscuously?

The matter has provoked fierce debate in the Knesset, where Naomi Chazan, of the Left-wing Meretz Party, and Naomi Blumenthal, of the Likud, have complained that public money is being used to subsidise sexual apartheid and that the segregation constitutes a denial of human rights.

It is reassuring to know that there are issues which transcend political differences in Israel. But there can hardly be a denial of rights where people are actually prepared to forgo them – as they patently are in this case.

It is true that the Bnei Brak Beth Din did not hold a public inquiry before reaching its decision, but it is obviously a popular one. In the few weeks since segregation was introduced, passenger traffic has increased by 20 per cent.

I am old enough to remember a time when there were 'women only' waiting rooms on British railway stations and 'women only' compartments on British trains. But there were no 'men only' compartments or waiting rooms.

Now that's what I call a denial of human rights.

28 July 1995

Internal combustion

ISRAEL HAS NO North Sea oil. It did have a bit of Red Sea oil, but that's going back to Egypt. It also had what it calls its 'Little Texas' near Kiryat Gat which, on closer examination, turns out to be very little Texas, for the area contains about enough oil to fuel a sizeable primus stove. It used to get most of its oil from Iran. (In the olden days, when you mentioned that fact, people would put a finger to their lips and whisper: 'Shah!')

In other words, the country has a fuel crisis. You wouldn't think so living here, because it has so many other crises (including the economic crisis – which is no joke – the immigration crisis, the *yerida* crisis, the stadium crisis, the fodder crisis, the Jesus crisis. The Jesus crisis? Well, that's another story about which I hope to write later) that one more crisis passes almost unnoticed. Nevertheless, various means have been proposed to combat it, one of which was a carless day. It received short shrift. Many Israelis have cars; some hire them; others steal them; and the rest regard themselves as prospective car-owners in temporary non-possession of a vehicle.

It is generally believed that the state religion round here is Judaism, but that's only a front. The local deity is the Internal Combustion Engine. When people come home after a day's work they will anoint it with various expensive oils, or prostrate themselves under it as a devout Muslim prostrates himself on his prayer rug, and face Detroit.

I may add that Chief Rabbi Ovadiah Yosef has given some thought to the matter and has, in his infinite wisdom, found that Jewish law demands safe driving, but he has yet to appoint a corps of *mashgichim* (supervisors) to enforce it and in the past four months 249 people have been killed on the roads. The number nearly grew to 250, and the *JC* was almost deprived of a valued contributor, when I stepped out of the garden and into the path of a Volvo which was reversing at about 70mph. I should perhaps point out that I live in a one-way street, and if an Israeli wants to go up a one-way street in the wrong direction – and he usually does

280

– he will do so in reverse. There are so many one-way streets, with so many vehicles reversing down them, that a newcomer to the country might feel that he is in breach of the law if he drives forward.

The immense reverence accorded to the Car (or, as the devout would have it, the C-r) in this country means that there is no such thing as an abandoned vehicle. When a driver finds that his brakes have failed, that his steering is faulty, that his doors won't shut, that his tyres won't grip and that his lights won't function, he doesn't merely leave his vehicle by the wayside, as he might in England; he continues to drive it – as long as the hooter is in working order. In other words, people are about as likely to accept a carless day as a foodless day, and in Israel there isn't even such a thing as a foodless hour (a matter to which I hope to return in a later week).

Another fuel-saving suggestion – and one which happily has even less chance of acceptance – is the compression of the working day. Israel's day is divided into three main watches: from eight to one, when everyone rushes round in a frantic fury to get things done or, more usually, undone; from one to four, when everyone sleeps (housing contracts have clauses requiring children to be kept silent during those hours); and from four to seven, when the country comes alive. It has been suggested that if people worked in one continuous stretch from eight till four, there would be no need to keep shops and offices open till seven, and thus (I don't know how) there would be an important saving in fuel.

The temperature around here has been in and around the 90s for much of the summer and has sometimes reached 100 and it isn't the temperatures which debilitate so much as the humidity. I work in an air-conditioned room and when I emerge into the street it's like being hit in the face with a warm, wet rag, but at about five in the afternoon – especially in Jerusalem, which I visit frequently – there is a sudden change in the air, as if a new soul has been blown into the atmosphere.

It is my favourite time of the day, even in England, tea time, when the world is at its most amiable and relaxed. A breeze springs up and smells of pine and eucalyptus come wafting in, distant laughter and distant snatches of conversation. People become less limp and less testy, their very clothing seems more crisp, their voices become softer and less raucous. The houses empty and the streets fill up, and if you stand at the corner of Ben-Yehudah (part of which has now been made into a pedestrian precinct) and George V at about six in the evening, you will meet everyone you have known in the past 25 years.

The shops are full, and cash registers ping away like sleigh-bells. The cafés are crowded and people dare contemplate a hot drink like café *hafuch* (literally, overturned, alias, expresso coffee: Israel is the last resort of the expresso machine and I, for one, am grateful for it).

Israel lacks the long, lingering twilight of the north and at about seven the day suddenly darkens, as if someone has pulled a blind, and people turn for home, the discomforts of the torrid day forgotten in the vivaciousness of the evening hours. I can't see the Israelis forgoing them for all the oils of Arabia. Nor, for that matter, can I see them forgoing their siestas – there would be a serious drop in what they call 'internal-*aliyah*' if they did.

17 August 1979

Vandalising bus shelters

ON FRIDAY, 11 JULY, 1986, on a day which will go down in infamy, Israeli feminists vandalised ten Tel Aviv bus shelters.

This, on top of the innumerable shelters vandalised by our black-coated brethren in Jerusalem and elsewhere, may make Israeli bus shelters an endangered species. It also suggests that, far from being torn apart by *kulturkampf*, Israel is united by a common hatred of bus shelters.

My suspicions on this matter were aroused some months ago. I was about to cross Herzl Boulevard in Jerusalem (always a hazardous undertaking) when an ambulance suddenly screamed out of nowhere and hurtled straight into a bus shelter, demolishing the shelter and almost demolishing the three people in its shade.

That same week, another shelter was demolished by a lorry and, as both shelters advertised a well-known brand of salad dressing, I wondered if the vandals were merely protesting that Israelis preferred their salads undressed. Further reflection, however, convinced me that a more sinister motive was afoot and that these were the actions of incorrigible shelterphobes.

Why should anyone hate bus shelters? They, after all, provide shade against the heat of summer and – albeit to a much lesser extent – against cold and the rains of winter, but it is possible that people hate them because they hate buses and it is easier to get at a shelter than at a bus.

And they hate buses because their very need to resort to them is a constant reminder either that they cannot afford a car or, worse still, that they can afford a car, but that they cannot afford to use it. (They may also hate bus drivers, but that is a perfectly natural sentiment which calls for no explanation.)

A more likely reason, however, is that Israelis have no blood sports. They don't go in for bullfighting or hunting and shooting, and they have little scope for fishing, if only because Israeli fish tend to be tame and domesticated and bred in ponds, and, as a result, people have turned upon bus shelters instead.

If this is the case, and the practice cannot be eliminated, it should at least be controlled. Bus shelter vandals should have to take out a licence (which could be an important source of revenue) and there should be a closed and open season for vandalising bus shelters, if only to allow time for new ones to be built.

In Britain, for example, the grouse-shooting season begins on the Glorious Twelfth, that is, 12 August. Israel could have the Glorious Fifteenth – that is, the fifteenth of Av, a wine festival which was the occasion for great jollification in the days of the Second Temple, but which, possibly because the jollification became too great, was allowed to lapse with the passage of time.

It would restore a colourful date to the common memory and bring some vivacity to an otherwise dull time of the year – and it could be a major tourist attraction.

Some difficulties might arise out of the fact that here is an area in which groups as diverse as feminists and the Neturei Karta share a common passion, and to avoid the dangers of mixed vandalising, one would have to set aside certain days of the week (or certain locations) for men, and other days and locations for women.

As the Neturei Karta were, after all, pioneers in this field, their religious susceptibilities should be respected. For the same reason, one would have to make sure that no shelters are vandalised on the holy Sabbath. (Is there, incidentally, a blessing to be uttered on putting a bus shelter to the torch? If not, one could possibly adapt the blessing for Chanucah lights.)

If the idea is taken up, the bus shelters would, I think, have to be moved from the main centres of population and set up by the nature conservancy in places like Galilee and the Arava. And, given the difference in climate between the two, one could even have a summer season in the former and a winter season in the latter.

In the meantime, while shelters are being destroyed indiscriminately without let or hindrance, and while the authorities seem helpless to do anything about it, I intend to set up a committee of Friends of Israeli Bus Shelters, to be known by its acronym, FIBS. Donations will be gratefully received.

25 July 1986

End of the line

I HEAR THEY'VE closed one of the most beloved of all Israeli institutions (beloved, that is, by me) – the Jerusalem – Tel Aviv railway line.

It was said to be losing money. There are few railways anywhere which aren't and, offhand, I can't think of any public institution in Israel which is actually making money.

It is also said that it is quicker to travel by bus. Well, there, I must confess, critics may have a point, for I suspect it may also be quicker to travel by bicycle and there are times when it could be quicker to go on foot.

Middle Eastern railways are not renowned for their speed, and it is possible that the Children of Israel took 40 years to cross Sinai because they took the slow train from Kantara, stopping at Rameses, Succoth, Etham, Baal-Zephon, Migdol, Pene Hahiroth-on-sea, Marah, Elim Spa, the Wilderness of Sin, Dophkah, Alush, Rephidim (the same is Bir Gaf Gafa), Kibroth Hatta'avah, Hazeroth, Rithma, Rimmon Perez, Libnah, Rissah, Kehelatha, Haradah, Makeloth, Tahath, Terrah, Mithka, Hashmonah, Moseroth, Bene Jaakan, Hor Hagidgad, Jotbathah, Abronah, Etzion Geber, Kadesh Barnea and Mount Hor (which, for Aaron, at least, was the terminus) and all stations to Jericho.

The Jerusalem–Tel Aviv train made scheduled stops only at Beth Shemesh and Ramleh. It sometimes made an unscheduled stop to let a camel cross the line or to allow a goat to browse on the greenery between the lines, and took about two and half hours to cover the 40 miles.

As buses take about 45 minutes, the railways are not a favoured means of travel for men in a hurry, but just in case they should be, the railway company located the terminus on the southern edge of Tel Aviv, miles from anywhere, so that even those who might be tempted to travel by train still had to take a bus to get to their destination.

It was a journey to yesterday, an excursion out of time, and although I must have made the trip (as far as Ramleh, at least) more often than I've had hot dinners, I made it yet again every time I was in Israel.

There is (or was), first of all, the railway station itself, an imposing edifice built by the Turks nearly 100 years ago and still in fairly good shape. Bus stations in Israel are like a grinding vortex, but the railway station, even in the rush hour, is almost like a retreat; one half expects to hear the sound of bells summoning one to matins.

The train, though by no means magnificently appointed, was never crowded and set off slowly, clattering through the streets of Baqa like a tramcar.

Once out of town it gathered pace and a few miles on, it moved gracefully through the charming Arab village of Beit Safafa. Before 1967, Beit Safafa was in Jordan while the railway line was in Israel, so that one had only to lean out of the window to be in enemy territory.

From there the train entered upon a biblical landscape as it wound its way, slowly and majestically, round the Judean hills, with the river Sorek gurgling below.

We were in what one might call the Samson country, for Samson 'loved a woman in the valley of Sorek whose name was Delilah,' and there was something along every inch of the line to beguile the eye and the imagination.

Closing the line is an act of wilful desecration – and worse. Tradition hath it that the Messiah will come to Jerusalem on a donkey. I must admit that I myself have a weakness for donkeys because, apart from anything else, they are easier to park and less expensive to maintain than horses.

The first of the many times that I lived in Israel I could not afford a car, bicycles were too hazardous, and I therefore acquired a donkey. I don't know what it would be like in Tel Aviv, but it is ideal for getting around Jerusalem especially the stepped narrow streets of the Old City, and one doesn't even have to feed it, for it helps itself to the vegetation in the surrounding gardens.

I used to think that what was good enough for the Messiah is good enough for me, but now believe that, if he will come at all, he will come by train (on a Pullman, probably). No train, no Messiah.

23 May 1986

Wandering Jews

OUR YOUNGSTERS ARE becoming wandering Jews.

In the beginning, they assembled in their multitudes in Golders Green, hard by the station, and tarried for many a long night, till they encamped up the line at Edgware which is in Middlesex, where they multiplied exceedingly and covered the station fore-court like the sands of the sea, to the discomfort and dismay of those who actually wanted to catch trains.

And their elders came beseeching them to move, but they moved not, and the police did the same, but still they moved not, until the

Lubavitch came upon them with a *mitzvah* tank, and threatened all who tarried with *havdalah* wine, whereat they fled in great disorder and pitched in Hampstead, by the heath (the same is the wilderness of sin), where they have remained unto this day.

I could not for the life of me understand why anyone with a roof over his head, or even without, should want to cross London to congregate in either Golders Green or Edgware station, and even the attractions of Hampstead have their limitations when the crowds descend and it's almost impossible to move – until it dawned on me that the crowds themselves are the attraction.

Jewish youngsters, while individualistic in some respects, are like sheep in others, and will travel any lengths and suffer any discomfort to be where the others are. The actual venue is immaterial. If it is Hampstead today, it could be Kilburn High Road tomorrow. Wapping the next day, and the Isle of Dogs the day after that.

Some youngsters, in their desperation for company, have been known to resort to synagogue, which is why so many synagogues are filled to overflowing three times a year.

The matter should, I think, be kept in perspective. The youngsters may be boisterous, but no one has suggested that they are drunk, violent or destructive. The police, it seems to me, have been a little high-handed, for the youth are not in breach of the law, and as long as they keep moving (if only in a circle), they cannot even be charged with causing an obstruction.

Their nuisance lies in their number. One is saddened by the thought that, in a metropolis which has so much to offer, so many youngsters should have nothing better to do with their time. It does suggest a certain emptiness of mind and vacuousness of character, but it does not amount to a social calamity.

Our rabbis and communal leaders have been wringing their hands over the phenomenon, and there have been calls for more money to build more youth centres. Money indeed seems to be regarded as the panacea of our age. One only has to mention a problem and immediately there is an appeal for funds.

We are not at all badly off for youth centres. There is a splendid one in Ilford, and another in Hendon; and, in fact, every major synagogue in the capital has extensive social facilities which could be easily adapted to the needs of youth, to say nothing of Maccabi and the various centres run by the Zionist youth groups.

If the community were to build an Albert Hall of a youth centre in the middle of Hampstead Heath, with discos and coffee bars and milk bars (and perhaps even a library), it might attract the crowds for a year, perhaps even two, and then gradually it would begin to echo with its own emptiness.

There is a paradox to Jewish gregariousness, and it is this. Everybody wants to be where everybody else is, as long as not everybody else is there. In other words, it must have a passing claim to exclusiveness, but once the *nochschleppers* (those trailing along behind) *schlep* along and the pubescents intrude upon the adolescents, the in-places are out.

The great advantage of the street is that it is free, and as one area falls out of favour and another comes into vogue, nothing is lost.

Unfortunately, English streets are not built for crowds. They allow for ingress and egress, but not for people who actually want to stop there, and I have every sympathy with the residents of Hampstead who have to suffer their incursions, or the motorists who have to inch their way through milling crowds which overflow into the roads.

What London really needs is a Dizengoff, which was built to cope with Jewish gregariousness, but Dizengoff is fortunate not only in its spaciousness, but in its climate. Such places call for sunny days and balmy nights. Here, alas, we only have cold nights and barmy youngsters.

24 October 1986

15
Around and About

There is no rush hour in Tel Aviv. They rush all the time and the more frantic their efforts to get around, the longer they stay in place.

Farewell to the Atarah

I HAD HEARD that Pizza Hut was looking for a central site in Jerusalem, but did they have to take over an institution as cherished and as venerable as the Atarah café? Could they not have settled for the Western Wall?

When I first lived in Jerusalem, in 1951, half the city seemed to derive its livelihood from selling beverages to the other half. And, at that time, every second shop in and around Zion Square was a mittel-European-style café set up by mittel-European immigrants who had been forced to make their homes in the mittel-East.

Their establishments did not quite fit into the local scene and those who hankered for an Oriental café or who were otherwise anxious to turn native had to take a bus up to Machane Yehuda, where they could get a Turkish coffee, thick as mud, in a tiny, chipped cup served by a chap in a fez (who was probably from Bialystok).

There was a shortage of everything in those days, certainly anything one might reasonably wish to eat or drink. The coffee was ersatz and, if its consistency and flavour were anything to go by, I suspect it was made of pulverised plywood.

One could also get cream cakes made with ersatz cream, and one went to the different cafés not so much for the food or drink, as for the company and ambience – though, of course, it was the company which made the ambience.

The oldest café, I think, was the Vienna, which had a large Mussolini-style balcony overlooking Zion Square from which politicians sometimes harangued crowds in the streets below. I never set foot in it because I was offended by its name.

A little way up Jaffa Road, near what used to be the Egged bus station, was the Navah, which is still there. This used to have a garden so large that one could spend a day there without catching sight of a waitress – or rather, the waitress never caught sight of you.

It had the best pastries – my favourite was something called *streusel kuchen* (crumble cake). It seemed to be patronised largely by German-speaking matrons in fancy hats and reminded me of the Cosmo café in Swiss Cottage.

Opposite the Vienna, in the shadow of the Zion Cinema (now no more), stood Kapulski's (now no more), which was the least expensive café in town, and which was the hangout of the Begin crowd. It could not have been a large crowd, for it was a small café, but their politics weren't mine, and I did not feel at ease among them.

At the other extreme – politically – was another café, known familiarly as The Kremlin, which is still in business, and which was the redoubt of unwashed, long-haired Bolshie types, who smoked Turkish cigarettes and spoke in conspiratorial whispers of the coming revolution.

Nowadays, I suppose, they are all friends of the Earth and smoke pot. All conversation would stop when I entered the place because, in those days, I was clean-shaven and wore a *kipah*, and I eventually became a regular at the Atarah. *Kipot* were also rare there, but not so rare as to cause alarm, and the politics at the Atarah were more akin to mine.

It was also, as I soon discovered, the favourite venue of the Anglo-Saxon crowd, most of whom were about as Anglo (or Saxon) as I was, but we passed for Anglo-Saxons in Jerusalem.

The Hebrew University had been exiled from Mount Scopus in 1948. The new campus at Givat Ram was still being built, and many students, and not a few dons, used the Atarah as a refectory and common room.

The old Knesset building was only a few yards up the road so that one also encountered the occasional professional politician. The rest of us were amateur politicians and we sometimes had heated debates lasting late into the night.

Life was earnest in those days, as were we. When I returned to the Atarah in later years, the atmosphere had become more relaxed, even frivolous, especially after the area was converted into a pedestrian precinct, and the cafés moved the chairs and tables into the street.

I suppose the open skies and the bright sunshine were partly to blame, but where we used to cogitate upon the future of Zionism, Israel and mankind, young couples sat around holding hands and rubbing noses as if they were in Paris.

Indoors, however, one could, in less crowded moments, still recapture the atmosphere of the old Atarah. And there were compensations. The coffee was real coffee, and the cream was real cream, though, alas, one had to pay for it with real money.

Everyone has his own particular vision of Jerusalem. The Atarah was part of mine. The place won't be the same without it. A curse on pizzas!

9 February 1996

Tel Aviv

I HAVE BEEN to Israel about 20 times (I've lost count) since the Yom Kippur War, and I generally stay in Jerusalem. Last week, however, the hotels were so full that I had to stay in Tel Aviv, which, to me, was a novel, and rather pleasant, experience.

I hate the sight of the great, grey slabs of concrete in what I call the Valley of the Hotels, on Hayarkon. Are they bunched so closely together in their own ghetto to insulate tourists from contact with the natives? But ugly as they are on the outside, they are well appointed and comfortable inside and, by European standards, offer excellent value for money. The standards of service are not all they could be, but standards elsewhere in the world have deteriorated so fast that those in Israel seem fairly high.

I am an early riser, at least in Israel, for I like to get my work done before the heat of the day sets in and I asked to be woken at five. But I was woken at 4.30, not by the hotel, but by a sound like heavy drops of oil falling into a barrel – plick-plock, plock-plick; plick-plock, plock-plock, plick . . .

I pulled open the curtain, walked out on to the balcony, and there on the sands, among the swirling mists of dawn, were the first of the beach-tennis enthusiasts swinging their rackets and thumping the ball, plick-plock, plock-plick; plick . . . And not only them. There were stocky white-haired figures doing a Ben-Gurion, with their heads in the ground and their legs in the air. Others were on their backs pedalling away furiously as if they were riding some invisible bicycle.

So much energy put to so little use. If they could only be harnessed to a generator they might go far towards solving Israel's fuel shortage. A woman like the Rock of Gibraltar emerged from nowhere and bore down upon the waves with such fury that the waters seemed to recoil at her approach, and for the first time I grasped the full meaning of the expression from the 114th Psalm *hayam ro-ah vayanos*, the sea saw, and fled.

By six the beach began to fill with figures running, jumping, skipping thumping, in the water, on the sands, wrestling with unseen adversaries like Jacob with the angel, glistening with sweat, panting, puffing, huffing, snorting. Large men with bulging biceps, like swarthy Popeyes; thin men with shrill voices and sunken chests, like Olive; short men trying to expand; fat men trying to contract; and all manners of men swinging their hefty trunks this way and that, that way and this, in an apparent attempt to detach their top half from the bottom – could they be Chasidim? And then the women again, each bigger than the other, a whole troupe of them, holding hands, and they remind me this time of the Irish song: 'Where the mountains of Mourne go down to the sea.'

As the morning progresses, the crowds change. The dawn brigade are the earnest brethren, the body-builders (though they sometimes give the impression of being body demolishers), who rush religiously to their morning exertions as a zealot rushes to his *beit hamédrash*, and who will be there every morning, come summer, come winter, and then go off to their labours.

About eight the dilettantes begin to descend. They toil not, neither do they spin, but arrive merely for pleasure, in towelled dressing-gowns and sunglasses, with little plastic shields on their noses, which make them look like birds of prey. And they come hauling whole pharmacopias of lotions and balms and hand-creams and foot-creams and face-creams and creams for other places, and a carton or two of yoghurt to fend off hunger, and a Thermos to fend off thirst, and a radio to fend off quiet.

And then a group of small children in yellow *kovahs* (floppy sun hats) and red tee-shirts, at first in semi-regular columns, then exploding in all directions with whoops of glee at the sight of the sea, with their harsh-voiced, hoarse-voiced escorts panting after them. 'Yigal, get out of the water or I'll break your arms and legs .... Yuval, get out of that dustbin ... Zvicki, not here, you're too big for that ... Yoram ...' The poor women seem at the end of their tether, though the day has only begun. In the meantime there are small flecks of red and yellow, darting everywhere, until somebody opens a hamper and they all swarm towards it like bees to a honey-pot.

The plick-plockers and plock-plickers have grown in number, whole lines of them, and disc throwers, and ball pitchers, and one cannot move without suffering their cross-fire, but the ice-cream vendors who weave among them seem to lead a charmed life. 'Artik!' 'Limon!' 'Limon!' 'Artik!' The market used to be dominated by small boys, but they seem to have been undercut by Arabs.

The family parties arrive, fathers, mothers, brothers, sisters, uncles, cousins, with here and there a crumpled ancient in a large straw hat, and tourists from the hotels with flowing kaftans and peeling skins, dusky belles with husky escorts, and by noon the Israelites have multiplied until they are as the sands on the shore.

A black pennant hangs limply from the lifeguard's perch, which suggests, presumably, that the sea is dangerous and swimming is forbidden. The lifeguard blows his whistle until he is blue in the face, but the sea is black with bobbing heads, one cannot swim for swimmers and if there is any danger at all it is from the congestion.

The hours pass, the crowds ease, the waters empty. The sun grows until it fills half the sky, a vast sphere of glowing scarlet. Then, as it begins to sink, it seems to melt in the water, and the waves lapping the shore turn red. The beaches fall silent. A slight breeze ruffles the sand, then suddenly, as if a blind has been pulled, it is night.

10 July 1981

Jaffa

TEL AVIV HAD but one public building of distinction, the Herzlia gymnasia at the top of Herzl Street, which they pulled down about 20 years ago to make way for the tallest and, almost certainly the ugliest, building in the Middle East – the Shalom tower. Well, the Society for the Uglification of Israel (SFUI), which seems able to sweep everything before it, plans to do the same for Jaffa harbour.

The northern coast of Israel has many attractive features, especially around Acre, but south of Caesarea there is nothing to gladden the eye, and a great deal to sadden it, until one gets to the towers and minarets of Jaffa, or Joppa as it was called in the olden days, a small port of great antiquity and infinite charm, built round a lofty promontory, and buffeted by the blue waters of the Mediterranean Sea.

It was the point of entry for the great cedars of Lebanon used in the building of both the First and Second Temple: 'And we will cut wood, of Lebanon, as much as thou shalt need, and we will bring it to thee in floats by sea to Joppa; and thou shalt carry it up to Jerusalem,' and when Jonah sought 'to flee from the presence of the Lord,' he 'went down to Joppa and he found a ship going to Tarshish.' (And a fat lot of good it did him.)

It is also the home of Andromeda's Rock, which should not, however, be compared to Brighton rock. Andromeda, an Ethiopian princess, was, according to legend, chained to a rock near the harbour mouth to assuage the wrath of a sea monster until she was freed by Perseus.

I am not sure if Andromeda ever existed and, if she did, whether she was chained to that particular rock, and if she was, whether Perseus swooped out of the skies to rescue her, but it's a good story, and in any case how many people would put their hand on their heart and swear, that, say, King David's tomb on Mount Zion actually contains the remains of King David? Antiquity should never be scrutinised too closely.

It is some years since Jaffa had any significance as a port but it still offers a livelihood to about 200 Arab fishermen, and it has all the bustle and colour which goes with the trade, the small craft bobbing in the harbour, the nets drying on the sands, the tarred warehouses, the cobbled quays, the shrill cries of seagulls, the pungent smell of fish, and the tanned, leathery features of the fishermen themselves.

For me, as many others, the pleasures of a visit to Tel Aviv lie mostly in Jaffa, and they are all under threat, for there is a $20 million conspiracy afoot to banish the fishermen and the fishing boats, to bury Andromeda's Rock itself under concrete, and to convert the ancient port into a vast marina for 800 yachts.

Eight hundred! As is well known, most yachts in Israel are owned by dentists. Could there be that many dentists in the country? And if so, are they all that prosperous?

People are now making strenuous efforts to save what there is left of 'old' Tel Aviv, by which they mean buildings which date back to the 1930s, but they seem to lack the determination to save Jaffa, which has real claims to antiquity, from the developers.

Large parts of the sea front are no longer accessible to visitors, and one area is defaced by a hideous high-rise building (with a penthouse at the top which was one of the several homes of the late Moshe Dayan). Old buildings have been demolished and replaced by expensive edifices in mock antique-style, housing expensive art galleries, boutiques, and plushy apartments, and the non-rich are being prised out and priced out of Jaffa. The plans for the port, however, have gone a little too far, and they have aroused local resentments to the point where Jew and Arab have made common cause to withstand any further depredations. They deserve the support of everyone who prefers the old and the mellow to the brash and the new.

Mr Shlomo Lahat, the mayor of Tel Aviv-Jaffa, though with impeccable Right-wing credentials, has found that what is good for the developers is not always good for Tel Aviv. I think he will find that the same is even more true of Jaffa.

Jaffa as Jaffa is unique. Jaffa, as yet another marina, would be commonplace.

14 August 1987

Glasgow

WHEN GLASGOW, OF all places was designated the 1990 Cultural Capital of Europe, it sounded like a joke. It was rather like designating Dublin the Sobriety Capital, or awarding Tel Aviv the annual prize of the Noise Abatement Society, but the choice has been triumphantly vindicated. For the past 12 months the city has been a place of pilgrimage for lovers of music, drama and the arts, and it looks as if it might remain so.

A friend of mine, the late Tom Honeyman, who was director of the Glasgow Art Gallery, loved the city, but sometimes despaired of it as the ultimate resort of the philistine, and he once said to me, 'the trouble with the place is that it hasn't nearly enough Jews.'

Nobody seems to be quite sure what the Jewish population of Glasgow is, and the most frequently quoted figure is about 8,000, but their impact on the cultural life of the city is out of all proportion to their number.

When the choice of Glasgow as the cultural capital was first announced the local Jewish community decided to make its own distinct contribution to the year with a festival of Jewish culture and the matter was taken in hand by a sisterhood of volunteers headed by three remarkably active – and remarkably attractive – young women, Louise Naftalin, Linda Goldberg and Ann Furst.

The festival lasted for about two weeks, but the preparations took nearly two years and not a few husbands I encountered had the woebegone look of men who had forgotten when they last ate a warm meal, or slept in a well-made bed, to say nothing of other, less-mentionable, services.

The sisterhood had to arrange events and book halls long before they could be sure of having the money to pay for them, getting artists to perform in them, and, most important of all, getting people to attend them.

It was an act of faith, but one which was abundantly fulfilled. They compiled a programme which included performances by the Israel Philharmonic, the Amadeus Trio, Giora Feidman, Ida Haendel; the Scottish premiere of Sobol's *Ghetto*, exhibitions of work by Jankel Adler, Josef Herman and Dora Holzhandler; and discussions between various Jewish writers, including David Daiches, Elaine Feinstein, Bernice Rubens, Frederic Raphael, Arnold Wesker, Chaim Potok, and another Chaim, a large bearded gentleman, the wisest and most genial of men, whom modesty prevents me from naming. The patron of the event was Jeremy Isaacs, director of the Royal Opera House, Covent Garden, who also presided over the writers' symposium.

Jeremy and I – in case I may not have mentioned it before – are both Glaswegians, and Glaswegians tend to be sentimental about their home town, especially after they have left it, and there is no danger that they may have to go back to it. So no doubt we are biased, but we both agreed that an event like this could not have been held in any other Jewish community in the country.

There was almost an element of *chutzpah* involved in dreaming up something so ambitious, but they got away with it, and almost every event attracted a full house. Chaim Potok, who has lectured all over the world, could not believe that something so large could have been staged by a community so small.

Glasgow has never been a hotbed of Jewish Orthodoxy and unlike, say, Manchester, or parts of London, it is not in the grip of a religious revival even now. Where there were a dozen synagogues it now has five, and the *yeshivah* I attended gave up the ghost when the principal gave up his post. Intermarriage was, and still is, rife and I recall any number of prognostications that the community would fade into oblivion in a generation or two.

It has certainly shrunk. Jews have a wanderlust, and so have Scotsmen, but there is nothing quite like the wanderlust of Scottish Jews. One finds them everywhere, in Israel, Australia, America and, above all, in London. As the festival has shown, however, Glasgow Jewry, even if smaller in size, continues to flourish.

There seems to be a general belief that provincial communities can survive only by retreating to the ghetto, but Glasgow has shown that, given social cohesion and intellectual vigour, one can remain an integral part of the host society without forfeiting one's Jewish soul.

7 December 1990

Beautiful Israel

I AM FORTUNATE in that my work takes me to Israel at least once a year and I always try and be there between Purim and Pesach, after the rains have stopped and before the heat of summer has shrivelled the greenery to a dusty brown. An Israeli spring is like an idyllic English summer: an English spring is but an extension of an English winter. Oh, not to be in England now that April's here!

Israel, if one avoids the large towns, is particularly beautiful this year, for the rains have been abundant and I found many a forsaken wadi tinkling with water like a mountain stream. The Wilderness of Judea, which is normally stark, barren and forbidding, was as green as the Pennines, though its fauna is infinitely more exotic. On a hillside near the Inn of the Good Samaritan (which, I should perhaps add, is not a place to quench a thirst) I came upon a conclave of storks, dozens of them, some pecking fiercely at the ground, some, with wings extended, jumping excitedly up and down, some moving dejectedly in ever-narrowing circles, like Cabinet ministers fretting over a budget cut.

Israel is an ornithologist's paradise and within its small orbit one can find as large a variety of birds as in the whole of Europe. In the Bet Shean Valley I took a stroll among the fish ponds of kibbutz Tirat Zvi. I am not, I am sorry to say, particularly light-footed (or, for that matter, light-handed) and at my approach a whole cloud of birds shot up from the reeds – storks, herons, pelicans, sandpipers, swallows, finches, grebes, warblers, wagtails, sparrows, white-headed gulls, black-headed gulls, moorhens, ducks, geese, and one particular creature about the size of a rook with a coat of so many colours that I was tempted to call it the Joseph bird. I even thought I saw a vulture but that may have been an apparition conjured up by my age and my state of health. They darkened the sun with their number, circled noisily at a distance, and returned as soon as I left. They may be bad for the fish, but they're good for the eye and they freshen the spirit.

I am told that the depredations of the birds are so heavy that some kibbutzim are talking about abandoning fish-breeding, but given the bird life the ponds attract, they would, as far as I am concerned, justify their existence even if they did not yield a single marketable fish.

The roadside verges in the Emek, the Bet Shean Valley and well up into Galilee were shrill with flowers, asphodels, hyacinths, wisteria, cyclamens, delphinium, lupins, irises in every conceivable variety (I counted at least six), wild orchids and, most common of all, bright red anemones. One can find them all in England, but rarely in such profusion, and never at the same time. The anemones especially show such an eager animation that they almost threaten to leave the ground. They are particularly abundant around Safed, and seen from a distance they gave the impression that whole hillsides were flickering with flames.

My own favourite is the orange blossom. One finds the flower and fruit on the tree at the same time, which strikes the English eye as somewhat incongruous. One expects the old generation to give way to the new, but not in Israel. They somehow manage to co-exist, and on a calm, balmy night, they exude a scent which is almost intoxicating.

Only one sight darkened my eye, and that was near Mayan Harod, in the Emek. Who, I would like to know, has been cutting great chunks out of the Mountains of Gilboa as if they were a Dutch cheese? There's God in tham there hills and one should hesitate to tread on them, let alone quarry them. Who allowed the desecration? I am not normally in favour of the death penalty (except for such crimes against humanity as watering whisky, or playing the radio full-blast on an Egged bus), but anyone scarring a hill open to the public view – and especially in so historic a range as the Gilboa – should be stoned with rocks from his own quarry. I am told that some of the kibbutzim in the area may be responsible. If true, it will confirm my suspicion that kibbutzim have merely replaced individual cupidity with collective greed.

And while I'm grumbling, let me grumble about something else – though the matter is a comparatively minor one. I went to Israel hoping for a dip. Even in Jerusalem the daytime temperature was in the upper 60s, which is the sort of temperature one hopes for in England on a decent summer's day. In the Bet Shean Valley it was nearly 80, which in England would be considered a heatwave, and I trudged from kibbutz to kibbutz hoping for a swim; but all their pools were closed in the apparent belief that anyone who sets foot in water before May will – or at least should – perish of cold.

Finally, I decided to suffer the heat until I came to the Sea of Galilee and there, among the reeds opposite Kibbutz Degania, I began to strip. A stout, motherly woman with a large handbag, noticing my convulsions (for it isn't easy to get into one's swimming trunks without taking off one's trousers – though I have nearly mastered the act) hurried over in alarm to ask what I was doing.

'I'm going to have a swim,' I said.

'A *swim*?' she said, in a tone which reminded one of Edith Evans in the role of Lady Bracknell.

'A swim.'

And satisfied that I was merely crazy, but not suicidal, she went on her way.

And she was right. The Sea of Galilee was like melted ice. I now feel equipped to brave the Serpentine on Boxing Day.

10 April 1981

Back in Jerusalem

SO HERE WE are, back in Jerusalem. Last time we were here, we lived in the centre, in Rehavia. This time, we had to have a larger flat and we had to go to the outer fringes of the city before we could find one, and I am at his moment sitting out on a balcony with a sun-umbrella over my head, a bottle of Chenin Blanc by my side, and a cat at my feet, overlooking the Jerusalem Forest.

It was worth coming out here just for the view – and the forest was handy, too, when it came to finding *sechach* for our *succah* – though tell it not to the JNF. On second thoughts, you can tell it. after all those seven bobs for trees I had paid out or collected throughout much of my youth, I felt entitled to a twig or two in middle age.

The flats themselves are nothing much to look at, but the beauty about living in them is that one doesn't see them. They are also more formidably built than any flat I had hitherto occupied in Israel, which is to say, one can pull a plug out of the wall without pulling away half the wall with it.

The neighbourhood we live in was completed only two or three years ago, which means it still looks like a building site, and the whole area is strewn about with rubble and timber and odd bits of machinery; and I feel tempted to use the building material I can see all around me to run up a villa on an adjoining site, which is what

302

a lot of the natives go in for.

The flats are built against the side of a hill, so that if one enters on one side, one goes *up* a flight of stairs, and if one enters on the other, one goes *down* two flights. I still haven't quite got my bearings and keep going up when I should be coming down, and coming down when I should be going up; and as the furnishings round here are fairly standard, I have sometimes wandered into a neighbour's flat thinking it was my own, and settled down for the evening until I noticed that the wife and children were different.

On the side of the flats overlooking the forest we have a ravine (into which I nearly toppled one dark night – do I hear cries of 'Why didn't you?'). On the other, we have 39 steps, which form our link with the rest of the city and which are a source of distress to some of our neighbours, not because of their number and steepness (which are a source of distress to me), but because they seem to trap every bit of paper and dirt flying about Jerusalem.

Jerusalem may be a heavenly city, but it has more than a few citizens who do their level best to bring it down to earth, and many of its streets look as if they have lately formed the route of a paper chase. And not only paper. There are plastic bottles and glass bottles, cans of every variety, old shoes, discarded mattresses and, most ubiquitous of all, melon rind.

Mayor Teddy Kollek has a council for the beautification of Jerusalem which has worked wonders round the Old City and elsewhere. Also, the trash-collecting services are better in Jerusalem than in London (and infinitely better than in Hampstead Garden Suburb, where the dustmen hold the public to ransom), but in the last resort, if the public is not interested in the cleanliness of its surroundings, they'll get dirty, and many a Jerusalem street is like an overflowing midden.

Anyway, one evening I was finding my way back down the 39 steps when who should I find but a neighbour – Mrs Daphne Leighton, late of Mill Hill – and what should she be doing but sweeping the steps, all 39 of them.

Prices have gone berserk in the past few months and I thought she might have taken a job with the municipality to help out with the housekeeping, but it wasn't quite like that. She couldn't stand the dirt and the mess, and as nobody else seemed disposed to do anything about it, she rolled up her sleeves, took out a broom, and set about cleaning the place herself.

She told me that a neighbour of hers, also from England, used to do the same, but had given up. Mrs Leighton has been here only two years and I suppose when she's been here another, and she and her family turn native, we'll have to take over (unless, of course, we should have turned native first).

I can't honestly say that I personally am too troubled by the mess in the neighbourhood, for what with the ravine on one side of us, and the 39 steps on the other, I rarely set foot outside and am waiting until they either build a road on one side of us, or a funicular on the other, or both.

In the meantime, I have the balcony and the view of the forest, and the view beyond the forest to the Jerusalem hills. One can see earth-movers and bulldozers busy in the distance and in another year or two every escarpment will be covered with flats as charmless as the one we occupy; but for the moment I can still lift up mine eyes unto the hills and see the hills, and luxuriate in my surroundings.

The drawback to it all, of course (and there is a drawback to everything) is that I'm so preoccupied by the scenery that I find it difficult to get down to work.

22 October 1982

Jerusalem in the rain

ADVICE TO ANYONE contemplating *aliyah*: don't.

No, I take that back. Come by all means, but bring an umbrella, wellington boots and, if possible, a rubber dinghy with an outboard motor.

Normally one wakes in Jerusalem to blue skies and bright sunshine. This morning I woke to black clouds, cold winds and a cloudburst, and as I watched the street outside forming into a muddy lake, I thought to myself: 'For this I've got to come to Israel?'

Different people come here for different reasons, but I should imagine that one factor which enters into the calculations of every Briton who makes his home in Israel is the weather. We had unbroken sunshine for the first six weeks of our stay and I began to feel almost nostalgic for the grey clouds and moist air of *der heim*. (I have many *der heims*. When I lived in Glasgow, it was Latvia; when I was in London, it was Glasgow; now that I'm in Jerusalem, it is Hampstead Garden Suburb.)

The feeling was deepened as I listened to an excellent programme on the poetry of John Betjeman on Galei Zahal one evening (Galei Zahal, incidentally, is the Israeli forces network. Could you imagine a broadcast on a foreign poet on BBC Radio One?) and I yearned for the gurgle of rain in the gutters.

Well, we've had it now with a vengeance, except that the rainwater, when it comes, doesn't gurgle here – it rages, and, as there would appear to be no drains, it rushes along the thoroughfares in broad rivers. An umbrella offers some shelter from the skies, but there is no escaping the splatter of mud (and latterly of slush) from the passing traffic.

But in a way I welcome the change, not merely because it is a change, but because a break in the weather can restore one to reality. While the sun shone and the skies were blue and noon temperatures were in the 80s, I couldn't escape the feeling that I was still on holiday, and that I would be abusing the beneficence of nature if I actually got down to work. But now, as the torrents splash about me, I can finally return to my labours.

Jerusalem was built for sunshine and does not look at its best in the rain, while Jerusalemites seem to double in size with jerseys on top of sweaters and sweaters on top of jerseys and flock-lined anoraks as bulky as quilts. Buses seem to be full even when they're half empty, and stranger begins to talk to stranger, both through a shared sense of discomfort and because the weather (as in England) gives them something to talk about.

Those who find the weather irksome can easily escape it. While Jerusalem shivered in the rain and the snow, Tel Aviv, which is only 40 minutes away, was basking in warm sunshine. Temperatures in the one were in the 40s, in the other they were in the 70s, while in Jericho, which is even nearer than Tel Aviv, but which is downhill all the way, they were in the upper 80s.

My favourite television programme is the weather forecast

which follows the nine o'clock news. Each region is depicted by a different scene. The scenes depicted, I may add, bear no relation whatever to the region in question. For the Golan Heights, for example, they have a pair of alligators basking in the sun, and for the seashore they have a pair of playful rhinoceroses (rhinoceri?), as if they were part of the natural fauna of the area and could be found browsing in Ashdod Park.

But the amazing thing about the forecast is the climatic variations from region to region. The Golan has one sort of climate, the northern valleys another, the Judean hills a third, the foothills a fourth, the sea-shore a fifth, the Jordan valley and the Dead Sea a sixth, the Negev a seventh, and Eilat an eighth; and anyone unfamiliar with the geography of Israel must feel, when watching the forecast, that the country is about the size of China, whereas one can comfortably traverse it in the course of a day.

There is, at most times of the year, a smaller range of temperatures between London and Athens, which are over 2,000 miles apart, than between Safed and Tiberias, which are only about 20 miles apart. What Israel lacks in size, she makes up for in variety.

Jerusalem is about the coldest, wettest and windiest place in the country, but before the *va'ad ha'bayit* (the house committee) has agreed to light the central heating, and before a mechanic is found who knows how to get it into working order, 'the winter is past, the rain is over and gone; the flowers appear on the earth; the time of the singing of birds is come; and the voice of the turtle is heard in the land.'

The truth of the matter is that the birds round here never stop singing. And when we went for a walk in the Jerusalem forest last Shabbat (it has become as much a part of our Shabbat ritual as going to *shul*, and infinitely more pleasurable), the pathways were bright with wild crocuses (though I'm still on the look-out for turtles). And in any case, the rigours of winter can never feel that rigorous when one knows that summer is but 40 minutes away.

11 February 1983

16
War Crimes

*One cannot redress the impotence of one age
with excessive zeal in another.*

The Western Front

THE FIRST WORLD WAR (1914–1918) was the bloodiest in
British history. Nearly a million men perished on the battlefield. A
further two million were seriously injured. The bombardments
were endless and the slaughter incessant.

In one campaign alone, the abortive attempt to dislodge the
Germans from Ypres in the autumn of 1917, Britain suffered more
than 300,000 casualties.

Life was cheap and, in such an atmosphere, any man who was
deemed to be shirking his duties could face execution for desertion
or cowardice. In the course of the war, 312 British soldiers were
shot by British firing squads.

It was a barbaric penalty and, for the families immediately
affected, it involved a double tragedy, not only the death of a
cherished son, but the shame surrounding the circumstances of his
death.

In recent years, attempts have been made to obtain a
posthumous pardon for the men involved, but they have got
nowhere. This is a pity, not only because the penalty was excessive
but because, in some instances, it was totally undeserved.

I know of one man who was almost certainly the victim of a
miscarriage of justice, because all the evidence suggests that he was
guilty of confusion rather than cowardice.

I came across his case while writing a book on the East End
some 20 years ago. He was 18, the only son of Russian-Jewish
immigrants living in Whitechapel. In 1915, at the height of the
slaughter on the Western front, he volunteered for the army
without telling his parents. At first, he was more worried by
the distress he caused at home than the dangers he would face
at the front. He was clearly an immature 18-year-old and his
letters were semi-literate, which somehow adds to their
poignancy:

> Dear Mother, I arrived safe and everything is alright. I was
> very sorry to leave you, and very sorry to see you cry as much as

you did, but never mind, I will be back one day, so be happy at home.

Dear Mother, do not forget my nineteenth birthday May 1st. Tell Father and Kate to be happy . . . from your loving son Aby.

Dear Mother, I would like your photo to hold on to me.

A few months later he wrote from the front: 'I have been in the trenches four times and come out safe.

Dear Mother, we go in the trenches six days, and then get relieved for six days . . . You write you was nearly going mad waiting for my letters. You know it takes two days to get to London or more . . .

Dear Mother, I know it is very hard to miss me from home, but still never mind, be happy and don't cry. I think you know I'm sorry I done that, but if I have luck I will come home . . . I might be home for the Jewish holidays.

But he did not get home for the holidays and months passed without a word from him.

Then, early in 1916, his parents received a letter from the War Office informing them that he was 'ill at 38th, field ambulance, suffering from wounds and shock (mine explosion).'

It is clear from his letters that he had no idea what had hit him. He spoke of injuries to his back and foot, and bed sores but he was, in the main, concerned to reassure his mother that he was being well looked after.

He made no reference to the mine explosion or the shock, but the extent of his injuries may be measured from the fact that he spent a month in hospital and subsequent events suggest that his recovery may have been far from complete.

On 20 January 1916, he was discharged from hospital and sent back to the front. At the end of February he was in difficulties:

Dear Mother, We were in the trenches and I was ill, so I went out and they took me to the prison, and I am in a bit of trouble now and won't get any money for a long time. I will have to go in front of a Court. I will try my best to get out of it, so don't

310

worry . . . I will let you know in my next how I got on.
Give my best love to Father and Kate.
From your loving son,
Aby.

There was no next letter. After two months of silence the family received a curt note signed by a Lieut-Colonel P. G. Hendley:

Sir, I am directed to inform you that a report has been received from the War Office to the effect that Number —, 11 Battalion, Middlesex regiment, GS, was sentenced after trial by court martial to suffer death by being shot for desertion, and the sentence was duly executed on 20 March, 1916.

11 November 1994

The bombing of Dresden

'FIFTY YEARS ON, the bombing of Dresden still haunts the conscience of the West,' declared *The Times* on 13 February.

It doesn't haunt my conscience, not for a minute. And it wouldn't have bothered me if the whole of Germany had been flattened. But then, I am still haunted by the newsreels of Belsen and Buchenwald I saw towards the end of the war, and by the knowledge of what my grandparents, cousins, uncles and aunts suffered at the hands of the Nazis.

I also lived through the Blitz, and I felt then, as I do now, that the Germans had it coming. From July 1940 until June 1941, German planes devastated almost every urban centre in the British Isles. London was battered by night and by day. Liverpool, Plymouth and Coventry were eviscerated. Coventry, indeed, was adopted by the Germans as a byword for obliteration.

There were few raids on Scotland but I still remember the Blitz

311

on Clydebank, some 20 miles from my home. The earth quaked, windows shook, and the fires burned so fiercely that they turned night into day.

News was heavily censored. The full extent of the damage inflicted by the Luftwaffe was withheld from the public, and I grasped what 'Blitz' really meant only when I visited London shortly after the war. In the City, St Paul's was like an island in a sea of ruins. In the East End, whole streets had vanished. Blackened buildings stood out amid the rubble like bad teeth among rotting stumps. The docklands were a wasteland and wild flowers grew in the desolation. Large parts of the West End were devastated.

It was the Germans who pioneered blanket bombing with the devastation of Guernica before the war, who developed it further with the destruction of Warsaw and Rotterdam, and who perfected it with the raids on London and Coventry.

It was the Germans, too, who developed the concept of total war which placed unarmed civilians in the front line. Over 23,000 men, women and children perished in the Blitz between July and December 1940. Over 35,000 were to perish in Dresden alone, but, in the words of Air Chief Marshal Sir Arthur Harris, the head of Bomber Command: 'The Germans had sown the wind, and reaped the whirlwind.'

Harris now features in the liberal imagination as a terrorist and war criminal, but both Harris and Churchill believed that the German war effort could be undermined by the destruction of the country's industrial centres. We now know with the benefit of hindsight that they were mistaken, but there was no mistaking the boost to public morale occasioned by the raids on Berlin, Hamburg, Bremen, Düsseldorf, Cologne, Frankfurt, Essen, Stuttgart, Nuremberg and other major cities.

The campaigns on land and at sea were all distant from Germany and it was Bomber Command which carried the war to the heart of the enemy. Things in Britain were fairly bleak and news of the bombings gave a good start to the day. The price in manpower and aircraft was heavy. Of the 795 planes which took part in the raid on Nuremberg, in March 1944, for example, 94 – each with a crew of seven – failed to return.

In all, Bomber Command lost more than 80,000 men and, in retrospect, one must ask whether the damage inflicted on the

Germans was equal to the losses suffered by the Air Force, but that is not a moral issue. Nor is the fact that Dresden was a beautiful city and a major cultural centre. So were Berlin, Cologne, Frankfurt and Nuremberg, but their ready acceptance of Hitler and Hitlerism had damned them all, as it had damned the entire Third Reich, including Austria.

The Bishop of Coventry, who attended the memorial service in Dresden to mark the fiftieth anniversary of the raid, showed commendable forgiveness, but I felt that, given the seat of his diocese, his breast-beating was excessive.

It is true that a smaller total of 400 people were killed in Coventry, as against the thousands who died in Dresden, but there is no strict accounting in total war. Or, as the German president, Roman Herzog, said: 'Life cannot be balanced against life, pain against pain.' If it could, Germany would remain eternally overdrawn.

It was left to the prime minister of Saxony to put events in their true perspective. He linked 13 February 1945, with 30 January 1933, the day Hitler came to power. The one, he said, was the outcome of the other.

17 February 1995

Holocaust studies

IN AMERICA, MOST universities are private foundations dependent largely on the benefactions of private individuals. Like universities everywhere, they have been going through hard times recently and have had to cut down some departments and close others, but there is still one topic which represents a growth area, the Holocaust, and one has the impression that one need only mention the subject for purses to spring open of their own accord.

In a recent issue of *Commentary*, Robert Alter, professor of Hebrew and comparative literature at Berkeley, California, mentioned that there are now no fewer than 93 courses in Holocaust studies being offered at American and Canadian universities. At least half a dozen Holocaust research centres, he added, have come into being, including such major foundations as the National Holocaust Resource Centre, New York, and the Wiesenthal Centre for Holocaust Studies (of which more later) in Los Angeles.

In some respects this is a welcome trend, for it could be argued that one cannot know too much about the Holocaust, and that one must dwell upon it in detail not only out of deference to the memory of the 6,000,000 dead, but to counter the suggestions that it never took place.

Yet, as Professor Alter shows, the subject is being approached with excessive zeal and insufficient discernment with results which, he believes, could lead to 'serious distortions of the Holocaust itself and, what is worse, of Jewish life'. A lot of knowledge, crudely dispensed, can be a dangerous thing and a course on the Holocaust unsupported by an infrastructure of general Jewish studies can, I believe, be harmful.

Of the 93 academic institutions offering courses on the Holocaust, nearly *half* do not touch on any other aspect of Jewish life, as if the Exodus, the wanderings in the wilderness, the giving of the Torah, the rise of the Jewish Commonwealth, the Babylonian exile, the golden age in Spain, the *haskala* (Age of Enlightenment) and all the other episodes of Jewish history were but stations on the road to Auschwitz. Jews have not only died, they have lived. To harp on the Holocaust as the central event of Jewish history to the exclusion, almost, of all others is to be guilty not only of imbalance, but of masochism.

There seems to be an ineradicable belief that by making people – and not only Jewish people – more fully aware of exactly what happened in Europe between 1933 and 1945, one is doing something to guard against a repetition, but, in fact, the more one is exposed to horror, the less one is horrified, for one becomes gradually deadened to enormities. Moreover, if one is at all a normal human being one does not need a PhD in Holocaust studies to be convinced that it is wrong to slaughter innocent men, women and children.

On the other hand, if one is an abnormal human being – and psychopaths lurk on the fringes of every society – one might not only take pleasure in the sight of such slaughter, but try to emulate the ways of the slaughterers. I suspect that the passion for swastika armbands and other Nazi regalia among skinheads was inspired partly by that unspeakable television drama on the Holocaust which, I believe, has also spread the idea that Jews may be humiliated and attacked with impunity.

Excessive concern with the Holocaust can also have a pernicious effect on Jewish attitudes to the outside world. It intensifies paranoia and the sense of isolation, and I believe that the extraordinary support which Mr Begin enjoys in the diaspora is due not so much to what the Arabs have done, or might do, as to what the Germans have done; or, as Alter says:

> . . . the effect of such Holocaust-centred thinking is to introduce at least a faint undertone of panic into political discussions by superimposing the images of past murderers on present adversaries . . . To invoke the Holocaust as the supreme paradigm of the historical experience of the Jewish people is to preclude the idea of political bargaining and concessions . . .

It also feeds the hatreds of extremist cliques like the Jewish Defence League.

But beyond that, the unique character of the Holocaust demands that its evocation be handled with sensitivity and imagination. Yet it is already clear that in some instances, self-appointed remembrancers have approached their task with the delicacy and tact of men trying to stage a three-ring circus.

Professor Alter quotes the handout of a multi-media project being planned by the Wiesenthal Centre in Los Angeles (for which, incidentally, funds are still being solicited):

> This multi-screen, multi-channel sound, audi-visual experience of the Holocaust will utilise a 40-foot wide and 23-foot high screen in the configuration of an arch, three 16mm film pro-jectors and a unique Cinemascope lens, eighteen 35mm slide pro-jectors and pentaphonic sound (five source), all linked to a central computer which will control all functions simultaneously. It will be a definitive educational medium on the subject.

To which Professor Alter adds:

Definitive, one might say, except for the omission of a computerised, convector-current olfactory unit to waft about in seven presequented patterns the odour of rotten bread, potato peels and scorched flesh.

31 July 1981

A time for justice

SZYMON SERAFINOWICZ, A Byelorussian carpenter, was arraigned before Surrey magistrates last week for the alleged murder of four Jews between October 1941 and March 1942.

The hearing excited comments in every paper. Nearly all of these included some reference to Bosnia, as if there were any comparison between what happened in Russia 54 years ago and what is happening in the Balkans now.

The civil war in Bosnia has been raging now for three years. It may continue to rage for a further 30. All wars are cruel, and civil wars are particularly cruel. The only difference between this and similar wars in earlier periods of history, is that this particular conflict, with its attendant miseries, is being fought out in front of the cameras – and sometimes for their benefit.

Both sides have been guilty of atrocities, though the Serbs, being the more powerful, have been the more vicious. Both have been callously indifferent to the plight of their own civilians where there was a good photo opportunity in the offing.

I half suspect that the Bosnian Muslims may have abandoned Srebrenica in the hope that the sight of long lines of hapless and bedraggled refugees might induce America, or the European powers, to take military action against the Serbs.

There were no cameras or cameramen about when Jews were being herded into death camps or slaughtered elsewhere. Nor did Jews represent an armed threat to any group. They were hounded down and wiped out wholly and solely because they were Jewish,

316

without the benefit of 'safe areas', however tenuous.

There have been many war crimes trials in the past 50 years. And, if recent events in Bosnia show anything at all, it is that there is no deterring the war criminal in his hour of triumph.

Which brings me back to Szymon Serafinowicz. Serafinowicz is from Byelorussia. So am I.

I was born in a shtetl called Breslev in what was then Poland, but is now Byelorussia – or to get my post-Cold War geography absolutely right, Belarus.

My grandmother lived there, and numerous uncles, cousins and aunts. They were all murdered by the Germans or local auxiliaries. I stayed with my grandmother shortly before the war, and left some weeks before the borders closed. I was lucky not to have shared her fate.

And yet I regret that Mr Serafinowicz has been charged.

I return to a point I made when the War Crimes bill was first debated. I said then that if anyone was brought to trial, the jury – and the wider jury beyond the court – would not see the innocent young victims mowed down in the forests, but the doddery old men hunched in the dock. Serafinowicz, frail, white-haired, with sunken cheeks, broken and bewildered, lives up in every detail to the vision I had then.

He is 84 and so far has only had to face committal proceedings. He will be at least 85 before he is brought to trial, 86 before the process is complete. If his looks are anything to go by, I wonder if he will live that long. Even if he does, of course, it can by no means be assumed that the jury will find him guilty. If it does, he will end his days in a prison hospital instead of his Surrey home.

Some will welcome his trial, noting that, whatever its outcome, justice will have been done. Yet to many people, the process will seem an assertion of brute vindictiveness. A new generation has grown to maturity to whom the war years are history and it could be argued that, even if Serafinowicz is exculpated, the trial would be a salutary reminder of what Nazism really meant.

The same was said when John Demjanjuk was hauled before the courts, but all the Demjanjuk trial did was to bring the whole judicial process into disrepute.

Distant events, however heinous, in distant places have not the same impact on human emotions as ones close to home. Had

Serafinowicz been brought before the courts 40 years ago, or even ten years ago, it would have been different.

But now the alleged culprit has already emerged as something of a victim. His arrest has caused loud resentment, which will grow louder if the trial takes place, and which will rise in a crescendo as it proceeds. We may owe it to the memory of the dead to demand justice, but should also give some thought to the interests of the living.

I return to the words of Sophocles which I have quoted before, but which are worth quoting again: 'There are times when even justice brings harm.'

21 July 1995

Trials and tribulations

ONCE AGAIN, HOW wrong I was.

When the possibility of war crimes legislation was first aired in 1989, I wrote:

> If a Bill enabling the authorities to act against alleged war criminals is tabled at the end of this year, it is unlikely to become law before the end of next year, and, given the pace of legal proceedings, the first case will not be heard before the end of 1991 . . .

Committal proceedings did not in fact begin until 1996, but I was, unfortunately right about everything else.

I said that the parliamentary debates would arouse a great deal of anti-Jewish feeling, which they did, and for good reason. The crimes in question were committed by foreign nationals, against foreign nationals, on foreign soil. Britain had the authority to extradite the criminals but not to try them in a British court, and retroactive legislation was therefore necessary.

318

Such legislation always creates a dangerous precedent, and can be defended only if there is a realistic prospect of any criminals being brought to justice. As I said at the time, there was none:

> Once the trials begin, the jury will see not the innocent victims who were slaughtered in the forests and swamps of Eastern Europe, but broken old men standing in the dock who were alleged to have slaughtered them . . . I doubt if any jury will come up with a verdict of guilty.

And I was right again, except that, in this instance, the jury, after hearing the testimony of three doctors, took one look at the 85-year-old Szymon Serafinowicz and dismissed the case before it began.

Professor David Cesarani, who was an adviser to the Home Office war crimes unit, believes that the whole effort was justified because, apart from other considerations, five cases are still being investigated and there is a good chance of a further trial succeeding because one of the prospective defendants is a mere 75.

The prosecution, however, chose to indict Serafinowicz not because he was the oldest, but because, in its view, the evidence against him was the strongest. They would obviously have alighted on the younger man first if they thought they had a strong case against him.

I cannot see the matter being carried further, and I cannot see the prosecution succeeding if it is. The 75-year-old would be nearly 80 by the time he is charged and it is not difficult for an octogenarian to convince doctors and a jury that he is unfit to plead.

Professor Cesarani comforts himself with the thought that Serafinowicz was not pronounced innocent, but then, neither was he pronounced guilty.

The war crimes legislation and the trials which ensued have proved equality futile in Australia and Canada. There has been no such legislation in America because the American constitution does not permit it, which is why the Los Angeles-based Wiesenthal Centre used its very considerable influence to press for such legislation in Britain.

There are two things that could be said – and were said – in favour of the legislation. The first is that no man should get away with murder, especially mass murder, no matter where and when it was committed. The second is that the laws would be a deterrent. Unfortunately, however, where there are wars there will be war crimes, and an armed thug with people at his mercy is conscious only of his power and not of the consequences he may have to face if his side should lose.

Even the Nuremberg trials, the most publicised in history, and the subsequent hangings, did not deter Pol Pot, Idi Amin and the other mass murderers who have emerged since the war. And they eventually lost. How many mass murderers are still at large in China, in the former Soviet Union and the former Yugoslav republic?

The first of these points remains unanswerable but, given the years which have elapsed since the crimes were committed, it is too late. There is no point in making more enemies if, at the end of it all, we will be doing nothing to further the cause of justice.

The beginning of wisdom is to know when to cut losses. It has been tried; it has failed. We should try no more. It is time we put the whole issue behind us.

As I have said before, and as I hope I will not have to say again, Jewish resources and emotional energies can be applied to better things.

We cannot forget the past, nor should we, but let us concentrate on the future.

31 January 1997

17
Celebrations
and
Anniversaries

I have no immediate plans to celebrate the second millennium, or even the third, and I find it difficult to understand the whole fuss about anniversaries.

Satmar wedding

I HAVE READ so many different, and differing, reports about that Satmar wedding that I am no longer sure if there were 25,000 guests at a cost of £415,000 or 415,000 guests at a cost of £25,000. But even if the former version is correct, it must have been the biggest wedding since the whole of Athens turned up for the nuptials of Theseus and Hippolyta.

And, like all true extravaganzas, it was held on ice, or at least in an ice stadium. Why, you may ask, an ice stadium? Why not in the Yankee Stadium, or Carnegie Hall, or the more than adequate Madison Square Gardens?

Well, at Chasidic weddings it is customary for the bride to circumnavigate the groom seven times with a flaming candle in her hand, which, to someone not used to walking, can be quite a *schlep* (especially if the groom is bulky), and presumably on this occasion the bride wore skates, otherwise she might have had to go on a bicycle, which can be awkward with a flaming candle in your hand.

It is also difficult, when catering for 25,000 guests, to keep the champagne adequately chilled, and about the only way of getting round the difficulty is to have both the drink and the drinkers on ice. It also ensured that the jelly that accompanied the *gefilte* fish stayed properly jelled and did not decline into a molten mess.

I should imagine that the freezing temperatures evoked warm memories of Satu Mare (or St Mary's), the Romanian *shtetl* from which the Satmar sect draws its name, and, for once, the fur hats worn by Chasidim on festive occasions were not out of place; one only hopes their wives wore fur coats.

It was, by all accounts, a jolly affair, and the men danced with men and the women with women. This custom, though hitherto limited to Chasidim, is now fairly widespread in America, especially on the West coast, and some rabbis are known to frown on it as a *chukas hagoy* (a Gentile custom).

The music was played by the Matzevoth (or Memorial Stones),

323

a well-known Chasidic ensemble, augmented on this occasion by the New York Philharmonic Orchestra and the Beadles.

The bride, Miss Bruria Sima Meisels (19), and the bridegroom, Mr Menachem Mendel Teitelbaum (18), are first cousins, and grandchildren of the Satmar rebbe. They had to marry each other, for if either, or both, had married outside the family, the wedding could quite easily have been twice, or even four times, as big.

It is possible to get even 50,000 people under one roof, but the seating plan would have posed insurmountable problems. There were, I gather, difficult moments even with the 25,000 guests, for they included 5,000 rabbis, each of whom was hoping to say 'a few words', and 1,800 *chazanim*, each of whom was hoping to recite at least one of the *sheva brachot* (seven blessings). Perhaps they got the rabbis to talk in unison and the *chazanim* to sing in chorus.

Not a few people have expressed surprise at the scale of the affair, for Chasidim have always been modest in manner, humble in bearing and frugal in taste, and a wedding for 25,000 does verge on the ostentatious, while the cost of it all could have paid for a *yeshivah*, fed the hungry and housed the homeless (a subject on which more than one Satmar Chasid can speak with authority).

But Chasidim were modest, humble and frugal only when they were poor, and when one is poor, one doesn't have much chance to be anything else. The Satmar Chasidim – in common with others – have come upon better times.

Some of the benefits which are normally stored up for the pious in the world to come have been vouchsafed them in this one, and the Talmud does say that a man should live, and be seen to be living, according to his means. Moreover, this was no ordinary wedding, but a *royal* one.

Now, we had a royal wedding in this country a few years ago which was also the focus of fairly widespread attention, and although the parents of both the bride and groom were, by most standards, fairly well off, they limited themselves to a mere 2,000 guests.

But then, Lady Diana Spencer was a commoner, whereas in this instance both the bride and groom are of the blood royal. Moreover, as a family spokesman explained, they were not only celebrating a union, they were acknowledging divine beneficence. A modest affair would, in the circumstances, have smacked of ingratitude.

Finally, I understand that not all of the 25,000 people at the wedding were, in fact, invited guests. A great many people had turned up in the belief that they were about to see an ice-hockey match.

21 December 1984

Oyez, oyez

IN *DER HEIM* it was easy.

The *shammas* banged the table two or three times to obtain silence and then announced that the entire congregation was invited to the barmitzvah or wedding, or whatever. It was all so simple and straightforward that I sometimes wonder how people made enemies in those days.

Here it is rather different, for we, of course, live in the land of the printed invitation.

I still remember the first invitation we received. It was in gold lettering on cream-coloured vellum and, but for the fact that it was printed in Hebrew as well as English, we might have taken it for a diploma and framed it.

In this country, by and large, invitations, if sometimes ornate, are fairly functional. In America, they have been getting out of hand. I have seen one barmitzvah invitation which came in the form of a slim volume, with photographs of the young man depicting the various stages en route to his reaching manhood.

First he was shown as a chubby infant on an alpaca rug, then as a plump youngster on the way to school, and finally as an overblown barmitzvah boy, with a *tallit* round his shouders and a prayerbook in his hand – probably the first and last time he would be seen holding such an object.

Wedding invitations are even more elaborate, for, of course, they have two lives to depict and prospective guests are sometimes presented with a historical family album, with the young couple

325

apart in the earliest photos, then together, each pose more intimate than the next.

In this country, as I have suggested, we are more reticent and more to the point, but even so I'm beginning to wonder whether we should not dispense with printed invitations altogether, for they are almost specifically designed to create enmities – and I speak as a veteran with many children, who already has one barmitzvah and two batmitzvahs behind him and who is now about to celebrate another barmitzvah.

I must say right away that batmitzvahs are not a problem, for although the girls look pretty enough, they are always processed *en masse* and one is reminded a little of the emperor who baptised his army with a hose.

It is quite otherwise when a boy celebrates his advance to manhood, and no matter how many lists one makes and consults, and no matter how one racks one's memory for everyone who should be invited, one inevitably forgets someone, like, say, one's father-in-law. Moreover, if one has a large family and many friends, one cannot always remember what has befallen them. We can all fail to forget somebody living, but a far more serious offence is to invite somebody dead.

Another more contemporary hazard is to invite Mr and Mrs X when Mrs X is by now Mrs Y; or worse, when Mrs X is still Mrs X, but cohabiting with Mr Y. And there are even more complicated relationships which I daren't mention in a family paper. The whole thing, I tell you, is a minefield.

Then, added to the vagaries of one's memory are the vagaries of the Post Office, and one can be fairly certain that at least five per cent of the invitations will go astray. At my last *simchah* (joyous occasion), I enclosed reply cards and was outraged at the number of people who lacked the courtesy to reply whether they were coming or not, only to discover that they were equally outraged because they had failed to receive an invitation at all.

This time round, being more experienced, I was much wiser, sent no reply cards, but added 'RSVP' and my telephone number at the bottom of the invitation. Most people, needless to say, did not bother to reply and I phoned them instead (am I glad I've got British Telecom shares), only to find that nearly ten per cent of them had not received an invitation at all. But I was at least able to avoid the misunderstandings of the earlier occasion.

It is, all things considered, unlikely that I shall have yet another barmitzvah to celebrate, but there is the possibility of other *simchas* and I hereby give notice that if and when they arise, I shall do as they did in *der heim*, bang the *shul* table (I shall have to do so myself because in our *shul* they can't afford a *shammas*), and issue the invitations by word of mouth.

6 September 1985

Nuptial nerves

I HAD JUST about finished paying for the barmitzvah of my second son, when I was suddenly faced with the prospect of paying for the wedding of my first daughter.

I had vague intimations that my daughter was growing up when I came home one evening and found a line of battered cars without, and a horde of scruffy youngsters within. Could one of those ghastly creatures, I kept wondering, end up as my son-in-law?

I need not have worried, for she left for Israel the moment she finished school and joined the army (my daughter the soldier!) and as she was frequently stationed in or near one kibbutz or another I toyed with the hope that she might marry into the landed gentry. Not out of snobbery, you understand. It was more crass than that. If you marry a kibbutznik they pay for the wedding. They even arrange for the band and the flowers, and you roll up half an hour before the event, a guest at your own daughter's nuptials . . . you don't even have to bring a present. Marvellous institution, the kibbutz.

Needless to say, it didn't work out like that. She is marrying a medical student (my son-in-law the doctor!).

I have at various times fulminated against the extravagance, size and vulgarity of Jewish weddings, and this I thought might be an opportunity to demonstrate what a Jewish wedding should be,

327

small, tasteful, intimate, inexpensive, a quiet little gathering of family and friends.

But again it didn't work out like that (it never does, does it?). First of all I have married into a vast and fertile clan which grows by the hour – I used to add, *v'ken yirbu* (and so may they multiply) but I've stopped doing it because it only encourages them – and we had to advance the date of the wedding, because the longer the delay the more relatives there would be to invite.

Secondly, my *mechutanim* (or the MacNaughtons, as one calls them in Scotland), have a vast circle of friends.

Thirdly, my daughter, in the course of her military service, made friends with half the army, while her young man made friends with the other half, to say nothing of the better part of the Hadassah Medical School. On top of which I have (or think I have) one or two friends myself, so that when we came together to consider lists I suggested it would be easier to get the census returns and score out the names of people we wouldn't invite.

We did eventually manage to boil down the numbers but, even so, the date of the wedding was a military secret because of the borders of Israel being denuded that night.

But first there was the matter of venue. My MacNaughtons (bless 'em) and most of my wife's relatives live in Israel, which seemed to me as good a reason as any for having the wedding in England, but the young couple settled the matter between them. They would have it in Haifa and, given the number of expected guests, there was only one place large enough to contain them, the Dan Carmel hotel.

They say it's a small world, but it's a very large one when you're living at one end and trying to arrange a wedding at the other, especially when phone calls to the other end are about £3 a minute – considering the length and the frequency of the exchanges between my wife and my daughter it would have been cheaper for them to commute, King David class.

My daughter's identity caused consternation. She still had her army ID card, which said she was Jewish. Her passport said she was Jewish, and our local minister Rabbi Eddy Jackson wrote to confirm she was Jewish. Lord Jakobovits phoned the chief rabbi of Haifa to say she was Jewish, but being tall, blonde and blue-eyed (when she lived at home visitors took her to be our Swedish au pair) she doesn't look Jewish. The Haifa rabbinate wanted further and better particulars and the matter was not finally resolved until she arrived with numerous female relatives, some *sheitled* (bewigged), some murmuring incantations, and all brandishing *ketubot*, who avowed on oath that she was the Jewish daughter of a Jewish mother – though they were a bit non-committal about the father.

Then there were the invitations, or rather the lack of them. The proof copy arrived full of misprints. The final copy – entrusted to the tender mercies of Israel's postal service – failed, for a time, to arrive at all, and we had to start phoning around.

We needed a vast open space for the reception, which the hotel was happy to provide, but it included the swimming pool, and I could see myself spending half the night fishing guests out of the water, and the rest of my life fending off damage suits.

Finally, there was the not inconsiderable matter of refreshments. 'The wine,' the banqueting manager assured us, 'will flow like water,' but my MacNaughton and I feared that it might also taste like water and arranged for a fully stocked bar, which I thought had more or less settled the issue. Our wives, however, insisted that guests might also want something to eat and so the problems continued, each of them magnified by distance.

It so happens that one of our closest friends, Naomi Greenwood, was having a wedding in Israel in the very same week. She too has a vast family and many friends, except that where our daughter is marrying a native, hers is marrying a fellow Brit, which has, if anything, added to her difficulties and when my wife is not on the phone to my daughter, she is on the phone to Naomi – I wish I had held on to my British Telecom shares – for prolonged sessions of mutual commiseration:

'Why did we have to have the wedding in Israel? Why could we not have had it in London? Why . . .'

The question I keep asking myself is, why couldn't they have eloped?

22 September 1989

We are a grandfather

WE ARE A grandfather!

The event didn't take me by surprise. I knew it was on the way. I even knew what was on the way. It was a boy.

I didn't ask, neither did my daughter, but we were told. Such are the surplus wonders of modern science. Not that I was displeased with the news, but I wouldn't have demanded a second opinion if it had been a girl. Half of my immediate progeny have been female and I have no complaints about either of them.

Achake lo bechol yom sheyavo, as they say in the old prayer. I awaited his coming daily.

There is all sorts of help for expectant mothers, and perhaps even expectant fathers, but no one spares a thought for expectant grandfathers. I was fairly composed during the early months, but things changed when the appointed day came and he didn't. Or the day after, or the day after that.

Talk about *chevlei mashiach* – the birth pangs of the Messiah. They're not a patch on what I went through. My daughter lives in Haifa, we live in London, and distance only magnifies one's trepidations. Every time the phone trilled I pounced on it, and as we have several phones, and they trill all the time, I did a lot of pouncing, until I went into protracted labour.

I did all my breathing exercises, but they didn't help. My wife, who was calm – even nonchalant – throughout, suggested that I be given an epidural. I was finally relieved by Caesarean section.

You will be glad to hear that I've made a good recovery. So has the father. Oh, the mother and child are also doing well, bless 'em.

So what now? Does one decline into cantankerous old age? Or does one feel bound to show that there is life in the old dog yet?

One of the disadvantages of having a long beard is that I have always looked old. But because I have always looked old, no one has noticed that I have grown older, least of all myself.

Any man can become a father, as not a few men have discovered to their dismay, but being a grandfather is another matter. Had I been mugged on Hampstead Heath yesterday, the headline would

330

have been: 'Man mugged on Hampstead Heath.' Should I be mugged tomorrow it would be: 'Grandfather mugged on Hampstead Heath.' One acquires a new status.

La Rochefoucauld said that old men like to give good advice because they are no longer in a position to give a bad example. Everyone likes to give advice, good or bad, even if not everyone likes to take it. I have been giving the world the benefits of my wisdom for the past 30 years, but with a slight sense of presumption. I now feel entitled to do so, which doesn't, of course, mean that I feel old.

Old age is psychosomatic, not so much a physical condition as a state of mind. My wife will confirm that, far from entering my second childhood, I haven't outgrown my first. And yet, and yet, while old age may be a state of mind, grandchildren aren't. They are a public declaration, not merely that one is geting on, but that one has got on, especially among Jews. I am not only a grandfather, but a *zeida* and, while one sometimes hears of young, or at least, youthful grandfathers, *zeidas* are presumed to be old, even ancient.

The *booba* is the more familiar figure in Jewish lore because she was around longer. The *zeida* was more cherished, partly because he was less commonplace. Fewer men survived to old age, and even those who didn't, looked old.

My maternal *zeida* died shortly after I was born, but I have vivid recollections of my paternal one. He was short with bright eyes, shaggy eyebrows and a long, white beard. I thought of him as *Jedushka maroszh*, Old Father Frost, the Russian equivalent of Santa Claus. Yet he could only have been in his fifties.

We are all enjoined to teach our sons diligently, but until the recent past such duties were left to the *zeida* because he was the sole repository of Jewish learning. Today most *zeidas* would have something to learn from their grandsons and perhaps even more from their granddaughters – and, where they were useful as teachers and guides, they are now useful only as babysitters.

In the past, the status of *zeida* came with a feeling of resignation, and one lived through one's children and grandchildren. Now, however, people not only have a greater life expectancy, but they expect more from life, and even great grandparents are confident that they have suffcient active years ahead to live for themselves. The *zeida* of lore is thus no more.

9 July 1993

331

VE celebrations

I WAS SURPRISED by my reactions to the VE celebrations of the past week.

I approached them with apprehension for, though sentimental about the past – and who isn't? – I was afraid we might drown in a sea of nostalgia. Instead I found myself constantly moved and sometimes overwhelmed.

One did not have to be Jewish to be moved by the thanksgiving service broadcast from Bevis Marks on BBC2 – though I dare say it helped. There was something sublime about the entire occasion, the dignity, the decorum, the pithiness of the prayers, the antiquity of the rituals, the beauty of the singing, the mellowness of the setting.

And thanksgiving was, of course, the dominant sentiment, especially for those of us who lived through the war, together with a sense of privilege in being part of a nation which, for a grim 12 months, stood alone under relentless attack in the face of a mighty and murderous enemy, and which finally triumphed over every adversity.

The further one moves from the war, the easier it is to see what a close-run thing it was. Where would we be now if Hitler had delayed his invasion of Russia, if Japan had not attacked America, or if Churchill had not been prime minister?

I was too young to be fully aware of the peril we faced, but children are always sensitive to the mood of the adults around them and I shared the cheerful stoicism of the country as a whole and, foreigner though I was – and foreigner though I am – I acquired a sense of belonging which has never quite left me. I became British, so to speak, through a baptism of fire.

I was fiercely patriotic, and in 1942, when I attended my first Bnei Akiva camp, we were all eager to grab a pike and 'lend a hand on the land' as part of our war effort.

The following year, I joined the Jewish Lads' Brigade, which had been reorganised as an army cadet force, and wore the insignia of the Cameron Highlanders. I very much hoped for a kilt but, sadly, they were issued only to the elite, the members of the pipe band – the only Jewish pipe band in military history – and I had to make do with breeks. But I still marched proudly with puttees round my ankles and a glengarry on my head.

A little later, I tried to join the Home Guard (better known nowadays as Dad's Army). They wouldn't have me, but the recruiting officer, after examining my birth certificate, suggested helpfully that I might have better luck with the Polish Army.

He obviously missed the point of the whole exercise upon which I was engaged. I was yearning to see active service as a true Brit. As a result, when my children ask what I did in the war, I hold my peace.

In recent years, I have sometimes wondered if the fractious, shabby, seedy, whingeing Britain I know now could be the same country as the Great Britain I knew then.

The thought hit me with particular force when a storm blew up over the sale of the Churchill papers to a national archive for £12 million. It is a pity the papers could not have been handed over as an outright gift, but Churchill had no private means. He wrote for a living and his papers were the only vendible asset he could leave to his heirs.

The furore would, therefore, have been tasteless at the best of times. Coming as it did on the eve of the victory celebrations, it amounted to a national display of mean-mindedness.

Yet something of the Britain which had stood out as a beacon to the free world 50 years ago re-emerged, if only fleetingly, in the course of the VE celebrations over the past few days. Most encouragingly, the young, whom one is sometimes tempted to write off, joined as fully in the spirit of the occasion as the old.

I was particularly touched by the extent to which Blake's 'Jerusalem' has almost become the alternative national anthem. I must have heard it about 20 times over this past week or so, but couldn't hear it often enough. The final lines still reverberate in the memory:

> I will not cease from mental fight
> Nor shall my sword sleep in my hand
> Till we have built Jerusalem
> In England's green and pleasant land.

I am, of course, aware that Jerusalem is evoked as a metaphor, but

333

it showed how far the prophetic vision of Jerusalem as a metaphor for heaven on earth has affected British thinking. And it suggests that the country is perhaps not as Godless, or as feckless, as we are led to believe.

12 May 1995

JC is 140 years old

THE JC AS you may have gathered is 140 years old this week, and I sometimes have the feeling that I have been writing this column for 139 of them. As it is, I have been writing, under various guises, for the past 20 years and if at the end of my days, or at the end of time (which ever should come first), I am asked to show cause why I should be allowed to enter the kingdom of Heaven, I shall only have to wave my clippings to be ushered right in past serried ranks of seraphim and cherubim and a heavenly host singing the Hallelujah chorus.

And I make this claim not because of the nobility of my sentiments, the quality of my style, the truth of my revelations, or even the infinite charity which I bring to my labours, but because perseverance also counts for something in this world and (I hope) in the next.

I come from a part of the world (Scotland) where there was little money and even less inclination to spend it, and people would queue up in the local library for a sight of the JC. At the head of the queue was an elderly red-eyed moneylender who would even forgo his Shabbat *schloff* (sleep, rest) to claim his place. He liked to get his money's worth even when he wasn't parting with money, and he would go through the paper from beginning to end, moving his lips as he did so.

The media in those days did not give the extensive attention to Jewish affairs that they do now, so that anyone who did not read the JC had only a limited idea of what was happening in the Jewish world. The foreign news coverage was particularly good; there were some interesting feature articles; and the correspondence columns were usually lively. But every paper leaves a residual taste in the mouth, and the taste left by the JC was that of embalming

334

fluid laced with saccharin.

An order seems to have gone out from on high: Let us now praise famous men, and our fathers that begat us. Rare it was for a figure to be singled out except for approbation, and column after column read like a prolonged vote of thanks.

And in 1958 there arose a new editor who knew not the ways of the old, and I felt emboldened to write an article on Glasgow Jewry which, though couched in less than sycophantic terms, was not only accepted, but I was invited to join the panel of three or four contributors who were at that time writing the opinion column.

At first it was easy. Everyone has a swarm of bees buzzing away in his bonnet and for a marvellous year or so I was able (if I may mix my metaphors) to swing every axe I had ground, every prejudice I had accumulated, every obsession I had nourished, and get paid for it – after a fashion – into the bargain. But then, when I had spent them all, the labours began.

A Fleet Street colleague who used to contribute a weekly column to a national paper had to give it up after a year because, as she put it, 'I was at my wits' end what to write next.' Have pity, then, on someone who has to confine his column to purely Jewish affairs – but not too much pity, for if there is one thing I have learned in the past 20 (or is it 139?) years, it is to find a Jewish angle to almost anything.

In the last resort, the very absence of a Jewish angle can in itself be an occasion for comment, and I have sometimes been tempted to begin my column: 'The chief rabbi has once again been left out of the English team to play against India in the next test match, and while one would not accuse the selectors of racial bias . . .' But it is still hard work, and for every hour spent on writing this column, I spend five scratching around for something to write.

It would have been impossible were it not for what I regard as the journalist's best friend – the short memories of the reading public. I sometimes sweat blood over this column, at other times it seems to write itself, but it leaves me with a *déjà vu* feeling. I look up the back numbers, and lo and behold, I have said it all before. (Come to think of it, didn't I say all this on the 130th anniversary?) But there is no prose so memorable as not to be instantly forgotten, and even if something rings a bell in my memory, I can rely on the forgetfulness of the reader.

Cassandra, of blessed memory, who in his day was the prince of my profession, once said to me: 'Never praise, you will almost certainly be proved wrong.' No reader will believe this, but when I find a genuine occasion to praise someone, I approach the Sabbath with a lighter heart; but on balance it is not so much easier to criticise as safer.

There is an old Arab saying: 'Beat your wife every day, because even if *you* don't know why you're doing it, *she* does.' The same principle can be applied to nobler figures. In the last resort, if one has done somebody an injustice, one can always apologise and retract; but if one has overpraised a man, one has misinformed one's readers and they stay misinformed.

I have had to apologise in my time, but my greatest regrets are less from things I have said than from things I have failed to say. They were all of public concern. In two instances I remained silent out of charity, in a third, I'm afraid, out of cowardice.

In retrospect, I can see that in one instance, at least, and probably in all, my charity was misplaced. In the third, I was fairly certain that if I had come out with it on the Friday, the nationals would have come out with it on the Saturday, and the Sundays would have made a seven-course meal out of it. The editor had all the details and if he had published the story I would have chipped in with my comments. But in the event we both had cold feet and, I believe, we were both in the wrong.

13 November 1981

Millennial bash

I HAVE NO immediate plans to celebrate the second millennium, or even the third, and I find it difficult to understand the whole fuss about anniversaries.

In fact, I suspect that the idea of the anniversary was invented by the press as an inexpensive way of filling newspaper columns, especially at the turn of the year when there is not much hard news, or even soft news.

In *der heim*, we celebrated circumcisions, barmitzvahs, engagements, weddings, but never ordinary birthdays, silver weddings, or anything like that.

There were certainly no such things as golden or diamond weddings, because nobody lived long enough to celebrate them. Or, if they did, they were not in a fit state to celebrate them.

The only anniversaries which we did commemorate with any regularity – as we still do – were not birthdays but death-days, *yahrzeits*, and insofar as I contemplate the passage of time at all, I do so with regret rather than jubilation. I sometimes feel like lighting candles for all the follies committed and opportunities missed.

I am aware that the words 'jubilation' and 'jubilee' come from the Hebrew *yovel* but the jubilee, as described in Scripture, had nothing to do with jubilation or jollification. If anything, it was a solemn occasion:

'And ye shall hallow the 50th year, and proclaim liberty throughout all the land unto all the inhabitants thereof; it shall be a jubilee unto you; and ye shall return every man unto his possession . . .'

In other words, it was designed for the restoration of forfeited property and the redistribution of wealth, something favoured by the old Labour Party, but not the new one. It is new Labour, of course, which is arranging the celebrations, and which has appointed Peter Mandelson as 'Mr 2000,' the planner and overseer of the entire event.

It could be argued that, given what the world has been through in the last 2,000 years – and especially the past 100 – it is a miracle that it has survived this long. Thus, the celebrations would be merely a form of thanksgiving, a *shehecheyanu* (part of a prayer blessing God for having kept us alive), so to speak. Yet, if the millennium, as a millennium, marks anything at all, it marks the two thousanth anniversary of the birth of Jesus.

The date is of deep mystical significance to devout Christians who associate the millennium with the second coming and the end of days, much as devout Jews speculate on the coming of the Messiah. But, to the rest of us, it is but a nicely rounded number.

We, as Jews, date our era back to the beginning of creation (or thereabouts) so that, according to our calculations, we are living in

5758, while the Muslim era begins with Muhammed's flight from Mecca in 622 so that they are approaching the year 1376.

I suppose if we had to start from scratch, a royal commission, mindful of the fact that we live in a multicultural, multiracial society, might be tempted to add up the dates, divide them by three, and arrive at the year 3044. There is, however, no need for that – thank God – because the Christian era has, by universal consent, been accepted as the common one. But it nevertheless does remain the *Christian* era and, if there are to be any millennial celebrations at all, they should obviously be of a predominantly Christian character.

I cannot speak for Muslims, but I would say that any Jew anxious to have a millennial bash should wait until the year 6,000. Dammit all, what's the hurry?

All of which makes me wonder if Mr Mandelson is the ideal man for the job. He is a brilliant political organiser and has been widely credited with the scale of Labour's victory in the last election. He is also well connected, for his mother was a daughter of Herbert Morrison, Home Secretary both under Churchill and Attlee and who, in his day, was also a brilliant organiser.

Mandelson is, however, half-Jewish, and his late father, Tony – a good friend of mine who often entertained me to drinks in the Cavalry Club – was for many years advertising director of the *JC*.

It is, of course, possible that Peter Mandelson was put in charge of the millennial celebrations in a spirit of ecumenism, but I suspect it had more to do with the fact that his grandfather oversaw the 1951 Festival of Britain. Which recollection may suggest that, while Labour may not believe in a hereditary House of Lords, it seems to favour the idea of a hereditary Master of the Revels.

16 January 1998

*This was Chaim Bermant's final column in the *Jewish Chronicle*.